The Process of Occupational Sex-Typing

In the series *Women in the Political Economy*, edited by Ronnie J. Steinberg

The Process of Occupational Sex-Typing

The Feminization of
Clerical Labor in Great Britain
Samuel Cohn

Temple University Press, Philadelphia 19122
© 1985 by Temple University. All rights reserved
Published 1985
Printed in the United States of America

Library of Congress Cataloging-in-Publication Data

Cohn, Samuel, 1954–
   The process of occupational sex-typing.

   (Women in the political economy)
   Bibliography: p.
   Includes index.
   1. Sexual division of labor—Great Britain—History.
2. Women clerks—Great Britain—History.
3. Women—Employment—Great Britain—History.
I. Title. II. Series.
HD6060.65.G7C64   1985   331.4'8165137'0941   85-14864
ISBN 0-87722-402-1

Contents

To my mentors,

Charles and Louise Tilly,

for their advice and for their example

Acknowledgments

This project would not have been possible without extensive financial and intellectual support from many people. A particular debt of gratitude is owed to Gayl Ness and the University of Michigan Sociology Department and the National Institute of Mental Health, who provided me with the funds for a trip to London to locate archival materials for a potential dissertation. Had this initial trip not been provided, I never would have discovered the Great Western Railway and Post Office archives, and this research design never would have been developed. Not enough can be said for the importance of providing graduate students early in their careers with funds for the investigation of archives; historical work in particular is entirely dependent on the discovery of new archives with new bodies of material.

The Russell Sage Foundation very generously provided an entire year of fellowship support, research assistance, and computer support to allow for the analysis and writing of this manuscript. This project required an extensive re-analysis and fresh conceptualization that could only have been accomplished with the leisure that a year of freedom from teaching could provide. The Horace Rackham School of Graduate Studies also provided a year of fellowship support that allowed for a rapid completion of the dissertation on which this book is based.

I owe a special intellectual debt to W. B. Creighton, Alberto Palloni, and R. W. Jones. W. B. Creighton, an Australian legal scholar, provided a historical summary of the British protectionist laws relevant to female employment and nightwork that became essential to the chapter on the legitimation of exclusion. Alberto Palloni, a demographer at the University of Wisconsin, developed the modifications of

vii

the stable population equations that are used to estimate the relations between organizational growth and the viability of boy labor. R. W. Jones, the former archivist at the General Post Office archives, provided a wealth of information on postal history and the location of sources. He was indispensable both in providing documentary material on the most recondite matters and in providing interpretations and explanations of postal esoterica.

The number of individuals who have offered helpful advice on various aspects of this project is enormous. Among the people who have read earlier drafts of this research or who have provided substantial assistance on problems encountered in writing and execution are Julia Adams, Robert Cole, Roberto Franzosi, Warren Hagstrom, Charles Halaby, Robert Mare, Ruth Milkman, Jeffery Paige, Richard Roehl, Aage Sorensen, Charles Tilly, and Louise Tilly. My sincere gratitude to them all. I have endeavored to follow their suggestions whenever possible; whatever errors remain in this text are my own responsibility. The last debt is to my wife, Lynn Wallisch, for editing, commentary, and infinite patience.

The Process of Occupational Sex-Typing

1

Thinking about Occupational Sex-Typing

One of the fundamental concerns in feminist social science has been specifying the relationship between capitalism and patriarchy. Since Heidi Hartmann's seminal essay "Capitalism, Patriarchy, and Job Segregation by Sex" was written in 1976, it has generally been accepted that the oppression of women by men is facilitated and maintained by the economic institutions of modern society. However, specifying the mechanisms by which this occurs has not been easy; within the 1970's and 1980's, there has been a resurgence of interest in generating a materialist explanation of patriarchy that is consistent with rational economic theory. This new scholarship has taken a wide variety of forms. There have been attempts to develop a theory of patriarchy that closely parallels the form and logic of Marxist theories of exploitation (Secombe 1974; Beechey 1978; O'Brien 1981; Power 1983). Economists have used neo-classical economics, human capital theory, and, more recently, dual labor market theory to explain women's concentration in low-paid employment and production within the home (Barron and Norris 1976; Blau and Jusenius 1976; Polachek 1979). There has also been excellent empirical research on the history of women's experiences in the work world that has attempted to uncover inductively the obstacles impeding women's advancement (Kanter 1977; Dublin 1979; Kessler-Harris 1982; Milkman 1982). Finally, there has been a flowering of demographic research and family history that has documented how larger economic changes affected women's domestic roles, occupational lives, and self-perceptions. (M. Anderson 1971; Zaretsky 1973; Tilly and Scott 1978). Each of these styles of work makes its own distinctive contribution towards answering the question. There is one phenomenon, however, that has such an overwhelming effect on women's status and opportunities that writers of nearly every theoretical persuasion have made at least tacit acknowledgment of its importance. This phenomenon is occupational sex-typing.

Occupational sex-typing is the process by which certain occupations are designated as being primarily male or female. Sex-typing has produced a virtual bifurcation of the labor market into male/female sectors; in 1960, fully 50 percent of all women were working in occupations that were over 70 percent female (Oppenheimer 1970). This division of labor has had enormous consequences for women's economic opportunities and prospects. Valerie Kincaide Oppenheimer has compellingly demonstrated that occupational sex-typing has placed an upper limit on the extent to which women can participate in work outside the home. Between 1900 and 1960, the increase in the number of female sex-typed jobs far outweighed any supply-side variable in predicting the increase of female labor force participation (Oppenheimer 1970).

Women's wages are also affected by occupational sex-typing. The most compelling explanation of women's inferior wage attainments is the overcrowding hypothesis. This argument claims that sex-typing forces a large number of women into a small, restricted set of occupations, while men may select from a much wider range. The limited demand for female labor intensifies competition among women for jobs, thus lowering their overall market wage (Fawcett 1918; Edgeworth 1922; Stevenson 1975a, 1975b). The combination of limited job opportunities and low wages also serves to promote women's subordination in the domestic sphere. The dismal economic opportunities faced by women in the marketplace induce many of them to drop out of the labor force to become full-time homemakers. Furthermore, their limited financial opportunities increase their dependence on male providers, which in turn makes them vulnerable to domestic and sexual exploitation. Thus, if one is to understand changes in women's work and family roles, it is essential to understand the process by which employers designate which jobs will be open to women and which jobs will be reserved for men. While occupational sex-typing may not be the only mechanism by which economic forces shape those of patriarchy, it surely is one of the most central and important.

Common Explanations of Occupational Sex-Typing

Thus far, however, no one has developed a clear and convincing theory of what makes a given job male or female. One of the major problems has been that discussions of women's work have been dominated by a series of propositions that are for one reason or another unsatisfying. The major issue that confronts any theory of occupational sex-typing is that both economic and patriarchical considerations affect the hiring decisions made by managers. Managers are basically businessmen, whose rewards and life chances depend to a large extent on the growth and profitability of their enterprises. As such, hiring policy should be a tool for lowering costs, raising productivity, and furthering the organization's economic goals. At the same time, the firm exists in a society in which patriarchy is pervasive; commonly held sex-role ideologies might be expected to affect the hiring decisions of managers who are being ostensibly objective. The intellectual challenge has been to develop an explanation of occupational sex-typing that incorporates both economic and ideologically based variables into a synthesis that is both theoretically coherent and consistent with the available evidence.

Most theories of women's work do deal with both types of factors, but the strategies for combining them have often left something to be desired. It has often been argued that patriarchy affects hiring decisions through one of two following intermediating mechanisms: restricting female labor supply or creating normative and cultural limits on female employment. Let us consider each of these in turn.

Restricting Female Labor Supply

Many models of occupational sex-typing argue that women voluntarily choose to limit their labor supply in order to spend their time as full-time mothers and housewives rather than as paid employees. These models are used by authors of many different intellectual persuasions, but they have been most systematically developed by human capital theorists (Becker 1964; Zellner 1975; Polachek 1979; Rotella 1981).[1] Human capital theorists start with the reasonable assumption

---

1. For examples of the use of such theories in more eclectic presentations, see National Manpower Council (1957). and Oppenheimer (1970).

that both employers and potential employees are economically ratio-nal. Employers do not discriminate, but instead fill their job openings in such a way as to maximize productivity and minimize cost.[2] Deci-sions about occupational sex-typing are based on employers' choosing between two types of workers: men, who are committed to long-term employment, and women, whose labor force participation is likely to be intermittent. There are two reasons why women supposedly choose to withhold themselves from the labor force. On the one hand, tradi-tional gender ideologies encourage women to stay home, thus giving them a greater taste for leisure. On the other hand, women are hypothesized as having a natural aptitude for home production and as having a comparative advantage in child care, cooking, and other domestic tasks. Thus, it will be rational for women to concentrate in home rather than market production, particularly in those stages of the family life cycle when there is a high demand for child care.

Human capital theorists argue that women's domestic obligations result in their being excluded from high-status jobs. High-status jobs tend to be relatively skilled and require substantial amounts of both formal education and learning on the job. Because women anticipate interrupting their careers, they will choose neither to spend money on formal education nor to select occupations that require extensive training in the early stages of the career.[3] Thus non-discriminatory employers of skilled labor will find relatively few qualified female workers applying for their vacancies, and they will be forced by default to give these skilled jobs to men. Furthermore, even if a supply of female candidates exists, employers will be reluctant to give these positions to women. There are many situations in which the employers themselves finance the cost of educating workers for high-level jobs. In

---

2. There are of course neo-classical theories of discrimination. However, none of them predict hiring regimes that show significant deviations from those expected under a system of rational self-interest. Becker explicitly argues that employers who discrimi-nate will be driven out of business by the rigors of the market, while Phelps and Aigner and Cain view discrimination as the result of profit-maximizing under conditions of imperfect information (Becker 1957; Phelps 1972; Aigner and Cain 1977).

3. The rationale for the latter is that, in human capital theory, a worker who is being trained is indirectly financing his education by taking a lower salary. Supposedly, when employers provide workers with skills that are of value to competing employers, they force the worker to incur the cost of the training. The long-term worker is willing to make this sacrifice because his education will raise his productivity and thus increase his market wage. However, a short-term worker pays for training costs without receiving a long-term benefit, and thus should be uninterested in acquiring human capital.

these cases, employers will choose to hire workers with long anticipated tenures so they can minimize the number of times they have to
provide basic training. If they hire short-term workers, such as
women, there is a risk that the workers will leave employment before
producing enough to cover the cost of their human capital.

There are several possible objections to this account. First, it is not
at all clear that women's domestic obligations keep them from wanting
to obtain good jobs; in general the obstacles to women's entering
high-status jobs have come from management rather than from
women themselves. Second, the evidence does not support the claim
that, controlling for occupation, women have higher turnover than
men. Women seem as likely as men to remain in responsible positions.
Third, even if women voluntarily choose to have discontinuous
careers, it does not follow from this that employers would choose to
bar women from jobs with high firm-specific training. There are countervailing advantages to hiring women that can outweigh the costs
associated with human capital loss. Let us consider each of these
arguments in further detail.

The proposition that female labor supply has been limited by
domestic considerations may have some validity for the early
nineteenth century, but it is indefensible for the modern period.
Valerie Kincaide Oppenheimer's work (1970) has compellingly shown
that supply-side theories do not convincingly account for changes in
American female labor force participation from 1900 to 1960.
Women's work rates during this period did not correlate in any
meaningful fashion with changes in fertility, the availability of labor-
saving home appliances, or changes in national attitudes on traditional
sex roles. Female labor force participation rose dramatically during
the 1950's, despite the countervailing forces of the baby boom and a
generally conservative social climate. In the fifties, women's economic
opportunities increased, as employment in clerical work, education,
and the female semi-professions expanded. Women responded to
these opportunities and left their homes for paid employment even as
the baby boom added to their domestic obligations (Oppenheimer
1970). Cynthia Epstein's research on law shows that even women who
had relatively conservative attitudes on sex roles entered law school
when law schools changed their admissions policies and began to
accept women. Despite traditional socializations, many women were
capable of making the ideological adjustments necessary to prepare
themselves for professional careers (Epstein 1981). Both these studies
suggest that women are willing and eager to enter market employment

and that the primary barriers to female labor force participation come from management.

Furthermore, it is not at all clear that women have desisted from obtaining human capital. Historically, women have been more likely than men to seek higher education. Between 1870 and 1930, between 55 and 60 percent of all high school graduates were women (Rotella 1981). If women invested in long-term job skills in the late Victorian era when traditional sex roles were quite prevalent, it is implausible that modern women would be unwilling to make such commitments when the potential economic returns to such commitment have been substantially improved.

There are similar difficulties with the claim that women are disproportionately likely to quit their jobs. This proposition has received only lukewarm support from the empirical literature on turnover and exit rates. Some studies do find significant differences between men and women in career lengths (Parnes 1954; Burton and Parker 1969; Pencavel 1970); however, far more studies have found no sex differences whatsoever (Stoikov and Raimon 1968; Fry 1973; Armknecht and Early 1972; Begnoche Smith 1979; Blau and Kahn 1981). The size of the relationship is not robust to minor changes in the control variables or to changes in the strategies of measurement. An example of the complexities involved in the relationship between sex and turnover can be found in an analysis of quit rates by K. P. Viscusi. Viscusi found that global rates of turnover for female employees were higher than the equivalent rates for men. However, there were no significant sex differences in tenure-specific exit rates; furthermore, women were far more likely to decrease their quit rates in response to organizational incentives than were men (Viscusi 1980). The evidence does not support the conclusion that there are no sex differences in turnover whatsoever. Given the lack of consistent findings on the very existence of a turnover differential, however, let alone any consensus that the size of this turnover differential is large, it would seem inappropriate to base the explanation of such a pervasive institution as sex-typing on such an ephemeral phenomenon.[4,5]

Even if women do systematically interrupt their careers to get married and raise a family, there are still critical logical problems with

4. For an even stronger position against the existence of gender differences in turnover, see the extensive reviews of the empirical literature on quit rates by Anderson (1974) and Price (1977).

most of these supply-side theories. It is not at all clear that the most rational economic response by either women or employers to short anticipated careers is the elimination of women from high-status jobs. Consider this problem from the point of view of a female worker first. The primary reason a woman supposedly chooses a low-status position is that the job allows her to minimize her loss of human capital when her career is interrupted. The gains that come from the preservation of deteriorating skills would seem to be trivial compared with the overall benefits involved in taking a high-paying rather than a low-paying job. Furthermore, once a person has received his or her basic training in an occupation, skills that have been lost through short- or middle-term absences can often be regained fairly quickly. Adult students who return to school after several years in the job market usually regain their academic skills within the first year. Job skills are likely to have a similar rate of regeneration. And even if the rate of skill loss were catastrophic, the wages received during retraining in a high-paying job are likely to exceed the wages a fully trained worker receives in a low-paying job. Thus, it is very difficult to explain the concentration of women in low-status jobs in terms of a model of voluntary choice.[6]

---

5. A reasonable objection can be made that most of the data presented above come from the twentieth century. Brenner and Ramas (1984) argue provocatively that supply-side limits to female employment may have been more important in the nineteenth century. Market employment would have been less attractive to women due to the lower prevailing rates of real wages, while high fertility was an economic necessity due to children's importance as a source of security in old age. It is true that there were more incentives for women to remain home in the nineteenth century. However, it is still unclear that these incentives were so great as to restrict significantly the supply of female labor open to employers. The evidence that is required to show an independent effect of labor supply would be for employers to attempt to hire women for lucrative positions but be forced to hire men after experiencing a shortage of female job applicants. If an occupation de-feminized after employers failed to find an adequate supply of female labor, or after suffering from excessive rates of female turnover, this would support the Brenner and Ramas hypothesis. Empirically, it is hard to think of examples that fit this model. Those cases where de-feminization has occurred seem to have involved women's mobilizing into trade unions, the passage of laws banning female labor, or significant changes in the technology of industry (Kessler-Harris 1982). This is not to say supply-based changes did not occur. No definitive settlement of this issue can be made until there is the same sort of rigorous test of supply and demand models for 1820 that there has been for 1970.

6. This argument implicitly assumes that wages are not purely a function of productivity but are affected by exogenous factors as well. The recent literature on dual labor markets, internal labor markets, and the effect of unionization on wages provides more than adequate support for this hypothesis (Parsley 1980; Kalleberg et al. 1981).

The argument is equally hard to justify from the employer's point of view. It is not clear that the benefits of conserving scarce human capital outweigh the costs of operating with a relatively inexpensive labor force. A woman will work at the rate of 59 cents for every male dollar. Even if the use of women requires higher levels of training costs due to more frequent replacement of personnel, retraining would have to be very expensive to exhaust the 40 percent wage subsidy associated with using cheap female labor. Admittedly, there are personnel who are so scarce as to be irreplaceable; the Manhattan Project would have paid anything not to lose Enrico Fermi. However, the skills of most workers are not so rare as to require conservation at any price. Many skilled workers are readily replaceable from the marketplace. If one loses a high school principal, one merely hires a new one from another system. Other vacancies can be easily filled from within. Most advanced positions are filled not by neophytes but by subordinates in the same workplace who have some relevant experience and need only a partial retraining. It is not implausible to imagine that, when an assistant is promoted to a position formerly held by her supervisor, she might work at 60 percent efficiency the first year, 80 percent efficiency the second year, and full efficiency for all years thereafter. From the point of view of the employer, this would represent substantial training costs, but hardly an overwhelming burden. In particular, it would hardly justify turning down a female candidate who was willing to work for 59 percent of a male salary. The benefits from exploiting women's inferior position in the marketplace would seem to far outweigh the benefits that accrue from the conservation of human capital.[7]

Even if one grants that women are likely to leave their jobs because of family responsibilities, however, *and* that the costs of retraining these workers is greater than the savings of using cheaper labor, it is still logically difficult to argue that such problems will induce employers to bar women from high-status jobs. This is because only

---

7. The savings from using women in high-status positions could be even greater than those associated with normal jobs. The logic behind the overcrowding hypothesis would suggest that since the supply of highly paid jobs for women is far more constrained than the general supply of jobs, employers could receive far greater savings in using women for superior jobs than they could by using them in average positions. The extreme scarcity of supervisory positions for women might induce women to work at 40 cents to the male dollar, instead of the normal 59 cents.

younger women are actually subject to the kinds of domestic pressures that could force withdrawal from the labor force. Older women can readily be hired for any job involving firm-specific learning and will have low rates of turnover, similar to those of men. The one domestic duty that might require withdrawal from the labor force is taking care of infants and children under five. Cooking, cleaning, and laundry may all be deferred or obtained through the market, but small children require constant attention and nurturance, which is not easily provided by market labor. Nevertheless, only women in their twenties and thirties are likely to have young children in their households. Because fertility tends to be concentrated in the years just after marriage, by age forty most women have completed their childbearing and most of their children are old enough to free their mothers for work outside the home. Furthermore, because pre-industrial mortality schedules closely resemble modern mortality rates for ages after twenty, historically a forty-year-old woman could have looked forward to good health until her late sixties or seventies. She thus could have entered the labor force anticipating an uninterrupted career of twenty-five to thirty years. Most jobs could be filled quite profitably by twenty-five or thirty-year workers, even if they required extremely long periods of initial training.[8]

Occupational sex-typing divides jobs into subsets that are either all male or all female; there are very few jobs that are given to men and older women, but not to younger women. If employers were primarily concerned about conserving scarce human capital, such patterns would occur relatively frequently as employers differentiated between long-term and short-term employees. In fact, employers have hired

8. It is true that many employers are reluctant to hire older workers. Some managers fear that older workers have suffered a deterioration in their skills because of the long period they have been out of school. This would not be an issue for a women who has gone back to school after completing her childbearing. Another objection is that older workers are often failures and cast-offs from other organizations. This again is not a problem for an older female labor force entrant. A third issue might be the higher chance of serious illness or diminished physical capacities among older workers. However, most middle-aged workers are in perfect health. Furthermore, although a forty-year-old worker only offers a prospective career of twenty-five to thirty years, while a twenty-five-year-old worker offers a prospective career of forty years, it is not at all clear that the extra fifteen years offer any advantage to an employer. Over a forty-year period, most workers will leave their original employer for non-health-based professional or personal reasons anyway.

girls in their teens and early twenties quite readily, while discriminating against older women; the labor force participation rates of teenaged women have always been high, while those of women over forty-five only increased in the 1950's (Oppenheimer 1970). Conservation of human capital does not predict a division of labor that lumps all men into one category and all women into another. The phenomenon of occupational sex-typing that treats all women as mutually interchangeable, though different from men, must be explained by a wholly different dynamic.

Labor supply can also affect women's work through mechanisms that do not involve human capital. It has been hypothesized that sex-typing is affected by prevailing rates of female labor force participation at the time at which a given occupation is created. If the initial job openings occur in a period when traditional sex-role ideologies are inhibiting female labor force participation, no women candidates will apply for the new vacancies and the occupation will become male. If the job is created in a period of increasing female labor force participation, it will be possible to staff the positions with women. In either case, once these first workers are hired, bureaucratic inertia and the development of self-reinforcing legitimating ideologies tend to perpetuate the sex mix of the original cohort.[9]

This model rarely appears in explicit theories of occupational sex-typing, but it is extremely common in empirical studies of particular occupations. Consider the standard claim that clerical work feminized because office work expanded in an era of rapidly increasing female education and labor force participation. These changes in women's work behavior ensured that a supply of women would be available to take these new positions (Davies 1975, 1982; Kessler-Harris 1982). Such an insight would not be terribly informative if occupations adapted instantaneously to changes in the labor supply. If this were the case, all types of jobs would have responded to these changes and there would be no such thing as occupational sex-typing. Increasing labor supply becomes an internally consistent theory of occupational

9. The presence of this last provision makes the theory what Arthur Stinchcombe would call an historicist model. See Stinchcombe's *Constructing Social Theories* (1968) for an excellent discussion of the potential uses of such theories. See also Stinchcombe's 1964 essay on the effect of period of creation on organization structure.

sex-typing only if older occupations such as mining do not respond to changes in the labor market and thus remain predominantly male.

Although there are examples that can be used to support the theory, the number of counterexamples is quite striking. The feminization of teaching, clerical work, retail sales, social work, and nursing have been explained in terms of the increasing female labor supply of the late nineteenth and early twentieth centuries. Between 1870 and 1930, however, employers also first began to hire accountants, life insurance salesmen, airline pilots, truck drivers, electricians, elevator operators, advertising consultants, radio announcers, and automobile mechanics. All of these jobs became overwhelmingly male. The expanding turn-of-the-century supply of female labor does not seem to have had the same effect on every occupation that was created during the period. In fact, supply considerations seem to have very poor predictive power in explaining what types of jobs become male or female. In order to understand how new occupations develop their sex types, it is necessary to understand the demand-side determinants of female employment.

Normative and Cultural Limits on Female Employment

Many discussions of women's work explicitly argue that employers' hiring decisions are fundamentally shaped by occupational norms derived from the division of labor within the home. Because of this, women are given jobs associated with traditional female tasks or attributes (Caplow 1954; National Manpower Council 1957; Oppenheimer 1970). The training women receive in the household as young girls gives them a natural aptitude for jobs with a domestic component. Likewise, women's personalities, which are shaped by early gender socialization, makes them more suitable for work that requires "female" psychological attributes. Thus, women work in textile factories because as young girls they receive training in sewing. Women work as waitresses because at home they are more likely than men to serve meals. Women work in the helping professions because they are socialized to be expressive rather than instrumental. Just as women are concentrated in those areas where they have special expertise, men are concentrated in those areas where they have a particular gender-related advantage. Thus men are more likely to work in jobs that require physical strength, are dirty, or demand leadership skills.

Not every writer would insist that men and women differ in their gender-related competencies. Whether women are truly weaker or more understanding than men is a matter of considerable dispute. However, cultural theories of sex-typing need not be based on actual differences in the skills or personalities of men and women. It is sufficient for employers to believe that these differences exist and to hire on the basis of this consistent gender ideology. In their most credible form, normative theories predict the sex-type of occupations in terms of commonly held ideologies that blind employers to the possibility of extending the domain of female employment. Traditional gender roles irrationally inhibit firms from hiring women for jobs characterized as masculine, making the occupational structure reflect patterns of patriarchy in the larger society.

Although these considerations can provide seemingly plausible explanations of particular cases, they nearly always fail to provide a general principle that will correctly predict the overall distribution of male and female jobs. It is very hard to find a norm or a cultural prescription that seems to have been applied consistently by employers in a wide range of occupations. Consider the argument that women take jobs similar to those tasks done within the home. Although women traditionally cook within the home, they have not always obtained such jobs in the marketplace. In 1970, the occupation of cook was roughly evenly split between men and women: just under 40 percent of the cooks were men and just over 60 percent were female.[10] Despite the fact that baking bread and cakes is done by women in the home, only 29 percent of all commercial bakers and 35 percent of bakers' assistants were female. Only 35 percent of food manufacturing operatives were women. Within this set of occupations, the only occupation that was more than 50 percent female was the canning and preserving of fruits, vegetables, and seafood. It is hard to see how the traditional division of labor in the home would lead women in the labor force to can salmon but not to make butter or freeze TV dinners.

Such incongruities can also be found in work resembling domestic labor. Women invariably do the housecleaning in most families. Nevertheless, only 32 percent of all cleaning workers were women. Likewise, although women made up 69 percent of all food service workers, they comprised only 38 percent of all dishwashers. Although

10. All data on the sex composition of current occupations come from the 1970 *Census Report on Occupational Characteristics* (U.S. Bureau of the Census 1970).

women have been traditionally associated with child care, and 84 percent of all elementary school teachers were women, only 49 percent of all secondary school teachers were women. In the home, women's responsibility for their children hardly ends at age twelve. In the professions, women do tend to be concentrated in specialties that emphasize child care. In medicine, women are disproportionately likely to be pediatricians, and within mental health, women are more likely to be child psychologists. Nevertheless, none of these jobs have ever been female sex-typed occupations. Women at best have made up a somewhat larger minority than was to be found in other medical specialties.

The same incongruities appear in textiles. The fact that women sew has been used to explain women's concentration in spinning mills and clothing factories. Nevertheless, only 32 percent of all commercial tailors are women. This is surprising, given that women make the clothing repairs in most households. Although many female jobs require skills similar to those women use within the home, there is a very substantial number of jobs involving domestic arts that traditionally have been monopolized and dominated by men. Thus, the household division of labor actually turns out to be an unreliable guide to predicting occupational sex type.

It is also difficult to find social-psychological correlates of male or female jobs. Although women are traditionally associated with nurturance, they have not always been used in jobs that involve care or sensitivity in dealing with people. Nursing and social work have been traditionally female jobs. However, psychiatry has remained a male occupation. Furthermore, most religions have traditionally provided only limited opportunities for women to act as clergy, despite the fact that this occupation specializes in the most profound emotional and spiritual concerns of human life. It is true that some religions have made use of women in specialized capacities. The Catholic Church has always permitted spiritually inclined women to serve as nuns, but nuns have been confined to a fairly narrow range of duties and rarely heard confessions or provided pastoral care.

It is also difficult to find any physical correlates of men's or women's work. Women's supposedly superior hand-to-eye coordination may be invoked in explaining their concentration in textiles and electronics manufacture, but these skills have never gotten them hired as jewelers, engravers, or surgeons. It is true that women have not tended to appear in occupations that require physical strength, such as baggage porters or freight and material handlers. However, they have also been excluded from manual occupations that involve very little physical exertion at all. Women made up only 3 percent of parking attendants, 11 percent of vehicle washers, and 6 percent of taxi drivers. None of these jobs are particularly physically demanding. Women made up only 2.9 percent of all gardeners and groundskeepers despite the fact that many women routinely garden at home. Since most occupations do not call for very much upper-body strength, it is unclear how much of the difference between men's and women's jobs can be accounted for by physical strength.

Although most cultural propositions can be contradicted with numerous examples, one can never prove definitively that ideological factors do not contribute to sex-types. There is no limit to the number of propositions that could be devised by a dedicated believer in sex roles. Furthermore, a cultural determinist could argue that the individual normative factors only work when considered in concert and that an ideological model must contain an enormous number of variables before it can obtain predictive power. Nevertheless, deriving a sex-role socialization model that would be measurable, non-tautological, and consistent with the complexity of most occupational systems is a formidable prospect. The task is made more discouraging by the poor performance most of the components of such a model have when considered individually.

A Framework for Thinking about Occupational Sex-Typing

It is necessary to develop an alternative to supply-side and normative theories that can explain the creation and persistence of occupational sex-typing. Such a theory should be capable of making concrete predictions of the sex-type of a given job, consistent with an assumption of economic rationality on the part of the employer and informed by the actual problems and concerns faced by real-world managers. There are many propositions that at first glance appear to satisfy these conditions. Some after closer examination can be shown to be flawed; others make important contributions to the overall theory. In order to organize the various alternatives to supply-side and normative models, it is helpful to place these models within a larger theoretical framework.

Most theories of occupational sex-typing attempt to specify what is distinctive or unique about women's work. Human capital theory argues that male workers are acceptable for all jobs, while female workers must be confined to a more limited subset. The theory then attempts to specify the properties of this female subset. Normative theories could concentrate on the attributes of jobs of either sex. In practice, however, they have tended to focus on women's domestic roles and personality and how these shape the universe of jobs that become defined as female. While there is nothing incorrect about proceeding in this fashion, it is more informative to proceed in the opposite fashion and ask what it is that is distinctive about those jobs that are defined as male.

Employers should prefer to hire women rather than men, all other things being equal, because women work for substantially lower wages. At the global level, this phenomenon is caused by occupational sex-typing and by the overcrowding of the labor market that results from discrimination. For an individual firm, however, national patterns of discrimination are a given. An employer deciding how to fill a particular vacancy knows that, because of the hiring policies of other employers, women can be forced to accept a lower level of wages; this should make women the employees of preference for all positions until occupational sex-typing completely disappears.

This argument was originally made in 1957 by Gary Becker in his *Economics of Discrimination*. Becker argued that any firm that chose to discriminate was arbitrarily restricting its labor supply and forcing itself to operate with a higher level of market wages. This economic handicap would restrict the firm's ability to compete effectively and could ultimately lead to the closing or sale of the firm. Becker thus concluded that discrimination was economically irrational; if prejudice persisted, it was because either the employer or the workforce had a "taste for discrimination." There are many grounds on which this argument can be challenged, such as its overreliance on the principles of neo-classical economics and its strong prediction that in the long run discrimination would disappear. Nevertheless, Becker's main argument that employers pay a premium to employ men is basically sound. The important theoretical task is to move beyond the vague term "taste for discrimination" in order to specify the economic basis for not making use of cheap female labor.[11]

---

11. In this light, it is hard to accept the argument that particular occupations feminize because of an employer's need for cheap labor (Oppenheimer 1970; Prather

Logically, there are four different categories of reasons for employers not to hire women. No one particular category has any intrinsic logical advantage over any other. Although each type of argument has the capacity to be the basis of a reasonable, internally consistent theory of occupational sex-typing, individual arguments within each category will vary in their logical adequacy and empirical support. The four different strategies for explaining the non-hiring of women are:

1. Identifying a countervailing economic advantage to using men.
2. Identifying some environmental constraint that prevents employers from hiring women.
3. Identifying some sector of the male population that will work for lower wages than the average salary demanded by women.
4. Identifying some factor that buffers employers from the requirement of minimizing labor costs.

Let us consider each of these in turn.

Countervailing Advantages

Employers could hire men because men are associated with countervailing advantages that can compensate for their relatively higher pay rates. Both human capital theory and cultural theory argue that men are inherently more productive than women in performing certain kinds of tasks, which justifies paying a premium to obtain male labor. These two specifications are the most common forms of countervailing advantage arguments; however, there are a variety of alternative specifications. Consider Michael Reich's theory of the racial division of labor markets. He would argue that by dividing the labor force into two hostile groups and carefully rationing employment between the two sectors, employers can lower the level of working-class militancy (Reich 1981).[12] Such a strategy requires the hiring of both white adult males and some other category of workers.

1971; Davies 1975). Since, at a superficial level, all employers have some interest in obtaining cheap labor, it is necessary that authors use this argument in tandem with other considerations that explain why feminization does not occur universally.

12. This argument is generally more convincing for race and ethnicity than it is for sex; however, it is a non-trivial theory of gender that will be examined in detail in Chapter 7.

A model will be presented in the analysis called the "synthetic turnover hypothesis" that links occupational sex-typing to motivation problems in internal labor markets. Under a narrow set of conditions, employers within a bureaucracy can find themselves forced to reduce the levels of rewards to some workers within the system arbitrarily, while maintaining these rewards for the rest of their labor force. Under such conditions, it is necessary to create a caste system within the organization in which differential placement and treatment are legitimated in terms of pre-existing social and demographic distinctions. Under such conditions, it is necessary to hire both a set of victims, such as women or blacks, and a set of elite members, namely white adult males. These conditions do not apply to all employers; in those settings where synthetic turnover operates, however, men are hired because of the countervailing advantage they provide in maintaining segmented reward systems within the firm.

Environmental Constraints

Even if employers prefer to hire women for a given position, they may find themselves prevented from using women and forced to use men. Labor supply arguments make use of such environmental constraints. In these models, employers wish to hire women because of their lower wages; however, because women are choosing domestic production over market employment, female job candidates are scarce, and employers are forced to use men as a more expensive alternative. Two other environmental constraints that are often discussed in theories of occupational sex-typing are exclusionary demands from organized labor and legislative limitations on female employment.

The exclusion of women from certain occupations can be caused by a strong, well-organized, sexist male union. Gary Becker argued that discrimination can come from two sources: employers and employees (Becker 1957). Employee discrimination is actually easier to account for than employer discrimination. The traditional worker strategy for increasing wages is to limit the supply of potential workers. Thus, organized labor has attempted whenever possible to enforce extremely restrictive limits on who may obtain employment, a policy that has encouraged racism, sexism, ethnic prejudice, and the development of barriers to exclude some categories of white men. The hostility of male workers to women has been fueled by patriarchical concerns as well. Thus, it is not surprising that historically there are many examples of male unions' actively agitating for the formal restriction or abolition of female employment (Hartmann 1976; Kessler-Harris 1979; Foner 1979, 1980; Milkman 1980).

While organized labor represents an important source of exclusionary pressure, its importance in determining sex-type is limited. Not all unions have the strength to impose a male workforce on an employer who is committed to resisting these demands. In most union-management confrontations, management has bargained from a position of strength. Union security is a very recent concession for many workers; obtaining economic benefits has often been problematic. It has been extremely difficult to win concessions on issues not involving wages, such as limits on the rate of work or protection from redundancy. Most unions have very little control over hiring decisions and only limited control over promotions and job assignments. Without such power, unions can contribute little to the process of occupational sex-typing, and gender decisions remain a matter of managerial prerogative.

There are, however, some exceptions to this. Workers in very strong positions, notably craft workers, professionals, and managers, have historically maintained tight control over recruitment into their occupations. The exclusionary powers of doctors, lawyers, and plumbers is well known. Thus, the concentration of men in the most skilled or powerful occupations can be plausibly explained in terms of the environmental constraint of male organized labor, as long as one compares average jobs with those of the very elite.

Many employers have been unable to use women because hiring them for a particular job was illegal. In the nineteenth century, women were barred from many manual occupations by protective legislation. In some cases, these laws limited the number of hours and times of the day that women could work when long night shifts were a substantive requirement for employment. In other cases, women were forbidden from workplaces that were legally defined as dangerous (Creighton 1979; Kessler-Harris 1982). The prevalence of these laws can be exaggerated. Most occupations were wholly unregulated by the state, and even within the most heavily regulated industries, women were barred from employment in only a limited number of localities (Brenner and Ramas 1984). Nevertheless, protectionist legislation provides an obvious environmental restriction on female employment that should have a measurable effect on occupational sex-typing.

Alternative Sources of Secondary Labor

The discussion thus far has assumed that there are only two kinds of workers, cheap women and expensive men. Thus, the theory of sex-typing devolves into a theory of what jobs can be filled with cheap labor. However, women are not the only source of secondary labor available to employers. An employer who is seeking inexpensive labor can hire blacks, hispanics, or local teenagers, all of whom work for less than the average white male. Some white males will also work for a marginal wage, particularly if they are unqualified, desperate, or looking for very temporary employment. Given that women do not have a monopoly on the market for cheap labor, it is necessary to specify the conditions under which secondary jobs will be given to women as opposed to members of other groups whose wages are depressed.

There are several factors that can determine whether women will be used to fill a secondary position. One consideration is the human capital requirements for the job. Some secondary jobs require few skills and little education. Others, despite their low pay, require substantial amounts of human capital. Virtually anyone can qualify to be janitor; nursing requires years of formal study and practical experience. Many workers would be unlikely to have the qualifications for the more demanding secondary positions. Juveniles can not take any position that requires advanced education; recent immigrants can not take a job that requires fluency in the host language. For many secondary jobs that require substantial human capital, women may be the only source of cheap labor having the necessary skills.

A second consideration of equal importance is the relative supply of alternative sources of labor. Many desirable sources of inexpensive labor are not available to particular employers. There are legal restrictions on certain kinds of workers. Child labor laws and school attendance requirements remove certain juveniles from the labor market entirely. Immigration policy restricts the minority labor supply. The juvenile labor supply will be affected by the availability and importance of schooling. Where higher education is open to the general public, many teenagers will voluntarily delay labor market entry in order to attain a degree. There may be regional strictures on the supply of labor as well. Very few communities aside from frontier communities have a shortage of women; however, some areas are ethnically homogenous and lack minority labor. In each of these cases, an employer may be limited in his options for filling the secondary positions within his firm. Women should be hired in those situations where alternative sources of labor are scarce.

There may be other considerations that affect the trade-off between competing secondary labor forces. The wages for these different groups are unequal. Juveniles make less than women, while the relative cost of ethnic labor depends on the amount of discrimination suffered by any particular group. The least expensive workers should be relatively more attractive to employers. Likewise, there may be differential psychic costs to employers in hiring women as opposed to hiring minorities. The theory of the competition between women and other disadvantaged groups is far less developed than the theory of competition between majority males and majority females. Nevertheless, both are important to a fully predictive theory of sex-typing.

Buffering from Labor Costs

Men are more likely to be hired into occupations in which employers are under little pressure to economize on labor costs. The prime consideration that makes women more desirable than men as employees is that women work for substantially lower wages. If wages cease to be a significant concern for management, then hiring can be based on other principles that can be either gender-blind or overtly discriminatory. Either way, fewer women will be likely to be hired under these conditions than would have been the case had the firm been trying to minimize labor costs.

There are several conditions under which employers can be released from the obligation of having to seek the cheapest possible labor. Most of these involve situations in which labor costs are relatively unimportant in determining organizational survival or rates of organizational growth. Consider the case in which labor makes up a relatively small proportion of costs within the firm. In labor-intense industries, staff expenses make up the overwhelming majority of operating costs. Employers in such firms must work aggressively to contain levels of salaries and wages or risk seriously overrunning their total budget. This problem is far less pressing for capital-intense employers. Although they may have total wage bills that are absolutely high, these expenses are relatively small compared to expenditures on raw material and technology. Technological increases in productivity or savings from obtaining cheaper sources of raw materials can all subsidize a relatively expensive staff.

The same argument holds for isolated subgroups of workers within a larger population of workers who are being managed efficiently. If an employer obtained 95 percent of his staff at the cheapest possible rates, he could afford to hire somewhat more expensive workers for the remaining 5 percent. Thus, if one could identify a set of positions that for exogenous reasons an employer might prefer to staff uneconomically with men, such positions might remain male so long as they represented such a small share of total staff that their cost would not significantly raise the total wage bill. Most firms do not control remuneration to executives with the same rigor that they control the other aspects of corporate expenditure. High salaries, generous expense accounts, and lavish fringe benefits have been justified in terms of the high productivity of top administrators. To some extent, however, the extremely generous executive remuneration found in most corporations stems from managers' choosing to reward themselves when they know that such payments will have little effect on the overall profitability of the firm.

Another case of buffering is when organizational success depends less on the conservation of costs than on other criteria of performance. A firm with a solid cost-plus contract need not worry about hiring female labor. Likewise, a firm whose profits depend on the irregular success of particular products may put all of their resources into product development and few into obtaining cheap factors of production. In Hollywood, where a single hit can finance the expenses of a studio for years, one would expect that film executives would emphasize artistic values and marketing and be less concerned with the costs of studio labor. Another example is the political organization that runs on patronage. The purpose of a patronage organization is to provide lucrative jobs for the supporters of the incumbent political party. Because of this, it is less important to economize on labor costs and more important to make salaries as attractive as possible. Women should appear in those firms that engage in price competition, and men should be hired in those firms that are protected from such considerations.

The Study of Occupational Sex-Typing

General Considerations

The preceding discussion of the theory of occupational sex-typing suggests two general conclusions. First, there are a very large number of variables that play a major role in determining the sex-type of a given occupation. Second, there are an equally large number of variables whose relationship to sex-typing is either non-existent or spurious. This implies that empirical studies of the economics of women's work need to use data of sufficient richness and detail to permit the identification of the complex historical and contextual factors that could be contributing to the determination of a particular sex-type. At the same time, the research methodology needs to be sufficiently rigorous and scientific to permit the testing of alternative hypotheses and the rejection of those variables that do not play a significant role.

In general, most of the recent research on women's work has been either historically detailed or methodologically rigorous, but rarely both. Great historical works such as Margery Davies' *Women's Place Is at the Typewriter* and Alice Kessler-Harris' *Out to Work* represent sophisticated treatments of women's economic life that are based on enormous masses of historical and archival material. These authors have, with good reason, emphasized intellectual and historical breadth rather than the niceties of social-scientific methodology. Their analyses are compelling because of the large number of examples they provide, but they rarely apply alternative models to their data to see if different perspectives provide a better explanation. In the interest of maintaining an integrated perspective, they incorporate as many variables as they can into their explanations, without attempting to test particular theories with an eye to disconfirmation so that a simpler, more parsimonious explanation can be extracted.[13] These accounts, while often convincing, leave the reader curious about how their implicit models would behave when subjected to rigorous quantitative examination.

The quantitative work on occupational sex-typing has been extremely informative, but limited in the types of questions it could address. Most of these analyses have used census data or other comparable national aggregate statistics to study inter-occupational variance in the use of women. David Snyder and Paula Hudis in the late 1970's and William Bridges in the 1980's have provided stimulating analyses using this technique. However, most national economic data do not provide information on many factors that could reasonably affect the

---

13. For an exception to this tendency, see Kessler-Harris's excellent discussion (1982) of the extent to which the impact of World War II on women's employment has been exaggerated.

feminization or de-feminization of an occupation. Union membership data are available, but little is known about which male workers accept or resist the extension of female employment. Statistical measurements of skill are available, but these hardly describe whether a given job requires upper-body strength. Salary data are available, but little is known about the effect of female employment on promotion chains or job queues. Most of the interesting questions concerning women's work require detailed information on organizational functioning that is hard to synthesize from national statistics.

An alternative strategy is to collect one's own data on the determinants of occupational sex-typing in a form readily amenable to quantitative analysis. Although it would be desirable to do this for an entire national occupational structure, in practice it is very difficult to obtain detailed information on more than a small number of related occupations at one time. In order to do sophisticated multivariate analyses, however, it is essential to have a relatively large case base. One solution to this problem is to abandon the occupation as a unit of analysis and investigate variations in the use of women within a single occupation. One can contrast firms versus firms, departments versus departments, industries versus industries, or periods versus periods, in each case contrasting those units that use men with those units that use women. The concentration on one occupation considerably simplifies the analysis, since it is far easier to grasp the underlying economics of staffing a small number of related positions than it is to understand the complexities of every single job in the economy. At the same time, the smaller units of analysis virtually force the investigator to become aware of the firm-level and workplace-level considerations that are affecting the use of women. Such immersion in the organizational micro-dynamics of the firm can produce unexpected and counterintuitive findings that can have implications for macro-level research. A study based on a single occupation does have the drawback of being of limited generalizibility. If scrupulous attention is paid to the ways in which the central occupation differs from jobs in other sectors of the economy, however, the research can suggest global propositions about sex-typing as a whole.

The Research Design

This is an organizational-level investigation of the feminization of clerical labor in Great Britain. Within the subject of occupational sex-typing, there are two reasons why clerical work is an especially important case to study. First, clerical occupations make up a very large proportion of female employment. In 1950, 15 percent of all American women worked in some sort of clerical occupation (Oppenheimer 1970). Second, clerical work is one of the few occupations that has undergone a drastic shift in sex type. In the mid-nineteenth century it was a virtually all-male occupation. Then, between the 1870's and the 1950's, it feminized so rapidly as to become virtually all female. This is a somewhat remarkable transition considering that most occupational sex types remain constant over time. Between 1960 and 1970, fewer than 25 percent of all occupations changed their sex composition by as much as 5 percent (Snyder and Hudis 1976). Clerical work represents a rare opportunity to study significant historical change in a field where most longitudinal changes are relatively trivial.

More specifically, this study is a contrast of the employment policies of two major employers of white-collar workers. One, the British General Post Office (GPO), was one of the first employers in England to use large numbers of female clerks, while the other, the Great Western Railway (GWR), was one of the last employers to maintain a clerical force that was overwhelmingly male. These particular firms are especially important because of their completely different solutions to the problem of clerical hiring. The Post Office was the lead sector of feminization (see Table 1.1). It hired its first women clerks in 1870, and by the late 1870's nearly a quarter of its clerks were female. By the onset of World War I, the Post Office was 40 percent female, and by the mid-1930's nearly half of the postal clerks were female. The Great Western Railway did not even begin to hire women clerks until 1906. It had considered hiring women in 1876, but explicitly rejected the possibility. In the pre-World War I period, while the Post Office was

Table 1.1

Percentage of All Clerks Who Were Female in the Great Western Railway and the General Post Office, Selected Dates

Date	GWR (%)	GPO (%)
1876	0	24.6
1896	0	22.0
1914	0	39.2
1933–36	16.2	46.6

Source: GPO Establishment Books (1857–1937); GWR Women (1906); GWR Staff Census (1933).

feminizing dramatically, the railway hired only a handful of women. The war period significantly increased the GWR's use of women so that, by 1924, 16 percent of all GWR clerks were women, but this number remained virtually fixed throughout the next fifteen years, so that by World War II, despite the national trends, the Great Western Railway still filled five out of six of its clerical positions with men.

The General Post Office and the Great Western Railway are typical of the behavior of the civil service and of railways overall. Table 1.2 shows the percentage of clerks who were female in various industries in Britain in 1901 and 1921. Following the example of the Post Office, the British civil service and local authorities feminized fairly rapidly. At the turn of the century, the public sector was the only industry in Britain whose clerical force was more than one quarter female. Many important clerical employers, such as insurance and banking, had not begun to feminize at all. By 1920, most of the private sector had caught up with government. A conspicuous exception was railways. The railways had hired no female clerks during the nineteenth century, and even after World War I they continued to be alone in maintaining a clerical force that was more than 85 percent male.[14, 15]

In order to test competing theories of occupational sex-typing systematically, it is necessary to go beyond a simple comparison of these firms. Because only two cases are being considered, it would be easy to identify many empirical differences between the Great Western Railway and the General Post Office and link them in some convoluted fashion to the use of men or women clerks. To differentiate effectively between the valid and invalid explanations, it is necessary to consider additional data. One strategy for doing this is to examine internal differences within each case. Each firm had several semi-autonomous

14. The London and Northwestern Railway experimented with hiring women in the 1870's, but seems to have abandoned the project soon thereafter (GWR Women 1906).

15. American industries closely resemble British industries in their history of using women clerks. The federal government was the first employer to hire women clerks. Women were introduced to the Treasury Department in 1862; by 1870, no other private employers had yet begun to hire female clerks, although the practice had spread to other federal offices (U.S. Bureau of the Census 1870; Aron 1980). By the 1930's, private industry had caught up with the public sector, and as was the case with Britain, government had an average ratio of males to females. Railways, however, lagged considerably behind. In 1930, fewer than 20 percent of all rail clerks were female, despite the fact that nationally the clerical force was 55 percent female (U.S. Bureau of the Census 1930).

Table 1.2
Percentage of All Clerks who were Female in Selected Industries
in England and Wales, in 1901 and 1921

Industry	1901 (%)	1921 (%)
Government	27	29
Commerce	15	37
Law	0	37
Insurance	0	37
Banking	0	26
Rail	0	13
Total	14	39

Source: Adapted from Klingender (1935).

departments with extremely different functions and technologies. These departments were responsible for setting their own hiring policies, with central intervention occurring only on a limited basis.

Furthermore, there is time-series data for each of the departments in the study. For the Post Office, there are observations of the percentage of females in each department for every year from 1857 to 1937. This is a remarkably continuous body of data that one rarely finds at the organizational level. For economy's sake, this study uses fifteen panels, spaced roughly five years apart, giving over three hundred usable observations. The railway data are almost as detailed. Since the GWR hired women in substantial numbers only after 1914, the only period of interest for departmental contrasts is the 1914–39 period. Although there are data available for many of these years, the use of women by the various departments is relatively constant over time. Therefore, the study confines itself to one year for which there are exceptionally good data: 1933. In this year, the Great Western Railway took a census of its entire staff, which provides department-by-department summaries of sex ratios, grade levels, and pay rates. This can be combined with the Great Western Railway staff chart of the same year, which provides sex ratios, grade levels, and detailed job descriptions for virtually every clerical work group within each department of the railway. This study will use both departmental and office-level railway data to test the theories suggested by the larger two-case comparison.[16]

16. See Appendix A for details of each sample.

This quantitative data can be supplemented by an unusually rich stock of archival materials drawn from the records of each firm. The papers of both the Post Office and the Great Western Railway have been preserved by the British government and are available for inspection at Post Office headquarters and the Public Record Office. These two main collections are remarkably intact, even by the relatively high standards of British industrial archives, and include the correspondence, reports, budget estimates, and memos that preceded most of the critical managerial decisions concerning female employment. These are combined with a wealth of material on the normal operation of the various departments within each firm that allows for the uncovering of the relationship between gender policies, personnel problems, and the concrete concerns of daily administration. Furthermore, there are several smaller archives that contain important additional material. The records of the unions of each firm have survived, as well as newspaper accounts of the major strike actions. Parliament made several investigations into both postal and railway operations and published detailed reports on the labor dynamics of each firm in the House of Commons Sessional Papers. Thus, the statistical analysis can be grounded in the historical context of the times; those hypotheses that are suggested by regression analysis can be validated from the actual writings of managers and observers who were intimately familiar with the operation of the firms.

The Historical Background: The Great Western Railway

Because these organizations are relatively unknown to the American reader, some background material on both firms is provided to clarify the material that follows. The Great Western Railway was an extremely large and successful railway that operated the line connecting London with Bristol, South Wales, and the West of England. The system has always been one of the largest in Britain, and effectively dominated inland transport over a significant portion of England. In the 1920's, it controlled as a subsidiary holding every coal railway and coal-loading dock in southern Wales; all the coal that was shipped out of South Wales after 1921 was transported on some form of Great Western facility. The scope of the Great Western Railway is best appreciated in the light of the events following 1921, when the British government consolidated all the private railways in the country into four private regional cartels. In most cases, this was done to eliminate the inefficiencies of duplication, and most of the holding companies consisted of the merger of two or three major systems. The western region, however, consisted of the Great Western Railway by itself. Although certain smaller lines were incorporated with amalgamation, the GWR had such hegemony over its region that the changes induced by the granting of a territorial monopoly were negligible (Nock 1964; Aldcroft 1968). The GWR was also a major manufacturer. It built most of its own locomotives and rolling stock and rolled many of its own rails. To this end, it operated an enormous complex of factories in Swindon, a rail junction in rural southwestern England. An additional minor holding was a chain of large hotels located near the major metropolitan depots. Furthermore, at various times, the GWR dabbled in bus transport, trucking, and shipping.

Railways represent the vanguard of modern-day business administration. As Alfred Chandler has argued quite cogently, railroads were the first corporations to hire large numbers of people in geographical settings that were dispersed over a number of widely scattered physical locations. Funds had to be collected from stations located all up and down the lines and safely delivered and accounted for at central headquarters in London. The enormous potential for fraud and embezzlement implicit in widely decentralized work settings was countered by the early development of a sophisticated coordinated system of financial checks and balances. Most of the modern bookkeeping and accounting procedures that we now view as the basis of sound business practice were first developed by the railways in response to their geographical vulnerability (Pollard 1965; Chandler 1977). Since an integrated accounting system required a clerical force to implement it, by the 1840's the Great Western Railway had become a national pioneer in developing a large, efficient, highly centralized administrative and clerical staff. Most of these employees were located in the company headquarters at Paddington Station, London. However, a substantial minority was located in the Chief Mechanical Engineer's Department in Swindon to deal with the western accounts, and many others were scattered among depots all over southern England and Wales.

Although the GWR was large and relatively monopolistic, it must not be thought that it was entirely free from the pressure to run efficiently or conserve on costs. Throughout the nineteenth century, it was perpetually fighting off challenges from aspiring competitors to siphon off traffic onto other lines. The traffic for the southwest of England was evenly divided between the GWR and the London and Southwestern Railway, while the London and Northwestern Railway built numerous feeders into GWR territory. The GWR had to engage in fare competition and invest substantially in subsidiary lines in order to defend its market against these rivals (Nock 1963; Macdermot 1964; Pollins 1971).

By the twentieth century, the GWR's position relative to rail competitors was essentially secured. However, maturity brought a new and far more devastating set of problems. The development of road transport created the defection of business to busses, trucks, and private cars, all of which operated with significantly lower levels of overhead. The demand for shipping declined even further with the slowing of the British economy, and the depression of the 1920's and 1930's especially lowered freight traffic. At the same time, operating costs began to rise significantly. Railway unions became established in the late nineteenth century and exerted a great deal of pressure on wages throughout the twentieth century. Furthermore, the physical capital of most lines had depreciated, requiring ever-increasing amounts of investment in order to maintain the quality of service. The result was that the railways became a high-cost provider of transport services in a period of declining market share (Nock 1964; Aldcroft 1968). Although the Great Western Railway enjoyed some competitive advantages relative to other railways, it was affected by these same adverse industry-wide trends and had to manage aggressively in order to preserve an ever-shrinking margin of profitability.

The Historical Background: The Post Office

The Post Office is one of the few bureaucracies that actually precedes the railways. Mail delivery has existed in England since the Renaissance. However, the nineteenth century gave rise to an expansion of national mail services that far outstripped the rate of change that had gone before. Part of this increase can be attributed to the Industrial Revolution and the general growth of commercial communication. However, the Post Office contributed to this expansion itself by dramatically dropping the price of postage in the 1840's. Furthermore, in the late nineteenth century, a wide variety of new functions were assigned to the Post Office. Its financial role was expanded by the addition of a money order system and the creation of a national postal savings bank. In the late nineteenth century, the Post Office expanded into telecommunications as well, as Parliament granted it a national monopoly on both telegraph and telephone service. The telegraph service was nationalized in the 1860's and the phone service in the 1890's. The Post Office became responsible for the construction, maintenance, and day-to-day operation of these services. As a result, the postal labor force became extremely diversified. Mail delivery required a staff of postmen and sorters, with a modest supporting staff of clerks. The financial divisions trebled the demand for accounting personnel, while the telegraph and telephone divisions created a demand for engineers, linemen, construction workers, telegraph signallers, messengers, and telephone operators. The rapid popular acceptance of both telegraphs and telephones led to dramatic growth in each of these divisions, while a simultaneous increase in the volume of mail produced a parallel although smaller growth in the more traditional postal occupations (GPO Establishment Books 1857–1937; Cohen 1941; Gladden 1967).

Like the Great Western Railway, the Post Office enjoyed some protection from price competition; however, it was still under pressure to conserve costs. The Post Office enjoyed a monopoly of mail, telegraph, and postal communications, which were under no significant pressure from alternative services. Furthermore, because the Post Office was a division of the British government, it could count on public subsidies if required to make up any financial shortfalls. Nevertheless, postal administrators still had to be budget conscious. Only a portion of total postal expenditures was financed by user fees, such as the sale of postage stamps. The remainder had to be requisitioned from the legislature, and Parliament was often reluctant to provide too generous a subsidy. To ensure that postal operations did not produce too great a drain on public revenues, a major check was provided on spending by placing the Post Office under the fiscal control of the Treasury. Every matter of postal policy that implied a change, either positive or negative, in the level of spending, had to be approved by the Treasury. In practice, the Treasury used its veto power frequently. In general, the Treasury rarely objected to technical considerations in the provision of service; the primary ground of contention was cost. Therefore, a major stage of the implementation of any innovation was the development of a proposal that would be financially acceptable to the Treasury authorities, and no staffing decision could be made without precise and defensible estimates of the implication of the new policy for overall costs. The tendency of the Treasury routinely to reject proposals introduced significant financial discipline into postal affairs.[17]

17. A second source of fiscal review came from Parliament itself. Parliament routinely held committee hearings on the postal budget and operations, in which the

Preliminary Considerations

The very nature of the cases being compared rules out certain preliminary explanations of clerical feminization. It would be difficult to argue that clerical work feminized as an automatic response by employers to the presence of cheap female labor. The staffing patterns of the Post Office are consistent with such a claim, but those of the Great Western Railway are not. Despite the availability of women clerks, the GWR waited thirty years before feminizing, and even then used female clerks sparingly. Labor supply can also be ruled out as an explanation for differences in these cases. Both firms recruited from almost identical labor markets. Both firms were hiring from 1870 to 1940 and both firms were headquartered in central London. Both firms also maintained a series of branch offices throughout Britain, in similar although not identical locations. The Post Office hired throughout Britain, while the Great Western Railway hired primarily in southern England and Wales. However, regional factors do not seem to have had any effect on hiring. The London offices of each firm show precisely the same differences in the propensity to use women that are found in the national organizations overall. Furthermore, differences in local labor markets do not seem to have had any effect on sex-typing within each organization. There were no significant regional differences in hiring within the Post Office. There were modest differences between English and Welsh offices in the Great Western Railway, but these invariably disappear when the substantive variables of the analysis are introduced. The distinctive hiring patterns of the Great Western Railway and the General Post Office were created by the firms themselves, not by the external supply of labor.

The reader should be aware that the clerical force employed by these firms was somewhat more diverse than is the case for the average office. These offices used large numbers of traditional clerks, but the Post Office employed a significant number of mail sorters, telegraph signallers, and telephone operators as well. Most commercial offices have used a handful of such workers. Most offices maintained mail-

administration would be expected to justify its expenditures. In practice, this was sometimes an easier forum than the Treasury, because fiscal conservatives were often counterbalanced with members whose primary concern was with the level of services provided. Nevertheless, many legislators were primarily concerned with reducing government expenditures, and parliamentary votes show significant opposition to a number of costly postal bills, in particular those that would have increased the level of wages.

rooms and telephone switchboards; in the nineteenth century, some firms had private telegraph lines for their most urgent communications. Nevertheless, the Post Office had a massive concentration of sorters, signallers, and operators that would have dwarfed the requirements of most private firms. This somewhat specialized labor force makes the so-called "clerks" of the postal analysis not at all comparable with the population of a modern office.

These additional workers provide an important analytical opportunity to test competing theories of clerical feminization. Each of these three types of exceptional workers differed from the more traditional clerks in important ways: the telegraphists were highly unionized; the sorters were in departments that were particularly prone to political manipulation; and the telephone operators had unusually low promotion opportunities. By systematically comparing these workers with those in more truly clerical offices, we can isolate the effects of unionization, patronage, and promotion chains in promoting clerical feminization. The semi-clerical workers increase the power of large sample tests using postal data by providing a larger range of variance in the independent variables. Including these extra occupations carries with it a small cost in generalizability; employers with a purely clerical force might not be subject to some of the processes observable in the periphery of this sample.[18]

The discussion that follows does not take the form of the theoretical discussion in the first part of this introduction. Rather, the main findings of the empirical analysis are laid out in terms of their own internal logic and then linked to the larger theory at the end of each chapter. In Chapter 2, the interrelation between the use of women and the need to conserve on clerical costs is explored. This leads to a two-part discussion in Chapters 3 and 4 of the relation between skill, internal labor markets, and female employment; Chapter 3 discusses the role of de-skilling in clerical feminization, while Chapter 4 provides a more broad-based attack on human capital theory. Chapter 5 discusses normative and ideological limitations on female employment and how they were related to exogenous economic needs. Chapters 6 and 7 provide a two-part discussion of the relationship between occupational sex-typing and class conflict; Chapter 6 describes the role of male unionists in determining sex type, and Chapter 7 describes the

18. For further details of the occupational base of this sample, see Appendix B.

extent to which women were used as a source of labor control. Chapter 8 describes the relationship between female employment and the availability of alternative sources of secondary labor. Chapter 9 restates the main findings of the analysis and discusses their implications for a larger theory of occupational sex-typing.

2

Buffering from Labor Costs

The last chapter argued that men are more likely to be hired into occupations in which employers are significantly buffered from having to economize on labor costs. In order to understand the rationale for this prediction, we need to consider the interrelation between patriarchy and the economic needs of employers.

Maintaining patriarchy is a secondary utility for employers. A secondary utility is a goal that an actor would like to attain but that can be overridden by more important concerns. For most employers, their primary goal is assuring the economic viability and profitability of their firms. For managers, secondary utilities might be the preservation of executive expense accounts, upgrading the food served in the company cafeteria, or providing corporate sponsorship for the arts. These goals are not essential to the economic well-being of the firm, although they may have mildly positive consequences for organizational functioning. As long as the company grows at a healthy rate, few people would question the allocation of funds for these peripheral projects. If these side activities came into serious conflict with the survival of the firm, however, most managers would eliminate the budget line for these items and concentrate their resources on more immediate needs.

Discrimination is a secondary utility for management when it does not provide an immediate economic return. There are certainly occasions when a policy of not hiring women is profitable, as would be suggested by many of the arguments in the introduction. Nevertheless, it is clear that many employers are openly sexist and would simply prefer not to work with women. There are several forms such overt sexism can take.

Some managers have moral objections to hiring women. They sin-

36

cerely believe that women should remain in the home, and they are reluctant to participate in arrangements that they perceive as having deleterious effects on the family. Other employers are concerned with preserving male employment; they don't wish to hire women when men have no jobs. In both cases, the manager in question is purchasing a public good; he is using corporate resources to maintain patriarchy in the rest of society. This is a secondary expenditure comparable to any other form of corporate philanthropy, albeit for a somewhat more questionable goal.

Other employers believe that women are inferior employees. As the examples below will show, managers in the Great Western Railway and the Post Office certainly perceived women as being sickly, physically frail, and incapable of performing tasks requiring intellectual sophistication or training.[1] While many of these statements can be dismissed as rationalizations, it would be hard to deny that the image many employers had of women was extremely negative and that these stereotypes exist to the present day. If women were in fact inferior employees, then the secondary utility argument would not hold; not hiring women would be consistent with a bona fide need to staff the organization with the most productive employees available. However, since women and men are equally productive in virtually every setting, these beliefs are the product of imperfect information. When managers consistently operate on the basis of faulty information, this suggests that their data collection and research has been less than authoritative and complete. Thus, the persistence of sexist beliefs among managers often reflects the secondary utility of not wanting to invest resources in obtaining accurate data about male and female capabilities.

A third form of sexism is the unwillingness by males to interact professionally with females. Rosabeth Moss Kanter has argued compellingly that managers prefer to surround themselves with colleagues

---

1. Citing all the cases I have found of managerial criticisms of women workers would be tedious and uninformative. The reader seeking particularly flagrant examples of belief in feminine frailty will find plenty of material in the writings of British civil service medical advisers. A good published source for these is the testimony given by medical personnel at the 1914 McDonagh Commission hearings. The 1881 Telegraph Controller's Report on the use of women for telegraph work contains an extensive discussion by local management of the physiological incapacity of women to work long distance lines (Telegraph Substitution 1880; McDonagh 1912–13).

similar to themselves. Employers prefer social interactions that are routine and unstrained; they attempt to achieve this by filling their environment with workers whose background is similar to their own. This provides a comparability of personal style that eliminates awkward "cross-cultural" contacts (Kanter 1977). This concern with homophily is an obvious secondary utility.

There is a last secondary utility that is germane to the exclusion of women that is not explicitly sexist in nature. Some employers might have resisted feminization because this would have produced administratively inconvenient changes in what was an otherwise satisfactory situation. The transition from an all-male to a mixed labor force does entail a number of minor adjustments. Rest facilities will have to be reallocated, or possibly redesigned. New sets of pay and benefit schedules will have to be developed. Offices and personnel may have to be reshuffled, especially if the women are expected to be segregated. None of these obstacles are especially time-consuming or difficult to overcome. However, managers are human, which means they are lazy. Delays in feminization may have been the product of procrastination and a concern with avoiding the nuisances associated with any type of major personnel change.

Firms can tolerate policies that are not in their best interests so long as the costs of such policies are reasonably contained. The best analysis of such suboptimalities comes from the work of the decision theorists. The decision theorists argued that firms do not attempt to maximize profits but merely to satisfice them. The rationale for this is that managerial energy and attention are not unlimited. Employers tend to work on a small set of problems at a time and turn their attention to other matters only as needed. This sequential problem-solving implies that many organizational matters are relatively neglected until they deteriorate into major crises: these crises produce dramatic interventions and responses by management, which in turn distract attention from yet another subset of problems. The result is that those matters that are central to organizational growth are often perceived as being at unsatisfactory levels and are constantly upgraded, while more secondary matters are administered in a relatively inefficient and negligent fashion (Simon 1957; Cyert and March 1963).

The cost of discriminating against women is a labor force that is overly expensive. Such a policy can be tolerated if labor costs are a relatively unimportant factor in determining organizational survival. There are a number of situations in which employers are buffered from the need to minimize labor costs. An important example is when firms are capital-intense. Although such firms may hire a large number of workers, their expenses are relatively small compared to their expenditures on raw material and technology. Such firms can afford to hire males if the extra labor costs are absorbed by savings in the management of the capital budget. No such subsidies are available for the labor-intense firm. Most of the working budget is committed to paying for personnel; the slightest upward drift in wages will have an immediate impact on overall operating costs. Therefore labor-intense firms should take advantage of every form of staff economy available, which implies an increased willingness to employ female labor.

This hypothesis has an obvious implication for the two firms in this study, the Great Western Railway and the General Post Office. The Great Western Railway was extremely capital-intensive, with its heavy investments in locomotives, rolling stock, permanent way, stations, and both the machinery and the raw materials used in the locomotive factory. The Post Office was far more labor-intensive. Mail delivery was virtually unmechanized; the telephone and telegraph services required surprisingly small amounts of physical plant relative to the armies of signallers and operators and required virtually no expenditure on raw materials. As would be expected, the labor force of the Great Western Railway was overwhelmingly male, while the General Post Office was heavily female.

Employers may also choose to hire men for certain occupations if these occupations make up a relatively small percentage of the total labor force. Just as high labor costs can be subsidized by efficient capital management, high labor costs for a minority of workers can be subsidized by efficient management of the majority. This principle has an important implication for clerical work. Clerical work should be more likely to be female in firms in which office work makes up a relatively large proportion of the total labor force. There should be a larger proportion of males in the clerical force of firms whose overall labor forces are blue collar. The Great Western Railway and General Post Office fit this pattern as well. The Great Western Railway hired mostly manual workers to run the trains, maintain the lines, and staff the factories. Clerical workers made up a far greater proportion of the General Post Office, which hired massive numbers of sorters, telegraphists, and telephone operators as well as pure clerks. The clerical force of the Great Western Railway was male while the clerical force of the General Post Office was female.

Another type of buffering occurs when organizational success depends less on the conservation of costs than on other criteria of performance. Most firms cannot allow their total overhead to become excessive; however, there are cases when objective criteria of economic efficiency become irrelevant to organizational survival and functioning. An important example is an organization run by patronage. The purpose of patronage is to provide lucrative jobs for supporters of the current political regime. Because of this, salaries are expected to be generous. Political hiring not only makes the savings from hiring women irrelevant, but it may disqualify women from employment totally if the administration decides to concentrate its rewards among its male followers. In general, the Post Office was not a patronage organization; however, there were particular offices and particular periods in which politics did interfere with the hiring process. An internal examination of the use of women within the Post Office clearly shows the impact of patronage in reducing female employment.

Four types of evidence will be presented to support the buffering model that has been presented here. First, the model will be used to account for variance within each organization in the use of female clerks. Longitudinally and cross-sectionally, men should appear in the least clerical-labor-intense departments and in those offices subject to political hiring. Second, the Post Office will be shown to be quantitatively more clerical-labor-intense than was the Great Western Railway. This difference in cost structure will be shown to outweigh the competing pressure from the small sector of the Post Office that was politically buffered. Third, it will be shown that managers sought to exclude women from their offices. This theory places the prime responsibility for excluding women upon management. If the historical record showed managers doings everything within their power to feminize, but being prevented by some sort of environmental pressure, then the buffering model would be incorrect. The arguments presented here claim that managers chose not to hire women due to their own personal preferences for a male labor force. Thus, there must be clear evidence of exclusionary sentiments among employers.[2] Fourth, non-clerical-labor-intense offices will be shown to be relatively inefficient in the handling of clerical matters not related to hiring. Most economic theories are based on the maximizing profitability and minimizing cost. This model follows decision theory in arguing that managers merely "satisfice" these utilities; they only reduce costs to levels that will avoid a crisis in profitability. Materialists should always exercise caution in using models that explicitly posit some level of non-rationality. What the analyst views as being inherently irrational may upon subsequent examination be discovered to have a sound economic base. If the hiring of men in non-clerical-labor-intense offices is the product of inattention to economic detail, this inattention should be manifest in a large number of areas besides hiring decisions. Record-keeping, office procedures, and the organization of the division of labor should all show signs of carelessness, neglect, and objectively low levels of operating efficiency.

Intra-Organizational Variance

In general, women were extremely underrepresented in offices that were not clerical-labor-intensive. Very few women worked in engineering, storehouse, or warehouse offices. Each of these administered a large number of factory workers and warehousemen. Women did not sort mail, because the same officers that administered mail-sorting also administered the mail carriers, a large blue-collar labor force. Women rarely did the clerical work in railway depots. The stationmasters in charge of the booking clerks also controlled the operating staff of the railway stations, an enormous force of freight loaders, train drivers, signalmen, and rail switchmen. The clerks were a very small proportion of the station staff.

Women appeared in very large numbers in the departments whose specialty was paperwork. Among the heavily female offices were financial offices, such as accounting offices, the Money Order Department, and the Postal Savings Bank. The labor forces in paper-collecting offices such as record registries and the Returned Letter Office were all primarily female.

Within the Post Office, an illustrative contrast can be made between, on one hand, the Telegraph and Telephone Departments and, on the other, the Engineering Department. All three departments

2. Note that, for the theory to apply, the amount of sexism need not vary across departments in any systematic way. The claim is not that clerical-labor-intense employers are intrinsically less opposed to women, but rather that such employers are organizationally less capable of acting on their non-economic preferences.

were involved in the general business of telecommunications. Both the telephone and telegraph services required extensive quantities of both capital and labor: a nationwide system of transmitting equipment and wiring with which to send messages, and a large force of signallers or operators with which to work the system. The Post Office bifurcated the administration of these systems, with responsibility for physical plant entrusted to the engineers and labor management entrusted to the telephone and telegraph departments. The engineers predominantly used male clerks. The telephone and telegraph clerks were overwhelmingly female.

This impressionistic account can be supported by more rigorous quantitative tests. Data for the analysis of the Great Western Railway come from their staff censuses. As we saw in Chapter 1, before World War I so few women were hired that there was no variance between departments in their sex composition. After World War I, departmental sex ratios were virtually constant. Therefore, the analysis considers only one panel: 1933. Departments were subdivided into the headquarters, the divisional offices, and the staff working in depots. Each of these subsections was treated as a separate unit.

There are two measures used for clerical labor intensity. The first is the ratio of clerks to total staff within each department. This is a literal measure of the degree to which clerks dominate the total budget for labor. As expected, this ratio varies inversely with capital costs: the departments with obvious raw material and physical plant expenses have very low clerk/staff ratios.

The second measure classifies the observed unit into office buildings or depots. The major concentrations of the blue-collar staff on the railway were found in depots. Even though the clerical staff in the depots could be large, it was always dwarfed by the operating staff. Most depot managers would have thus concerned themselves largely with blue-collar matters. The headquarters and divisional offices contained the clerical-labor-intense enclaves of the department, the central bookkeeping offices being an example. Thus we would expect to find lower percentages of female clerks in the depots, despite the clerical labor intensity of the whole department.

Table 2.1 shows that both measures are effective predictors of the percentage of clerks that are female. The zero-order correlations with the dependent variable are .43 for the percentage of clerical workers and −.46 for being a depot. When combined, the two variables explain almost 30 percent of the variance after adjusting for the small sample size. Both coefficients are significant at the .03 level. Overall, then, the clerical-labor-intensity model seems to be supported by the railway data.

The Post Office data come from the Postal Establishment Books. The sample consists of those years for which there were women hired by the Post Office: 1876 to 1936. The postal analysis uses two measures of buffering from labor costs. The first is the clerk/staff ratio that was used for the railway analysis. The second is the degree to which hiring was done on an economic rather than a political basis.

Before 1870, most civil service positions, including those in the Post Office, were filled by patronage. Members of Parliament and other notables would receive the right to nominate various individuals for government posts. Since government jobs were designed to be political rewards as well as positions of responsibility, salaries were set at fairly high levels, usually substantially above prevailing market rates. For comparable reasons, job holders were also given lifetime job security. It should be no surprise that, before 1870, the Post Office never made any attempt to feminize.

The patronage era came to a partial end in 1870, when a major program of civil service reform was instituted. There had been extensive parliamentary agitation for the abolition of patronage throughout the 1850's and 1860's, sponsored by such reformers as Sir Stafford Northcote and Sir Charles Trevelyan. In 1870, a set of Orders in Council were passed that completely overhauled recruitment proce-

Table 2.1

Regressions of Selected Variables on the Percentage of Female to Total Clerks in The Great Western Railway, 1933

Model	Clerk/staff	Depot	Adjusted R^2
Clerk/Staff Only	.176 (.018)	—	.16
Depot Only	—	−14.2 (.011)	.18
Both	.148 (.031)	−12.3 (.020)	.29

Note: $N = 30$. The Top figure is the unstandardized regression coefficient. The lower figure is the significance level.

dures for civil service jobs; the nomination system was abandoned in favor of a system of nationwide, open, competitive examinations (Cohen 1941; Richards 1963; Gladden 1967). Subsequently, new hiring was based on the relatively economic criteria of merit, *except* in the case of offices involved in the sorting of mail. Here patronage continued, albeit at reduced levels, until its demise in the 1890's (Hanham 1960; Richards 1963).

It is significant that, the very year that the Orders in Council were passed, the Post Office began to hire women. Furthermore, the period of the most rapid feminization of the Post Office was the 1870's. Some of this was purely coincidental. In 1868, the Post Office absorbed the private telegraph companies. The introduction of female telegraphists in 1870 was in response to a shortage of trained male telegraph operators (Scudamore 1871). In 1870, the Accountant General's Office began hiring women and in six years had become nearly 15 percent female. In 1872, the Returned Letter Department introduced women, and thereafter it feminized so dramatically that merely four years later it was 48 percent female. In 1875, the Savings Bank introduced women, and in 1876 a new Postal Order Division was created that was virtually all-female. These were all departments that were vigorously growing in both the 1860's and the 1870's. Before the Orders in Council, new positions had been filled with male political appointees, but after 1870 new openings were filled with women.

There was a second form of political hiring that affected women's opportunities. This was the use of government positions to support the unemployment policies of the welfare state. In the early twentieth century, the British government was advocating National Unemployment Exchanges and preferential hiring for veterans. In each case, the government decided to act as a model employer and itself reserve a substantial number of positions for both registered exchange users and veterans. Nearly all of the reserved openings were for postmen and sorters, including both permanent positions and the seasonal positions used for the Christmas rush. These political considerations undoubtedly restricted women's access to employment as sorters. Throughout the entire 1857–1940 period, sorting remained an all-male occupation. In 1912, the Huddersfield postmaster experimented with using women to assist with sorting during the Christmas pressure. He reported that the women performed their duties completely capably and at costs substantially below those associated with temporary male labor. His superiors ordered him to dismiss the women immediately. They acknowledged that using women was cost-efficient, but it would undermine the official policy of giving these positions to male labour exchange candidates (Christmas Pressure 1912).

In 1921, the Post Office systematically considered the future of female employment within the department. A substantial number of temporary women had been hired to replace men serving in the armed forces. The government had to develop a systematic policy as to whether such temporary women would be allowed to staff any of the permanent positions that had previously been held by men. Among the most important areas that had been feminized during the war had been mail sorting. The central administration avoided making any commitments about women in general. Women were to be used in situations where female employment was "appropriate." However, the relevant committees did make one consistent policy recommendation: that it was important to give some preferential consideration to the claims of ex-servicemen. Subsequently, the Post Office dismissed all of the women who had worked as mail sorters during the war. This created a manpower shortage that was partially filled by exams that were open to veterans only. The remaining vacancies were filled with an open all-male exam similar to those normally used for sorting recruitment (Whitley Council 1919; Ex-servicemen's Employment 1921). The national campaign to provide for ex-servicemen undoubtedly contributed to the de-feminization of post-war sorting. By removing economic criteria from hiring from some positions not only was a special enclave created for male hires but the general disregard for cost efficiency was extended to other positions in the department. The non-veterans' positions could have been filled with women. However, the administration exploited the laxity encouraged by veterans' hires to indulge their uneconomic pre-war male preference.

The measure of economic hiring is an adjusted estimated percentage of jobs that are recruited by open competitive hiring. Before the Orders in Council, this percentage is assumed to be zero. For all offices that were created after the Orders in Council, the score is 100 percent. For other offices, this figure is the percentage of all employees that were hired after 1870. This figure is adjusted for sorting offices to reflect those positions whose sex composition was determined by welfare state considerations.[3]

---

3. The percentage of post-1870 hires was estimated by calculating the number of employees working in 1870 and then estimating retirements per year based on Post Office actuarial data (War Cabinet 1919). The average male postal career was approx-

One control variable was added, namely the percentage of non-entry-level jobs in each department. Most writers on occupational sex-typing argue persuasively that women are confined to jobs with low pay and status. As Chapter 4 will show, in both the Post Office and the Great Western Railway, women were disproportionately represented in entry-level jobs, for reasons that are different from those discussed here. The percentage of high-status jobs was measured by the percentage of positions attainable only through promotion.[4]

The analysis is presented for each panel separately. Such a presentation is somewhat unwieldly when compared with pooled equations, but it possesses a number of statistical advantages. It is absolutely free from autocorrelated error and allows for the most explicit delineation of period effects. This removes most of the time-based disturbances that distort pooled ordinary least squares analyses of cross-sectional time-series data.[5]

There are two types of findings presented in Table 2.2: those that are essentially the same in all periods and those that change over time. The first general finding is that the model does a good job in explaining the variance within each panel in the use of women clerks. The adjusted R^2 is greater than .30 in every period, and in most of the early twentieth century it is over .50. Second, both the control variable, percentage of non-entry jobs, and the substantive variable, percentage of non-

imately forty years in length. In each year from 1871 to 1910, one fortieth of the number of workers in 1870 were estimated to have retired. Once the number of survivors was calculated, it was possible to calculate the percentage of staff not in this survivor pool. In sorting offices, all postmen were coded as having been hired through political channels. Other occupations were treated normally. This overestimates the political hiring of postmen, but underestimates the political hiring of sorters, providing a roughly accurate overall score.

4. This control was also included in the preliminary analyses of the GWR. As Chapter 4 shows, on the railway men were ten times more likely than women to hold non-entry-level jobs. However, this control does not predict office sex composition in this case. Due to the high percentage of male clerks overall, low-status offices contain large numbers of low-status male clerks along with the women. This weakens the ecological relation between status levels and gender.

5. The analysis begins in 1876. The Establishment Books generally reflect hiring practices two years before the observed date. This is because there was bureaucratic delay in formalizing and recording staffing levels. Typically, when new employees would be hired, they would not be recorded in the Establishment Books until the details of their long-term salary scales were determined. Thus the first observation point in the data that contains women is 1876, rather than 1871.

Table 2.2
*Regressions of Selected Variables on the Percentage of Female
to Total Clerks in the British Post Office by Date*

	Zero order correlations			Regression coefficients from quadrivariate equation				
Date	% non-political	Clerk/ staff	% non-entry	% non-political	Clerk/ staff	% non-entry	Ad-justed R^2	N
1876	.46	−.05	−.44	.572 (.000)	−.051 (.766)	−.794 (.001)	.58	19
1881	.33	.20	−.45	.313 (.021)	.241 (.071)	.474 (.006)	.36	24
1886	.43	.25	−.44	.581 (.005)	.235 (.138)	−.727 (.002)	.46	23
1891	.31	.27	−.46	.588 (.085)	.214 (.271)	−.626 (.026)	.32	15
1896	.30	.36	−.49	.411 (.038)	.212 (.116)	−.618 (.002)	.42	25
1901	.31	.37	−.38	.400 (.107)	.305 (.084)	−.619 (.012)	.31	24
1906	.35	.33	−.41	.451 (.169)	.339 (.213)	−.629 (.007)	.31	25
1911	.41	.45	−.46	.481 (.053)	.417 (.024)	−.676 (.000)	.52	25
1914	.41	.51	−.48	.461 (.067)	.504 (.005)	−.741 (.000)	.56	30
1918	.45	.56	−.48	.466 (.063)	.543 (.003)	−.924 (.000)	.59	30
1921	.48	.55	−.47	.515 (.044)	.504 (.011)	−.900 (.000)	.57	29
1926	.40	.51	−.42	.572 (.168)	.538 (.034)	−.789 (.107)	.43	20
1931	.44	.51	−.42	.622 (.120)	.541 (.041)	−.828 (.016)	.46	19
1936	.56	.34	−.44	1.204 (.047)	−.123 (.794)	−.762 (.041)	.44	13

Note: The top figure is the unstandardized regression coefficient. The bottom figure is the significance level.

political hiring, perform as expected. In most cases, the zero-order correlations with the dependent variable are in excess of .40, and the regression coefficients are highly significant.

The behavior of clerical labor intensity is somewhat more complex. The size and significance of the coefficients for this variable increase monotonically over time. In the nineteenth century, clerical labor intensity is a weak predictor of sex composition, the raw correlations being only in the twenties, with the regression coefficients being insignificant. By 1911, however, the effect of clerical labor intensity has doubled, with the regression coefficients being both significant and strong.[6]

The steady increase in the predictive power of clerical labor intensity reflects the slow implementation of cost efficiency in the Post Office. In the nineteenth century, there was no tidy relationship between office economics and sex composition because sex composition was determined in part by pre-existing policies of patronage. Every office contained a number of male employees hired before 1870 who were doing jobs that might otherwise have been done by women. The number of these holdovers declined steadily throughout the nineteenth century until they disappeared completely in 1911. The strength of the clerical labor-intensity coefficient directly reflects the decline of this confounding factor; as the hiring policies of the Post Office increasingly came to resemble those of the private sector, clerical labor intensity increasingly affected sex-typing.

These equations show a consistent correlation between clerical labor intensity and sex-typing. However, there has been little evidence presented to rule out alternative interpretations of this data. Women were relatively underrepresented in sorting offices, engineering offices, factory offices, and depots. There could be some other distinctive quality about these offices that may have contributed to excluding women.

The most plausible alternative explanations of the clerical-labor-intensity correlation involve the presence of physical labor, manual laborers, or unusual skills. It could be that the non-clerical-labor-intense offices involved some sort of dirty or physical work. Women might not work in factories or depots because such clerks might be

---

6. An exception to this trend is 1936. There are severe missing-data problems with this panel, producing an N of only 13.

expected to do non-clerical tasks as part of their duties. Second, working in non-clerical-labor-intense offices might involve social contact with blue-collar workers. Males employers might have kept women from such positions out of a paternalistic sense of gentility and class prejudice. Finally, it could be that non-clerical-labor-intensive offices involved some sort of special skills. If the work was highly technical or involved unusually high proficiency in math or science, women may have been educationally unqualified to take these positions. While each of these theories sounds plausible initially, they are inconsistent with the historical data on actual job content.

Few of the clerical jobs in these organizations actually involved physical, dirty labor. There were exceptions to this generality, such as shipping clerks, who occasionally had to handle their own packages, and inventory clerks, who often examined merchandise in unsavory surroundings. However, the majority of clerks in blue-collar settings actually did work that was clean and sedentary. Shipping clerks were a trivial proportion of the clerks in the analysis. Most goods and stores divisions used blue-collar workers to do much of the physical inspecting. The number of clerks who would have had such double duties is small. Depot clerks rarely got involved in the physical work of the station; they remained behind their windows, selling tickets and keeping accounts. Even mail sorters did not carry their own mail; the Post Office kept a special force of porters and bagmen to do the moving of heavy mailbags. Thus, in any of these offices, the physical demands of the jobs would have been extremely modest.

These findings are not likely to be the spurious result of managers' unwillingness to allow women clerks to mingle with blue-collar labor. In the non-clerical-labor-intensive offices, most of the work was done in offices physically removed from the shop floor. In the Chief Mechanical Engineer's Department, only 26 percent of all clerks actually had jobs requiring contact with manual laborers (Staff Charts 1933). Depot clerks would have worked in the booking windows and the accounts offices, while the physical work of handling freight and trains was done in the yards and on the loading quays. Of the workers in non-clerical-labor-intense offices, only sorters would have had sustained interactions with manual laborers. This is because they worked in mailrooms shared with porters and postmen.

Furthermore, despite the enormous amount of paternalistic concern many Victorian employers showed for their female employees, it is not clear that managers particularly objected to women's working in proximity to blue-collar workers. There was substantial concern about shielding women from unsavory members of the general public. When the management of the London Post Office was determining what sex of telegraphist to put in what branch, they explicitly took into account the quality of the neighborhood; women were explicitly kept out of the Bethnal Green and Crystal Palace branch offices. Both offices were in slum areas with a lot of street crime (London Branches 1914). However, nobody seems to have cared about lower-class employees. Most London Post Offices were sex-segregated. If women worked in a branch, then that branch was usually all female. However, the physical labor, such as hauling mailbags, was always entrusted to men. Thus the female offices would have had a blue-collar male staff that not only interacted with women but would have taken all of its orders from women.

These findings are probably not a spurious result of unmeasured variations in skill or human capital requirements. In the postal equations, differences in status have already been taken into account by the control variable, percentage of non-entry jobs, an imperfect but nevertheless valid measure of human capital stocks. Furthermore, although the non-clerical-labor-intense offices had distinctive types of workers doing tasks dissimilar from those performed elsewhere, the characteristic tasks of these offices were not particularly challenging. Mail-sorting was done in non-clerical-labor-intense offices. Mail-sorting, however, is quite simple, requiring merely good hand-to-eye coordination and an ability to read addresses. Temporary assistants hired during the Christmas season were able to perform quite competently after receiving only minimal training. Depot work was probably simple as well. Although the content of work cannot be measured directly, depots had the highest concentration of entry-level jobs of any type of office in the GWR. This suggests either that depot work was comparatively unskilled or that depot jobs were not highly valued in the railway status system. Either way, it would be unlikely that depot jobs were reserved for men because of their reputation for difficulty.

The only case in which unusual technical skills would have been required would have been in early engineering offices. There was often little differentiation in such offices between the actual engineering force and the clerical establishment; engineering trainees served their apprenticeship doing clerical work, while their superiors often took on some of the clerical work themselves (Engineering Clerks 1904, 1919). Early Postal Establishment Books made no semantic distinction at all between engineers and clerks; both were called "engineering clerks" (GPO Establishment Books 1857–1900). Thus some of the workers nominally called "clerks" would have been doing work of an advanced technical nature.

While technical skill somewhat distorts the equations in Table 2.2, eliminating scientific workers from the analysis has a negligible impact on the overall findings. Later twentieth-century Post Office data permits the division of engineering workers into two categories: those who did work we would now consider to be engineering and those whose duties were purely clerical. Eliminating the technicians from the data does not significantly increase the percentage of engineering clerks who were female. In 1921, only 6 percent of the pure clerks in engineering offices were female. Including the scientific personnel would only lower this figure to 3 percent. Both figures were among the lowest of any department in the Post Office. Running the regressions in Table 2.2 with either figure produces equations that are virtually identical.[7]

The robustness of the analysis can be explained by the high proportion of purely clerical positions within technical offices. The engineering offices did more than just design production processes. They also supervised the routine administration of large factories, docks, and communications networks. As such, they had to do many of the clerical tasks associated with any business: maintaining personnel files, paying wages, ordering raw materials, keeping records of stock, constructing budgets, keeping accounts, and corresponding with the outside world. Many of these tasks are fairly standardized and use the same procedures in both scientific and commercial settings. Thus, while the technical nature of engineering work may help explain why technical offices were female, this can not comprise the whole explanation. Clerical labor intensity helps to explain the use of men for tasks that do not have distinctive human capital requirements.

7. The analysis in Table 2.2 includes technical personnel to allow comparability between the equations for different dates. Engineers can only be excluded from engineering offices for selected dates in the twentieth century. Combining technical and clerical personnel was the only way to create a standard sample that could be used for every panel in the analysis.

Inter-Organizational Variance

The Post Office feminized before the Great Western Railway because the Post Office was more clerical-labor-intensive. The Post Office did suffer from the effects of patronage and political hiring. It can be shown, however, that the enormous gross differences between the two organizations in overall cost structure outweighed the distortions that came from the public sector.

The Great Western Railway had a much lower ratio of clerks to total staff than did the Post Office. Although clerk/staff ratios are only available for the GWR for 1860, 1919, and 1933, it is remarkable that three independent sources working over a span of seventy years produced exactly the same clerk/staff ratio: 11 percent exactly (Railway Report 1860; GWR Staff Census 1919; GWR Staff Census 1933). Estimates of the postal clerk/staff ratio are approximately 50 percent. The ratio was 57 percent in 1876, 49 percent in 1896, and 52 percent in 1921. By these estimates, the Post Office was roughly five times as clerical-labor-intensive as the railway, a differential that was both substantial and constant over time.

However, the clerk/staff ratio is only one component of clerical labor intensity. Clerical labor intensity is the product of the clerk/staff ratio and overall labor intensity, the ratio of labor costs to total costs. Although the intra-organizational analysis did not incorporate labor intensity, the data being unavailable at the departmental level, this variable can be included in an inter-firm comparison. In 1906, 41.5 percent of the Great Western Railway's operating budget went towards paying labor. The comparable figure for the Post Office was 61.6 percent. The ratio of labor to total costs in the operating budget slightly underestimates levels of capital expenditure, because large-scale capital acquisition was usually financed out of a separate budget. Furthermore, the purchase of telephone lines and equipment was not included in the operating budget. However, including these items only lowers the postal labor/cost ratio to 59.0 percent, a figure virtually identical to the original estimate. The entire cost of a year of phone construction, in the period of the most rapid growth of the network, was less than 10 percent of the wage bill for mail delivery alone. Thus both measures of clerical labor intensity strongly favor the Post Office.

Economic efficiency in the Post Office was somewhat impaired by political hiring. The effect of this dropped dramatically after 1870, however, and thereafter political hiring was concentrated in a small subpopulation of offices. By 1890, half of the pre-Orders-in-Council employees had retired, and they had completely disappeared by 1911. Thus, by the twentieth century, 92 percent of all office hires were economically based. In a large minority of offices, those that had been created after the Orders of Council, political hiring had never had any impact at all. Among these were the telegraph offices, the telephone offices, the engineering department, and the factory departments. In the nineteenth century, patronage would have had an impact on postal hiring. However, the burden of the railway's massive capital and blue-collar labor obligations probably provided a far more substantial buffer against clerical costs than did the limited degree of postal political hiring.

Managerial Opposition to Clerical Feminization

The previous analysis was predicated on the assumption that the primary responsibility for excluding women lies with management. Male managers are assumed to prefer an all-male labor force, but are frustrated by economic factors that compel feminization. It is easy to imagine an alternative model in which managers prefer an all-female labor force, but are constrained by forces that compel de-feminization. This might be the case if employers face strong sexist unions or vigorously enforced female labor laws. An employer seeking to use women to reduce costs might find his plans frustrated by strike action or by the fear of prosecution. One strategy for addressing these counter theories is to test them directly.[8] Another is to examine the actual behavior of managers considering feminization, to determine if they are supporting or opposing the use of women. Both the GPO and the GWR left extensive archival records of the policy decisions concerning their female employees. Within these files is a rich assortment of letters, reports, and memoranda in which supervisors openly discussed their opinions of women as workers. Using these letters, we can reconstruct the managerial ideologies of the period and determine whether employers facilitated or limited women's economic options.

In general, managers bitterly opposed the introduction of female workers. The overt objections took two forms: the claim that women

8. See Chapters 5 and 6 for explicit discussions of the roles of law and labor.

were physically and mentally incapable of doing a particular kind of work, and the claim that feminization would pose prohibitively complex administrative difficulties. The vigor with which these arguments were pursued suggests that managerial resistance was sincere. These objections were fairly thin, however, in that they were based on gross misperceptions of feminine incapacity or on exaggerations of problems that could be overcome with very minor levels of inconvenience.

A typical case of the posing of thin objections and their subsequent easy resolution occurred in London Postal Sorting during World War I. Late in 1914, the Women's Institute had written to the Postmaster General suggesting that since the military was quickly absorbing the supply of available male labor, women should be used as temporary replacements of men on leave from sorting offices. The letter was referred to the head of the London Postal Service, who considered the idea entirely unworkable. First, according to the Controller, major structural alterations would be required to provide restrooms for the women. Second, women could not work side by side with men, but would require completely separate offices. This would require fundamental alterations to the design of the main building. Third, sorting mail was too arduous for women. Men traditionally sorted while standing up; women would require chairs. Since the sorting boxes were at unusual heights, standard-issue chairs would be inadequate, and the Post Office would have to invest in specially ordered equipment. Furthermore, women could not be expected to work at night, a problem since a substantial percentage of mail-sorting had to be done at four or five in the morning. Given the enormous costs in construction and supplies, and the difficulties of scheduling inherent with an inflexible workforce, it would be far more economical to raise male wages and attract a larger pool of job applicants. The Postmaster agreed with the substance of the analysis, and the female sorter project was abandoned.[9]

A mere five months later, the situation had altered. The labor

---

9. Note the use of this opportunity by the Postal Controller to put in a plug for higher wages. In general, postal administrators were always advocating better conditions for their staff, exploiting any issue to refer to the need for higher pay. Since budgetary control was centralized outside of the individual departments, it cost the department heads nothing to make these requests, which facilitated good relations between management and labor.

shortage had become so intense that the Post Office could not find suitable males at any price, making the use of women unavoidable. Once the commitment to use women had been made, the supposedly insuperable obstacles of a few months before were easily overcome. Women were given their own floor at the sorting station, providing them with separate offices and lavatories at no construction cost whatsoever. Women were supplied with standard-issue chairs, which they rarely used, preferring to sort standing up like the men. Women were also quite willing to cover the late night shifts. The experiment in feminizing was so successful that the Post Office used women in increasingly large numbers throughout the war years (WWI Sorters 1915).

A similar story can be told about the upper management of the Great Western Railway. In 1876, a mere six years after the introduction of women to the Post Office, the board of directors of the GWR suggested an inquiry into the viability of using female clerks. The initial response from the department heads was overwhelmingly negative. Virtually every administrator raised the same objections, the non-availibility of lavatories and the impropriety of women's working side by side with men. Most of the reporting offices were located in the firm's headquarters at Paddington station, a very large multistory complex, making it hard to believe that these difficulties could not have been resolved with a modest amount of shuffling.

The board felt the accommodation argument was persuasive and ruled out the use of women in already-existing facilities. However, the argument was hard to justify in the case of offices currently undergoing construction for expansion. In these cases, the structural features necessary for the segregation of women could be obtained at nominal expense. Therefore, the board approved the use of women in a facility undergoing complete renovation, the goods department in Birmingham. However, before the plan could be implemented, managers from all over the system started submitting remodeling requests using as their rationale a desire to incorporate women workers. The same individuals who had opposed feminization were willing to accept women if this was the cost of having their offices redecorated. The board feared that granting these requests would set an expensive precedent and, rather than embark on a firm-wide construction project, canceled the plans for feminization. This suggests an extremely weak commitment to feminization by the board. Neither the option of mixing men and women nor the option of dividing pre-existing offices between the sexes was ever considered as an alternative to remodeling. On the basis of this very superficial analysis of the use of women clerks, the issue died entirely for twenty-nine years.

In 1905, the question of women clerks was renewed, after the General Manager of the company had taken a tour of American railways. At the time, the United States was considered to be in the vanguard of progressive railway administration, and the General Manager had noted that the Americans used female clerks. He took a poll of department heads, and as was the case in 1876, the response was overwhelmingly negative. The traditional complaints about sex-mixing and bathrooms re-emerged. These were buttressed with a variety of individual objections. The Relief Cashier argued that women could not take a job involving travel and thus could not go to out stations to perform relief duties. The Rates and Taxation Office, which had a wide variety of clerical and accounting positions, declared at the outset that women would only be suitable for messenger positions and then provided a long discussion of why messenger work is inherently better performed by men.

This time the General Manager was in favor of feminization, so he used his position to override the objections of his subordinates. However, he did acknowledge the legitimacy of the accommodation arguments. Therefore, he ordered the hiring of women clerks, but made remodeling funds generally available throughout the system to provide for segregated offices and facilities. As before, women were first placed in an office that for exogenous reasons was undergoing physical renovation, in this case the clerical section of Paddington Goods Station. The remodeling stricture severely impeded the rate of feminization, since the delays in implementing and completing construction could often be substantial. Therefore, by World War I, only a small number of female clerks had been hired, and these were concentrated in a select set of remodeled offices (GWR Women 1906).

In the Great Western Railway, a strong central executive had to force the introduction of women over the initial objections of upper and middle management. A similar set of incidents occured in the Postal Savings Bank. The debate over women in the Savings Bank began in 1874, by which time several other clerical-labor-intense departments, such as the telegraph offices, the Receiver and Accountant General's Office Department, and the Returned Letter Department, had already feminized. The Secretary of the Post Office observed that the Savings Bank was still all male, and suggested to the Controller of the Bank that he consider hiring some women clerks. The Controller's response was extremely negative. His main objection was a lack of "suitable accommodation" for women. Subsequent correspondence clarified what he meant by "suitable accommodation." Not only would women need to have separate lavatories and offices, but they would require separate lunchrooms and kitchens as well. The use of women would thus require a complete duplication of Post Office facilities.

The Secretary of the Post Office was unimpressed with these arguments. He ruled by fiat that the next sets of staff increases for the Savings Bank would consist entirely of female clerks, with the Controller left free to use these women as he saw fit. Because the Bank was very severely understaffed, the Controller could not afford to turn down the help. After several futile pleas for additional men, rather than women, he was forced to take in the new female clerks.

However, the battle was not over. The Controller next sought to demonstrate that women could not do bookkeeping. Since bookkeeping comprised the main activity of the Bank, barring women from the ledgers would guarantee that some fraction of future replacements would have to be male. Therefore, the Controller put all of his women to work addressing envelopes and copying receipts. Receipts were printed forms in which one filled in the name of a depositor with the date and amount of the deposit, as simple a job as could be found in the office. He then commissioned a set of pseudo-scientific tests to demonstrate that women lacked the mental capacity to keep accounts. Several women sorters were borrowed from the Returned Letter Department. These were basically filing clerks, who were hired with comparatively little skill or education and whose work did not involve any computational tasks. They were then given a one-morning crash course in calculating compound interest by hand. This involves some fairly complex arithmetic and requires practice to obtain proficiency. That very afternoon, the women were given several trial passbooks and told to balance the accounts and calculate the interest. About two-thirds of the women did very poorly at this exercise. The remaining third were given a second test with more difficult passbooks, and they too failed the exam. The Controller then sent the results of both tests to the Secretary of the Post Office as clear evidence of women's lack of quantitative skills. The Secretary criticized the unfairness of the makeshift exams and sent an explicit order to put the women on ledger duties.

The Controller then attempted to demonstrate that women were physically incapable of doing bookkeeping because they would be unable to lift or handle the heavy ledgers. This sounds outrageous to the modern reader, but would have been easier to justify in Victorian times. Before modern filing systems were invented, accountants kept related records together by writing them on the same page of a ledger. If the account was complex, this could require a very large physical document. The Savings Bank kept some record books that weighed over twenty-five pounds and stood over four feet high. The Controller argued his case successfully before the Chief Medical Officer, who in turn filed a report claiming that allowing women to lift ledgers would seriously impair their health. This argument the Secretary found convincing, but he decided that, rather than get rid of the women, he would have the ledgers redesigned so that workers of both sexes would find them more portable. The Medical Officer was then told to produce a signed statement giving full approval of women's doing ledger work, and the Controller was ordered to provide a comparable signed statement announcing his intention to put women on bookkeeping duties. The entire debate, from the Secretary's first suggestion to the receipt of the final signed concessions, had taken over a year and four months (Bank Introduction 1875).

Several points are illustrated by these stories. Managerial opposition to clerical feminization was quite widespread. This vigorous resistance to feminization was not merely confined to non-clerical-labor-intensive offices. It was endemic to managers as a whole, even in such clerical-labor-intense enclaves as the GWR Accounting Office and the GPO Savings Bank. In each of these cases, women were only introduced after the exertion of pressure from outside forces, usually central management. Cost structure did not cause local managers to change their preferences concerning women so much as it introduced pressures from organizational gatekeepers not to discriminate and instead to emphasize cost efficiency. The effect of cost structure can be clearly seen in the differing policies of the 1906 GWR General Manager and the Secretary of the Post Office in 1874. The GWR General Manager exerted significantly less pressure than his counterpart for the implementation of feminization. He never advocated the reshuffling of offices to attain segregation; he never redesigned normal work procedures to facilitate women's employment; he permitted the preliminary remodelings to occur at a very slow rate, significantly delaying the introduction of women to many offices. In distinct contrast to the Postal Secretary, he never accelerated feminization by banning male hires in particular offices. The greater capital intensity of the GWR decreased the urgency of achieving clerical cost controls, producing a far less intense commitment to implementing feminization over managerial resistance.

The substance of the objections the department heads raised is also important. In many cases, the administrators were clearly trying to avoid having to make adjustments in their normal procedures that would have been required by the addition of new types of employees. An example of such an objection is the binder reform, which, though precipitated by the introduction of women to the Savings Bank, was nevertheless a long-overdue rationalization of record-keeping. However, not all of the resistance can be attributed to bureaucratic inertia alone; some represents sexist ideology and a genuine preference for male colleagues. Both in the railway and in the Post Office, employers insisted that women be segregated from men. Segregation came to serve latent functions in the Post Office; however, the initial justification of this policy in both organizations was the normative impropriety of men's and women's having informal contact in an office setting. That such a factor dominated the discussion of an issue that had enormous implications for the lowering of operating costs suggests that Victorian sex-role ideology still played an important part in managerial decision-making. This can be seen as well in the continual references to feminine frailty in the debates over women's suitability as employees.

There is also evidence that men really wanted male offices and were willing to work quite hard to get them. The sixteen-month campaign of the Controller of the Savings Bank is an excellent case in point. A more dramatic example can be found on the Irish railways. When the Post Office nationalized the telegraphs, railway telegraphs were explicitly excluded. Subsequently, special arrangements were made to allow them to remain in private hands. In most cases, this merely formalized the railways' existing control over their own lines. In Ireland, however, a large number of telegraph lines on railway property had been built and operated by the Post Office. In these cases, the telegraphs were to be transferred to the appropriate private railways. When the Post Office operated these telegraphs, they were operated by women. After the transfer, the railway companies fired all of the women and hired men to do the signaling (Telegraph Report 1876).[10]

10. Fortunately, in the transfer the women were legally guaranteed employment, so the Post Office had to hire them back at considerable expense. Because the rail

This expulsion is remarkable for several reasons. First, telegraph operators took a long time to train, and the nation was suffering from a shortage of telegraph workers. Dismissing a fully functional operating crew and replacing them with raw recruits would have been an extremely substantial upheaval. Managers could not have been avoiding administrative complexities, for in this case clearly the simplest solution would have been to maintain the status quo. The railways voluntarily gave themselves an enormous organizational problem as the price of a male labor force. Second, ignorance about female capacities is not likely to have been a factor. Female telegraphists were now well established in both England and Ireland. Railway management would have had ample opportunity to see how well women worked when the Post Office was running telegraphs on the railways' own lines. This suggests a solid commitment by management to a male labor force, even when presented with good information on objective criteria favoring female employment.

Variations in Attention to Office Management

The main argument of this chapter is consistent with the earlier claims that patriarchy is in contradiction to the needs of both individual and collective capital. Discrimination is not wholly dysfunctional for capitalism; the GWR and the GPO used sex discrimination to solve problems involving their internal labor markets, as subsequent analyses will demonstrate. When employers chose not to use cheap female labor, however, their reasons were often cultural rather than economic, and the profitability of their offices often suffered as a result. The offices that chose not to save money on clerical labor took other liberties with office management, ignoring other economies in the administration of the clerical work itself. The fact that the most discriminatory offices were particularly inefficient lends support to the proposition that discrimination can run counter to the logic of capitalist rationality. There is unlikely to be an ulterior materialistic logic to

---

telegraphs had been a substantial proportion of postal employment, the Dublin office, which absorbed the women, was the only telegraph department in the country with a labor surplus.

the exclusion of women, if discrimination is correlated with inferior economic performance.[11]

The Post Office Engineering Department, which used a predominantly male clerical force, was notorious for its disorganized and inefficient office management. The paperwork fell into such overwhelming disarray that two separate formal inquiries had to be made into the department's clerical procedures. In 1904, investigators reported that the administrative work of the office was in extensive arrears. There was widespread confusion as to who was processing what materials and what actions the department had taken previously. The committee diagnosed the problem as largely self-induced. First, the engineering department had never made any attempt to create a division of labor among the clerks. There had not even been a clear division of labor between technical and clerical duties. Paying the staff and keeping accounts sometimes devolved upon technicians hired to design telephone systems. Second, the filing system had completely broke down. Part of this was a simple backlog in returning documents to the files; however, this was compounded by a system of file organization that was archaic and inefficient, resulting in very difficult document retrieval. Third, there had been little attempt to provide an overview of just what records were being produced. Many of the assignments that were clogging the office workflow were duplicates of tasks that had already been done elsewhere. No attempt had been made to eliminate redundant paperwork. Finally, the committee noted, the department was severely understaffed.

This last consideration was beyond the control of the engineers, staffing levels being determined exogenously by the Post Office Secretary. But these personnel shortages only intensified the problems; the basic inefficiencies of the system had been created by the engineers themselves. The relationship between the engineering department's capital intensity and its poor administrative practices was probably not coincidental. When the Post Office Secretary sought experts in office management who could rationalize the engineering department's procedures, he turned to the heads of the clerical-labor-intense depart-

---

11. In this section of the study, the term "office management" will be used in a very narrow sense. Office management here refers to the administration of data-processing and paperwork within the office. It includes accounting, filing, and the processing of correspondence, but not the administration of substantive policy. This usage is consistent with that of the literature on office administration.

ments. The filing system was assigned to officials from the Registry and the Returned Letter Office. The other procedures not handled by the Secretary's own staff were assigned to the Receiver and Accountant General's office (Engineering Clerks 1904). These were three of the most clerical-labor-intense departments in the Post Office, so it is significant that they were viewed as models of efficiency in data management.

Despite the objective shortcomings of their administration, the engineers were not personally criticized for their inattentiveness. The explanation of this is consistent with the clerical-labor-intensity model. In a post-crisis report of 1919, the Engineering Work Committee wrote:

> The position of the Engineering Department is peculiar in this respect that while the clerical work is of course ancillary to the engineering work and must to some extent be under the control of the principal engineering officer, it has at the same time so special a character that it is impracticable without loss of efficiency to require of a technical officer more than a general knowledge of the clerical procedures which he controls. . . . It is imperative that technical matters should make the first and by far the greatest demand upon his time and that any change of procedure which may tend to encroach upon the time which he gives to engineering questions is in our opinion strongly to be deprecated [Engineering Clerks 1919].

The Post Office thus explicitly encouraged its engineers to concentrate on matters other than the administration of clerical work. The presence of capital responsibilities allowed upper management to tolerate some inattention to office management per se. This toleration can be exaggerated, since the mere presence of a commission on clerical work in engineering suggests a certain amount of overall concern. The Post Office at various times did authorize high-level accountants and office managers to concentrate exclusively on the administration of the engineers' clerical labor. However, these officials were always subordinate to the Chief Engineer, who retained the ultimate control over staffing decisions. Engineering clerical policy continued to be treated as a secondary matter.

In this particular case, lax office management produced a crisis of serious proportions. Most administrative inefficiencies do not result in such dire consequences. The Great Western Railway seems to have handled its office work with dispatch and efficiency. Data collected in the 1870's by both the Railway Clearing House and the GWR itself suggest that the error rates in freight returns and accounts were typical of those of other railways (Staff Statistics 1870; Northern Recruitment 1904). Taylorite investigations of clerical performance in the 1920's reported adequate levels of overall efficiency (Clerical Work Committee 1916–28; Goods Stations 1922). Nevertheless, there is suggestive evidence that the railway did not devote its full attention to reducing clerical costs.

In 1879, a national recession severely reduced the GWR's traffic and revenues. The railway could not respond to the recession by reducing services and thus found itself under great pressure to reduce the costs of its fixed operations. The GWR introduced a program of labor austerity that cut pay rates for newly entering employees and imposed a stretch-out on existing staff. Most manual workers were paid by the day, with the hours of labor left up to the discretion of management. The GWR began imposing eighteen- and twenty-hour days upon most of the operating staff, compounded with consecutive shifts merely two or three hours apart. Workers could be on duty continuously for several days with only a couple of hours allotted for sleep. These abuses were so blatant and widespread that the eight-hour day became the central issue around which railway unionism crystalized (Bagwell 1963).

The Great Western Railway left written plans on the precise means by which these economies were to be obtained. They list pay cuts for several types of employees including guards, brakemen, switchmen, signalmen, porters, and police.[12] Clerks are conspicuously absent from the list. There was no discussion at any time of achieving cost reductions in the offices. A subsequent analysis reported the economies in total staff that had been made by each department. All of the staff cuts had been made in departments that hired predominantly blue-collar labor. Traffic, goods, signalling, and engineering all reported significant savings. In the offices that hired only white-collar labor, no staff reductions or pay reductions were made at all (Staff Expenses 1879). Such a policy could be justified economically in terms of the greater savings available from the numerically predominant blue-collar force.

---

12. Engine drivers and firemen were excluded from wage cuts, although not from hours abuse. Engineers and firemen were the craftsmen of the railroad, being highly skilled and, more significantly, highly organized.

However, the presence of such a source of savings did buffer the clerical force from cost-cutting and allowed for relatively lax office management.

Male office workers were thus associated with inefficiency in clerical administration. However, this was not the consideration affecting the use of men as opposed to women. The postal equations show that, net of variables associated with buffering models, the status and promotion prospects associated with an office had a critical impact on determining the sex-typing of its jobs. The next two chapters will explore the relationship between women and low-status jobs: Chapter 3 will discuss whether clerical feminization can be explained by deskilling; Chapter 4 will consider the relation between sex, turnover, and patterns of promotion within firms.

3

De-Skilling and
Technological Change

Many discussions of clerical feminization have put a great deal
of emphasis on the ways in which office technology and strategies for
organizing the labor process produced changes in the skill composition
of the clerical force. Most discussions of office work claim that clerical
jobs de-skilled during the nineteenth and twentieth centuries (Klingender 1935; Mills 1951; Lockwood 1958; Braverman 1974; Davies
1975, 1982; Glenn and Feldberg 1977). The argument is that clerks
evolved from a set of management trainees in small personalized
counting houses to proletarianized employees in large impersonal
bureaucracies. The increase in the size of clerical staffs forced management to reconsider the administration of office work, leading to the
development of various strategies for rationalizing and reorganizing
the labor process. This resulted in the development of office machinery, the creation of detailed divisions of labor, and the introduction of
Taylorite strategies for monitoring output, all of which served to lower
the autonomy and promotion prospects of office workers. The end
result was the creation of the semi-skilled clerical operative, who
makes up the majority of the workforce of modern offices.

This process has been linked, although with some reservations, to
the explanation of the origins of clerical feminization. Historically,
women have been confined to low-status occupations characterized by
low levels of responsibility, inferior rates of pay, and limited prospects
for promotion (National Manpower Council 1957; Oppenheimer
1970). If clerical work had systematically been de-skilled, the increasing undesirability of office jobs would have facilitated the use of
women for these positions (Davies 1975, 1982; Glenn and Feldberg
1977; Rotella, 1981). However, those who have linked feminization to

the degradation of office work have been very cautious in advancing their claims. One reason for caution is that de-skilling cannot provide a complete explanation of sex-type change. Davies, for example, argues that clerical feminization was a complex phenomenon that was caused by a number of different factors, such as changes in the female labor supply, the demand of employers for cheap labor, and changes in national gender ideologies. These would have contributed independently to the assignment of women to office tasks, weakening the overall importance of skill dynamics. This new caution can be seen in the work of Davies and of Evelyn Glenn and Roslyn Feldberg in which unfavorable technological change is treated as a burden affecting female occupations as well as a factor creating female occupations.

However, there is a more fundamental problem with such an analysis. It is not at all clear that clerical work has been de-skilled to any significant extent. There are both theoretical and empirical reasons for suggesting that office skill levels may have been more stable than is customarily acknowledged. The theoretical reasons involve the relationship between capitalist rationality and skill levels. Since Harry Braverman published *Labor and Monopoly Capital*, it has been customary to argue that managers seek to reduce overall skill levels in pursuit of the lowest possible labor costs (Braverman 1974). However, there is no necessary logical relationship between the goal of economizing on personnel and the use of an unskilled labor force. This point has been made quite cogently by Michael Piore and Peter Doeringer in *Internal Labor Markets and Manpower Analysis*. Piore and Doeringer argue that most managers attempt to economize on labor by substituting capital for labor to eliminate jobs entirely. Interviews with engineers showed that the criterion used by systems designers to evaluate the impact of technological change on profitability is not the extent to which an innovation will use a cheaper form of labor but the extent to which it will lower the overall size of the labor force. Managers were so unconcerned with the impact of technology on skill levels that they not only neglected to make projections of the type of labor that new innovations would require but used only one base salary for all workers regardless of skill in their calculation of overall labor costs (Piore and Doeringer 1971).

Furthermore, the use of technology to destroy jobs has important implications for skill distributions. An innovation that eliminates positions in the lower end of the status hierarchy will by default raise the average skill level of those workers who remain in the establishment.

An innovation that eliminates jobs at the upper end will lower the aggregate skill level. Job elimination thus can have varying effects on the resulting ratio of skilled to unskilled labor. To some extent, menial jobs are easier to eliminate by mechanization, since the work is simple, repetitive, and involves routine physical manipulations. Thus, there should be a slight bias for low-level jobs to disappear first, producing a net trend of upgrading. Since different technologies will have different effects, however, the overall impact of technical change should be somewhat random, producing no consistent pattern of downgrading or upgrading over time.

The empirical basis for the clerical de-skilling hypothesis has come from the historical work of sociologists studying white-collar labor such as C. Wright Mills, Francis Klingender, and David Lockwood. These authors argued that white-collar work had suffered a catastrophic loss of status. However, these conclusions are based on an overromanticized conception of the quality of clerical life in the nineteenth century. According to these accounts, nearly every Victorian clerk was a management trainee who in return for personal loyalty to an entrepreneurial patron could expect job security, future advancement, and job assignments with challenging substantive responsibilities. Gregory Anderson's work on nineteenth-century offices provides a serious challenge to these accounts by documenting the existence of a large clerical secondary sector. Much of the work in early offices was done not by clerks but by copyists. Copyists were temporary workers, comparable to modern Kelly Girls, who were paid by the piece to do tasks involving writing. The work consisted of simple duties such as making copies of correspondence, addressing receipts, or making entries in ledgers. The job security, pay, and prospects of these positions was marginal. The skills required were negligible, since transcription requires few skills other than literacy and penmanship. The status of permanently established clerks was often not much better. Nineteenth-century commerce was extremely cyclical, and many firms were forced by business conditions into bankruptcy. Small firms of the type Lockwood discusses would have been especially vulnerable to failure during the great financial panics. Anderson documents extremely high levels of immiseration among Victorian British clerks. Unemployment was a persistent problem. Many clerks only avoided unemployment by taking marginal jobs and living in poverty (G. Anderson 1976). When one compares the modern typist with the Victorian clerk, the modern typist compares quite favorably. The typist enjoys far greater job security, and although her duties may not be as complex as those of the semi-managerial trainees, they are certainly more complex than the duties of the copyists.

Just as the traditional account tends to overstate the status of the nineteenth-century office worker, it understates the status of the modern office worker. This is because most comparisons are made between those workers in both periods who are nominally called "clerks." In the Victorian era, the word "clerk" referred to anyone who worked in an office. The GPO Establishment Books use "clerk" for everyone lower than a department director but higher than a copyist. Many of the superior clerical positions would nowadays be referred to as "administrators," "accountants," or "middle-level managers." The claim that de-skilling has occurred because clerks no longer do the jobs involving supervision and responsibility that they once were assigned is based largely on a semantic difference rather than a substantive change. The real question consists of whether there has been a loss of skill or status among the entire population of office workers, whether the ratio of true managers to true clerks has declined over time. Measuring changes in the status of office workers as a whole is not easily accomplished with national census data. The population of office workers contains multiple occupational titles, whose meanings change in subtle ways over time. For example, the population of individuals called "managers" includes many proprietors of small firms, such as stores or family businesses, that do not use clerks in a formal sense. Such petty bourgeousie would have to be excluded from the analysis. Given the complexities of doing a methodologically rigorous study of national changes in office status, the white-collar historians can scarcely be criticized for confining their attention to the population of nominal clerks. Nevertheless, consideration of the whole population of office workers is critical to the assessment of whether office work de-skilled.

This chapter is an attempt to estimate the extent to which office work de-skilled between 1870 and World War II. If a significant amount of de-skilling occurred, it would not be unreasonable to suggest that this would have facilitated the feminization of clerical work. If the skill required for clerical work increased or remained constant, this would suggest the need to explore alternative explanations for the introduction of women to the office. The data that would allow for a completely rigorous assessment of the national evolution of office skill structures are unavailable. The fragmentary evidence that can be used consists of those materials previously examined in the literature on changes in clerical status in England and America as a whole and materials from the archives of the Great Western Railway and the General Post Office that allow for a discussion of status changes in two particularly important firms.

There are two types of data that have been particularly important to the discussions of national status trends. First, there are data on clerical wages. Large sample surveys of clerical incomes for different dates have been used to identify trends in remuneration. The postal and railway archives provide somewhat similar data. Both organizations left extensive documentation on salary levels. The firm censuses allow the reconstruction of detailed pyramids of pay levels within each organization, along with the number of individuals who were found at each level. These pyramids can be studied over time to determine trends in levels of remuneration. The data also allow the identification of entry-level and non-entry-level positions. Such data can be used to evaluate the prospects of upward mobility within these firms.

The second source of data is the writings of Taylorites and other advocates of scientific management. The usual way these materials are used is as chronicles of the attempts of the scientific managers themselves to impose rigorous regimes of work discipline on the labor force (see Davies 1982). Such a reading can be extremely informative. However, these works can also be read in their own right as descriptions of the skills required to do clerical work. In the process of attempting to reform the office, the Taylorites left a large number of technical discussions of the right way and the wrong way to do a wide variety of clerical tasks. One can use these descriptions of job contents to make an informed assessment of the actual difficulty of performing various office duties. By comparing earlier and later technologies for doing comparable clerical tasks, one may do a subjective assessment of whether such work was upgraded or de-skilled. As in the case of the salary data, there are parallel bodies of material for clerical work at the national level and clerical work within the firm. The latter materials are provided by scientific managers' in-house analyses of clerical work on the Great Western Railway.

National Trends in Salaries

The most systematic data available on long-term trends in clerical skill level comes from the traditional measure of status levels: salaries. Salaries are a useful index of changes in skill; however, these data must be treated with caution due to the presence of many potential sources of measurement error. Pay levels can increase because of general labor scarcity or because of a peak in labor demand within a particular industry or occupation. Institutional factors such as an increase in union activity will produce non-skill-related raises in wage rates. Salaries have a component that is skill-related. Artisanal workers tend to be highly productive, which raises the ceiling on the range of pay rates that would be economically justifiable. Furthermore, since skilled workers tend to be relatively scarce, they can command premium salaries through market competition for their services. Salaries are thus predictable from skill levels and a number of exogenous variables. One can use salaries to measure skill provided one pays explicit attention to the likely impact of these contaminating factors.

The data consist of a 1909 survey of British clerical salaries conducted by Cannon and Bowley and a 1929–30 survey of clerical salaries in London included in the New London Survey. These were the materials from which Klingender (1935) and Lockwood (1958) drew most of their conclusions for this period.[1] These two sets of data are not fully comparable. They refer to different geographical areas and used inconsistent sampling strategies and definitions of their industrial classifications. Furthermore, the periodization is not ideal. There is no information on any changes between 1929 and 1945, a period that included the clerical wage cuts of the Great Depression. Even worse, there is no data for any period before 1909. Not being able to measure differences in status between 1870 and 1909 truncates a very important period in the evolution of office work.

Despite these severe limitations, it is possible to draw some useful conclusions from the data. The findings suggest that the period from 1909 to 1929 saw very little deterioration in clerical standards. Since feminization occurred primarily between 1870 and 1945, with 1909 to 1929 being a critical period in this transformation, this suggests that the level of clerical de-skilling may not have been pronounced.

Table 3.1 is a recalculation of material originally presented in Klingender (1935). The figures presented here are methodologically superior to those in the original; however, a comparable analysis could be made of the published figures. The estimates of average industry-

---

1. For the period 1946–56, Lockwood also used reports from the Office Management Association.

specific levels of salaries in shillings per week come directly from Klingender. Real wages were calculated using the 1909 Sauerbeck-Statist price index.[2] The figures generally show clerical salaries remaining constant or improving during the period. Men maintained their economic position, while the women clerks made substantial percentage gains.[3]

There is one condition under which these data would be consistent with clerical de-skilling. If some exogenous force had independently

Table 3.1

*Average Weekly Salaries of British Clerks in Selected Industries,
1909–10 and 1929–30*

Sex of clerk	Commerce and industry		Transport		Banking*		Insurance*	
	Money	Real	Money	Real	Money	Real	Money	Real
Male								
1909–10	40	40	36	36	53	53	53.5	53.5
1929–30	65	41	75	47	90	56	75	47
Female								
1909–10	15.5	15.5	—†	—†	—†	—†	23	23
1929–30	40	25	45	28	60	38	45	28
Total								
1909–10	31.5	31.5	32.7	32.7			54.2	54.2
1929–30	57.9	36.3	71.6	44.9			70.5	44.2

*Sex Ratios for banking and insurance merged in the original.
†No females hired in this period.
Note: All figures are shillings per week. Real wages adjusted to 1909 shillings using the 1909 Sauerbeck-Statist price index.
Source: Adapted from Klingender (1935). Industry-specific clerical sex ratios from Klingender (1935) and the British Census. These sex ratios are used to create weighted averages of male and female salaries.

2. The figures on total combined salaries were calculated by weighting the male and female salaries by the percentage of male or female clerks within each industry.

3. It is also significant to note that the introduction of women to clerical work did not significantly undercut total wage levels. Women worked for significantly less than men, their salaries generally being only 50–80 percent of those of their male counterparts. However, the secular increase in both male and female wages counterbalanced the gender differential. Feminization helped to contain spiraling clerical costs but did not allow management to lower overall absolute levels of pay.

raised office salary levels, it is conceivable that de-skilling could have dampened the effect of this externality, producing a modest increase where one would have expected an increase that was more dramatic. Office work expanded dramatically during this period; the explosion of new jobs could reasonably be expected to have increased labor demand and thus contributed to an overall inflation of salaries. The effect of such market forces can be exaggerated, however. The expansion of clerical occupations produced a simultaneous increase in female labor force participation. The increasing supply of women would have eased the competition among employers for clerical workers and thus would have dampened the effect of occupational growth on rates of pay. Conceivably market forces could have produced increases in clerical salaries that were anywhere from massive to negligible. It is thus very difficult to examine a specific empirical case of an increase in the pay of office workers and judge whether such an increase is likely to have been caused by expansion, de-skilling, or some combination of the two.

In the light of this ambiguity, the following conservative conclusion seems warranted. The data do not show any patterns that positively support the contention that clerical work de-skilled. Had real clerical salaries declined during this period, this would have been a very strong confirmation of the de-skilling hypothesis. Since the natural factors affecting pay rates had an upward bias, the observed declines could only be attributed to the negative effects of skill. This data is also inconsistent with any claims of clerical immiseration. The standards of living of both male and female clerks were generally improving, due to a favorable mixture of market mechanisms and skill dynamics. These findings cannot disprove the hypothesis that a strong expansion in the demand for clerical workers was capable of compensating for a weaker tendency for office jobs to de-skill. Nevertheless, these data provide little support for the bleak picture that is usually painted of changes in the prospects of office workers.[4]

4. Both Klingender and Lockwood acknowledged the robust character of clerical salaries between 1909 and 1929. Both authors attempted to bolster their conclusions by arguing that, although white-collar salaries had risen absolutely, they had fallen relative to blue-collar wages. The blue-collar argument is irrelevant to the issue of skill. The relative decline argument was based on the assumption that clerks experience deprivation by losing their customary pay differential over manual workers. As Bain points out, this assumes that blue-collar workers are a meaningful reference group for clerks.

Lockwood (1958) does provide data that suggest that some de-skilling may have occurred after World War II. This finding is of definite interest, but is less important than the data he provides from earlier periods. The usual arguments about clerical de-skilling maintain that the downgrading occurred during the transformation of the offices from small personalized enterprises into large, bureaucratically administered, corporate firms. Furthermore, in these arguments, Taylorism is identified as being central to the process by which de-skilling occurred. Both arguments strongly suggest that the lowering of clerical standards should have occurred in the early twentieth century; this is the period in which Taylorism was at its height and the personalized offices of the nineteenth century became transformed into large centralized establishments. By 1945, the fundamental bureaucratization and redesign of clerical work had already occurred. If salaries were robust throughout the early twentieth century and only declined after World War II, this disconfirms most of the traditional accounts. Furthermore, clerical feminization occurred in the late nineteenth and early twentieth centuries. By World War II, the sex-typing of office jobs had been long established. The timing of the decline of clerical salaries is inconsistent with the proposition that the feminization of clerical work was caused by de-skilling.

Salary Trends within the Great Western Railway and the General Post Office

The discussion of national salary trends concentrates on the period 1909–29. While 1909–29 is important in its own right, the absence of the earlier material diminishes the utility of the national data for the discussion of long-term trends. Fortunately, both the Great Western Railway and the General Post Office have excellent data on salary levels that span the period from 1870 to World War II. With these

---

Manual workers are probably significantly less important in this regard than the clerk's family, his former schoolmates, and other members of his occupation (Bain 1970). Furthermore, the psychological well-being of white-collar workers is not an index of the objective conditions of white-collar work. What is at issue is whether the human capital requirements of clerical work declined and whether this would have affected the economics of hiring women. The perceptions and world views of clerical workers have little to do with corporate hiring policies.

data, one can replicate the analysis and the findings of the previous section. In both cases, clerical salaries rose, although there were exogenous factors that would have predisposed salaries to increase. Evidence exists for some departments that suggests de-skilling, but outside of this subset, clerical skill levels probably did not decline.

Tables 3.2 and 3.3 show the evolution of clerical wages in the Great Western Railway as a whole and in selected departments of the General Post Office. The rail data come from the two staff censuses of 1870 and 1933. The postal data comes from the Establishment Books. The sample used in Tables 3.2–3.5 is slightly different from that used in the rest of the book. The usual analyses exclude managers and professionals to allow for the study of the determinants of clerical sex-typing. In these analyses, however, the ratio of managers to clerks is what is at issue, so all white-collar workers are included.

Table 3.2 shows that real clerical wages more than doubled between 1870 and 1933. The trends in real wages were actually more favorable than the trends in money wages since prices declined during the period. Table 3.3 shows that real wages also improved in the Post Office. However, there was considerable diversity among the offices in the rate of improvement. The most dramatic wage increases came in the telegraph offices. Between 1876 and 1931, real telegraph wages more than tripled. The situation in sorting offices is almost as impressive: sorting salaries more than doubled. There was a set of intermediate offices such as the control offices, the Registry, and the Savings Bank. Lastly, there were offices whose salaries showed very modest improvement, such as RAGO, (the Receiver and Accountant General's Office), the Money Order Department, and the Returned Letter Office.

Table 3.2

Trends in Mean Salary on the Great Western Railway, 1870 and 1933

Population	1870 (money = real)	1933 Money	1933 Real
All clerks	78.7	202.8	243.4
Adult clerks only	98.6	204.1	244.9

Note: All salaries are given in pounds sterling per annum. All real wages are calculated in 1870 pounds.
Source: Staff Statistics (1870); GWR Staff Census (1932).

The figures in the middle columns of Table 3.3 actually underestimate the extent of salary improvement. That is because most of these offices feminized between 1871 and 1931. Because of the overcrowding hypothesis, women would have worked for less than men, even if they were doing precisely the same tasks. Correcting for such a bias produces even greater increases in salaries over time. Appendix C describes the procedure by which the sex-adjusted pay rates were calculated. The figures in the right columns of table 3.3 represent an estimate of what wages would have been in the absence of a change of sex in the Post Office. The estimating procedure uses the properties of a small set of occupations that are extrapolated to the dataset as a whole. Therefore the reader is advised to view the sex-adjusted figures as very rough approximations of the true rates. Nevertheless, when sex discrimination is taken into account, most offices can be shown to have

Table 3.3

Trends in Mean Salary in Selected Departments
of the General Post Office, Selected Dates

Department	1871 Observed (money = real)	1876 Observed (money = real)	1931 Observed Money	1931 Observed Real	1931 Sex-adjusted Money	1931 Sex-adjusted Real
Returned Letter	132	—	136	164	187	226
Savings Bank	144	—	202	243	246	297
London Post Control	297	—	289	348	296	356
East Central Sorting	77	—	209	252	210	253
West Sorting	79	—	156	188	156	188
Registry	109	—	179	216	205	248
RAGO*	245	—	239	288	276	332
Money Order	187	—	157	189	211	255
Central Telegraph Control	—	275	364	494	368	500
Central Telegraph Signal Room	—	62	156	212	N.A.	
West Telegraph	—	64	152	207	N.A.	

*Receiver and Accountant General's Office.

Note: All salaries are given in pounds sterling per annum. All real wages are calculated in 1871 pounds in the first half of the table and in 1876 pounds in the second half of the table.

Source: GPO Establishment Books (1871, 1876, 1931).

doubled their pay rates. The superior gains of the telegraph offices remain unchanged in these calculations. These offices had already feminized by 1876, so the impact of further sex change would have been negligible. However, the dramatic improvements of the telegraph department now appear in most of the other offices as well. Out of all the departments in the Post Office, only RAGO and the Money Order Department show modest rates of salary increase, and even here real wages went up 30 percent.

There were both upward and downward exogenous pressures on salaries in these firms. The Great Western Railway and the postal sorters and telegraphists were highly unionized. Although this unionism was of mixed effectiveness, there was undoubtedly some impact on pay rates, leading to the relatively favorable increases for all three groups of workers. Likewise from 1870 to 1930, both the firms and the British economy as a whole expanded, creating some inflationary pressure through increased labor demand. On the down side, the Post Office eliminated patronage in many of its operations. During the period the civil service moved from a regime of premium wages to one based on market rates. The main device for lowering pay rates was to transfer work being done by higher job classifications to workers with pay scales more in line with private rates. For example, in telegraph work, it was fairly common to transfer work customarily done by supervisors to rank-and-file signallers (Hobhouse 1906). A related development was the consistent introduction of new job titles lower than those that had existed previously with a concomitant knocking down of work assignments one level. Financial offices saw the introduction of male assistant clerks and female writing assistants, who did work previously done by male and female second-class clerks (Evans 1934). These semantic changes would have produced a lowering of pay that was not due to any real reduction in the true complexity of office tasks.

All things considered, the exogenous factors affecting salaries would have had a mixed effect, although those that raised wages probably predominated. Nevertheless, every office in the sample shows a very strong increase in real levels of remuneration. Thus, the conclusions for the GPO and the GWR parallel those made for the clerical force of Britain as a whole. The data consistent with de-skilling—an absolute decline in salaries or a modest wage increase coupled with overwhelming external wage pressure—do not occur. Although there can be no certitude, the best estimate would appear to be that skill levels in these firms remained constant. If there was any noticeable de-skilling, it is most likely to have occurred in the GPO's Receiver and Accountant General's Office or the Money Order Department, where the pay raises were markedly inferior to those found elsewhere in the sample.

Non-salary Measures of Status in the Great Western Railway and the General Post Office

Salaries provide a useful measure of clerical status. However, they are subject to factors external to the dynamics of the firm, such as changes in the labor market or in price rates. An alternative approach is to study the distribution of relatively good and bad jobs within the firm, as measured by hierarchical position. The skill distribution plays a key role in determining the overall ratio of superior to inferior positions. Entry-level work is considered to be relatively simple compared to non-entry-level work. Presumably, an individual equipped merely with the skills available to the population as a whole can do an entry-level job, while jobs reachable only by promotion require some level of firm-specific knowledge. A highly skilled firm may have a rectangular status pyramid—that is, one in which there are roughly equal numbers of individuals at every level of the hierarchy. A highly unskilled organization will have a small number of supervisors and a large number of subordinates. This will produce a triangular status pyramid, with most of the workers located at the bottom.

The advantage of such a measure is that it actually reflects the ratio of managers to subordinate workers, a critical concept in a claim that there is a relative proliferation of inferior jobs in clerical work. Furthermore, the rate of promotion is largely determined by the shape of the status pyramid, with promotions being relatively more frequent in rectangular firms. Lastly, the measure is independent of global exogenous factors that complicated the analysis of the salary data. The interpretation of these figures is much less ambiguous, which permits the generation of simpler and more straightforward conclusions.

The shape of the status pyramid will be measured by the percentage of workers who are non-entry-level. Where multiple ports of entry exist in a given job ladder, the highest port is considered to be entry-level even if it can be reached by promotion. The percentage of non-entry-level jobs does not capture all of the inter-office variance in skill levels. Differences in skill that come from moving to advanced entry-level tasks are not reflected in the measure, nor does the measure make any distinctions among the superior levels of the hierarchy. There are semantic problems as well. Skill is a continuum in which many conceivable cutting points are possible. Firms with identical human capital requirements could have different percentages of non-entry workers if one firm had a slightly lower cutting point in defining the first promotion.

Furthermore, status and skill are not identical phenomena. Sometimes a high-level worker can be less skilled than the individual he supervises. A hotel manager may be less skilled than the French chefs in his kitchen. A production manager may know less about his machines than the repair personnel. Even when these types of errors are taken into account, however, the percentage of jobs that are non-entry-level still captures a basic split between those workers at the bottom and those at the top of the status hierarchy. Since on-the-job learning and skill represent a significant proportion of the difference between the superior and inferior jobs, the crude perentage of non-entry-level jobs is still useful as a measure of the overall distribution of job complexity in the organization.

The measurement of the percentage of non-entry-level jobs on the Great Western Railway poses some minor methodological problems due to the differences in job classification schemes used in 1870 and 1933. In 1870, sixteen-year-old boys were hired as junior clerks. In two years' time, they could take an examination to become senior clerks. Thereafter, jobs were formally unclassified, although managers had explicit ideas about the maximum pay and natural ladders of progression associated with different positions. In 1933, the same junior/senior clerk distinction still existed. However, the senior clerks were divided into six grades—special and 1–5—with 5 being the lowest senior position. There were also three grades of adult women clerks, grade 2 being entry-level and grade 1 and special being advanced. There was a grade called "junior female clerk," but this was not a common port of entry as was the case with junior male clerk.

There are two ways to conceptualize the definition of entry-level positions in the GWR. In one sense, the only entry-level positions were the junior clerkships of both sexes and the women's grade 2, since the grade 5 male positions were attained by promotion from junior clerk. This definition of non-entry-level is called Assumption A; it explicitly treats the male grade 5 as a superior ranking. However, such a procedure creates an inequity between men and women. A male could become a grade 5 virtually automatically by waiting two years and then passing a test. The overwhelming majority of men passed their senior exam on the first sitting, while many of the remainder passed on the second or third examination. Leaving grade 5 was substantially more difficult. Over half of the adult male clerical force were employed as grade 5's, and many workers kept this status throughout their careers. Grade 2 was the equivalent job title for women. The overwhelming majority of women worked in grade 2 clerkships with only a small elite being promoted to grade 1. Thus, there is a sense in which grade 5 represents an automatic promotion, with grade 4 being the first discretionary screen. Assumption B treats grade 5 men as entry-level, an interpretation that captures the trivial nature of the senior promotion. There is no literal equivalent of grade 5 clerk in the 1870 data, so a false grade 5 was constructed using salary as a proxy for job grade. (See Appendix D for details of the calculation of the grade 5 equivalent.)

Table 3.4 shows the trend in the percentage of non-entry over time in the GWR. Assumption A and Assumption B both produce very similar findings: clerical work upgraded between 1870 and 1932. Using Assumption A, jobs on the Great Western Railway went from 71 percent high-status to 83 percent high-status. Under Assumption B, the improvement is especially striking. The number of superior jobs grew from 4 percent to 40 percent, a dectupling. The estimate for any given year of the absolute number of high-status jobs changes depending on the methodological procedure used. The number of grade 5

Table 3.4
Trends in the Percentage of All Clerical Jobs in the Great Western Railway That Were Non-Entry-Level, 1870 and 1933

Method	1870 (%)	1933 (%)
Using Assumption A	71.2	83.3
Using Assumption B	4.5	39.1

Note: Assumption A is that grade 5 men and their 1870 salary equivalents are non-entry-level. Assumption B is that grade 5 men and their 1870 salary equivalents are entry-level.
Source: Staff Statistics (1870); GWR Staff Census (1933).

men was so enormous that shifting the definition of grade 5 has an overwhelming effect. Nevertheless, there clearly was a trend for the relative share of inferior jobs to decrease and the share of superior jobs to increase.

Estimating the percentage of non-entry-level jobs for the Post Office poses few methodological problems since the job titles were essentially comparable throughout the period. However, the empirical findings are much more complex.

Table 3.5 shows an enormous diversity of patterns, with some offices de-skilling, some offices maintaining their status, and some offices showing dramatic improvement. Among the offices whose relative share of non-entry-level jobs rose were the Returned Letter Office, the Savings Bank, East Central Sorting, and the telegraph signalling offices. The West Signalling Office showed the most dramatic improvement, with a near quadrupling of superior positions. Among the offices that lost status were RAGO, the Money Order Department, the Registry, and all control offices. RAGO and Money Order were offices that also received comparatively minor increases in salary. This further supports the claim that de-skilling may have occurred in these particular sections. The registry lost status despite its relatively robust pay levels. The status data probably provide a more accurate picture of this office. The prime function of the registry was

Table 3.5

Trends in the Percentage of All Critical Jobs in Selected Departments of the General Post Office That Were Non-Entry-Level, Selected Dates

Department	1871 (%)	1876 (%)	1931 (%)
Returned Letter	16.4	—	22.6
Savings Bank	5.4	—	8.4
London Post Control	71.4	—	20.3
East Central Sorting	6.0	—	9.1
West Sorting	12.8	—	12.1
Registry	40.0	—	6.3
RAGO	22.4	—	10.0
Money Order	11.6	—	6.2
Central Telegraph Control	—	45.4	19.4
Central Signal	—	7.3	11.8
West Signal	—	3.1	11.5

Source: GPO Establishment Books (1871, 1876, 1931).

the maintaining of the postal archives, a job that required an extensive amount of filing. As will be argued below, filing and records management was one of those aspects of clerical work where Taylorism did produce significant de-skilling. The control office cases are more difficult to interpret. The Establishment Books show that, over time, there was an increasing proportion of clerks to managers in these offices. However, it is unclear whether this represents a de-skilling or a permanent assignment of staff to the control offices to do work formerly done by the general force of the supervised offices. Given the dramatic declines in the percentage of non-entry-level jobs, it is quite likely that both processes were occurring.

The data on the percentage of non-entry-level jobs support the findings of the pay discussion. The railway showed a dramatic improvement in clerical pay and status. While exogenous factors could account for a secular increase in pay, a change in the status pyramid from triangular to rectangular is harder to account for by such factors as unionization or a tightness in labor markets. Both of these factors would be expected to raise wage rates globally, rather than altering the distribution of pay within the firm.

The experience in the Post Office was more diverse. Some offices did show strongly suggestive signs of de-skilling, in particular RAGO, Money Order, and the control offices. However, others showed levels of non-entry-level jobs that are constant or rising. As in the case of pay, the opportunities in sorting offices were good and the opportunities in telegraph offices were excellent. Note that "truly clerical" offices did not show a general tendency to de-skill. On both pay and non-entry-level status measures, the Savings Bank and the Returned Letter Office showed signs of significant real improvement. The picture of the Post Office is complex and undoubtedly some de-skilling did go on, but the most reasonable interpretation of these data is that the skill level of clerical work remained constant, with gains in some departments being offset by losses in others.

Mechanization, Scientific Management, and Rationalization

These findings have important implications for the reader with a general interest in skill and technological change. At the beginning of the chapter, two conceptualizations of the evolution of skill were identified, that of Braverman and that of Piore and Doeringer. In the Braverman model, managers use technology to reduce labor costs by subdividing jobs into their simplest components, allowing management to hire the cheapest form of labor. In the Piore and Doeringer model, managers use technology to eliminate jobs. Because job elimination can occur among jobs with a wide range of skills, technological change should have a neutral impact on skill distributions. Some Bravermanian transformations can occur, but they are balanced by upgradings caused by the automation of unskilled positions.

This finding can be supported another way. Within the study of skill, there are two methodological traditions. One approach is to measure skill quantitatively, using measures of job complexity derived from the *Dictionary of Occupational Titles* (Horowitz and Herrnstadt 1966; Dubnoff 1978; Wright and Singelmann 1982). The second approach is to use case study material to examine the impact of particular technological changes. Some of the most impressive support for the Braverman hypothesis comes from the collection of essays put together by Andrew Zimbalist in which experts in a large number of industries provided an overwhelming array of examples of how capitalist technological change had undermined skill levels (Zimbalist 1979). Likewise, Piore and Doeringer's own insights grew out of participant observation of a Route 128 firm (Piore and Doeringer 1971). In the case of clerical work, it is extremely informative to turn to qualitative materials and consider the actual impact of the specific technological transformations that affected office work. A consideration of the content of clerical work will show that the effect of technological change on skill was extremely complex and that the present findings are no statistical artifact.

This section attempts to review as comphrehensively as possible the major technical changes in office procedure that were introduced in the late nineteenth and early twentieth centuries. The primary source for most of this analysis is a set of book-length Taylorite works on office management.[5] The scientific managers wrote extensively on

5. Since the contents of these works are extremely similar, I have dispensed with citations of individual authors in the following section. Appendix E contains a list of the more useful and general references. The reader seeking to validate the argument of the next section can find detailed descriptions of the skills required to operate various kinds of office equipment in any of the books in this bibliography.

office technology. Their descriptions of job processes are explicit, detailed, and based on years of acute observation. Given these descriptions, one can often reasonably estimate the skills it would have required to master these various procedures. Another source of information are the documents in the GWR and GPO archives. In the course of doing the research, it was necessary to examine original documents and ledgers that were written in different periods between 1840 and World War II. The records of the mid-nineteenth century are completely different from those found a hundred years later. Victorian records are hand-written in ink; they are kept in ledgers or piles of loosely related, pinned papers; statistical analyses are rare, based on small populations, and not highly disaggregated. Records from the 1920's are either printed, typed, or mechanically duplicated; the use of ledgers has declined, while the file classifications have become much more refined and detailed; statistical analyses are now common, cover the organization as a whole, and are available at very fine levels of disaggregation. It is not hard to examine a document, determine how it was made, and estimate what skills would have been required in its production. Thus the Taylorite descriptions of the cognitive demands of differing office technologies have been supplemented by my own assessments, based on a subjective interpretation of the physical properties of the papers containing the records of this study.

An examination of such materials can really change one's perception of scientific management. Ever since Braverman (1974), it has been customary to associate Taylorism with time-motion study and the speed-up. Braverman makes explicit reference in his discussion of clerical work to automated typewriters in which work is passed from clerk to clerk in assembly-line fashion. However, the office management literature paints a picture of Taylorism in the office that is both more mundane and more profound. Time-motion study and the development of micro-controls over the physical motions of workers played a trivial role in the scientific reform of clerical work. The contribution of the Taylorites was the invention of virtually every piece of office equipment we are familiar with today. Their contribution to the typewriter and the adding machine is well known. But few people stop to consider that file cabinets, rolodex cards, hanging manila envelopes with alphabetical tabs, postage meters, loose-leaf notebooks, swivel chairs, staplers, paper clips, carbon paper, and duplicating machines are all inventions of the Taylorite era. They were all absent from the Victorian office; they were all developed to deal with inefficiencies of early offices; and they all are basic to clerical functioning today. Some of these innovations represented de-skilling. Others, however, were labor-saving devices designed to keep clerks from wasting their time on tedious, menial, and time-consuming tasks. The postage meter, for example, eliminated the licking of stamps. Licking stamps cannot be said to be one of the rare and valued skills of a traditional clerical artisan.

One of the more important technological changes in the office was the simplification of arithmetic calculation; the Taylorites were fairly successful in reducing the necessity of doing arithmetic operations by hand. Adding and calculating machines reduced the need for book-keepers to do complicated manipulations such as adding long, repetitive columns of numbers or doing long division with unwieldy units of analysis such as tons, hundredweights, pounds and ounces, or pounds, shillings, and pence. Basic arithmetic skills could be found in the general population and did not require special training. Being able to do hand arithmetic for hours on end without making a mistake, however, requires a level of patience and special concentration. The loss of this would have represented a modest de-skilling. There existed other alternatives to hand calculation that would have had different impacts on skill levels. The use of published tables such as interest tables would have been an absolute de-skilling since the need for calculation would have been eliminated entirely. On the other hand, the Taylorites often recommended the use of slide rules. Learning to operate a slide rule would have been a wholly new skill that represented a significant upgrading.

There were at least five major innovations in the processing of business correspondence. These were the development of shorthand, dictating machines, the typewriter, mechanical duplication, and the addressograph. Each of these had very distinctive effects on the skill required to produce, record, and mail a business letter.

Shorthand was one of the major artisanal accomplishments of the turn-of-the-century clerk. Although shorthand was not extensively used in the early nineteenth century, over time employers realized the advantages it offered so that, by the late nineteenth century, fluency in shorthand was expected of any professional stenographer (Pitman 1891). The GWR, for example, required all male clerks to learn shorthand within the first few years of the senior clerkship (Salaried Recruitment 1912). Shorthand represented a very significant skill acquisition, since not only did the clerk have to learn the various symbols, but he had to develop speed and accuracy in taking dictation while using the symbols. The competent practitioner benefited from the fact that neither the general public nor the average employer could read a communication written in shorthand. As such, it could be used as a secret language to generate a certain feeling of exclusiveness. The British Museum has an extensive collection of shorthand journals dating from the turn of the century. These are magazines written entirely in different shorthand systems catering to the clerical community. The circulation and importance of these journals is unknown; their readership may have been confined to a small number of hobbyists, or they may have been distributed throughout offices nationally. However, the presence of such journals demonstrates that shorthand represented a body of knowledge that was sufficiently complex and involving that some people took an interest in the system for its own sake. Thus the diffusion of shorthand literacy that took place in the mid-nineteenth century would have represented a major upgrading of the clerical population.

The dictating machine was designed to undercut the artisanal base of shorthand writers by allowing the direct transcription of letters from voice. Had dictating machines been universally accepted, which in general they were not, the dependence of employers on shorthand clerks for dictation would have been completely broken. Before World War II, there were relatively few Ediphones in active operation. Taylorites remarked on the difficulty of working the machines and the preference of many employers for interaction with a live stenographer. Only in the 1970's—with the development of convenient, high-quality cassette recorders—was shorthand effectively removed from the working skills of the professional clerk.

Typing represented a significant upgrading of clerical work. Most discussions of office work treat typing as a menial occupation because it compares unfavorably with managerial positions. Such a position fails to recognize that the introduction of the typewriter represented a significant upgrading over what had gone before, which had been hand-copying. The only skill required in hand-copying is basic penmanship. Typing represented a quantum shift in the training requirements of copyists by demanding the acquisition of a whole new set of motor skills.[6] Not all of this new human capital was provided by the

---

6. To give the Victorian clerk his due, it should be noted that many clerks had excellent handwriting. Many of the account books and letters of the GWR in the nineteenth century are filled with striking examples of professional calligraphy. Such

firm; much of the introductory typing training was done by professional business schools and by the typewriter companies themselves
(Davies 1982). However, the Taylorites argued quite forcefully that
typing schools only provided a rudimentary familarity with the
keyboard. Many typists did not know the touch system. Those who did
were often extremely slow and inaccurate, requiring long hours of
on-the-job practice to develop reasonable standards of speed. The
Taylorites devoted a great deal of attention to increasing the rates of
production for typists. Time-motion studies were done to discover the
fastest way to feed paper into the machine, the best posture for rapid
typing, and the most efficient positioning of the material to be copied.
Competitive typewriting contests were held every year, and the techniques of the winners were studied carefully. The time-motion studies
were attempts to identify, codify, and publicize the procedures used by
the most artisanal typists, and they represented a conscious attempt by
office engineers to de-skill by shifting the locus of expertise from
workers to management. Nevertheless, what is important is that typing was poorly understood by both Taylorites and typists alike. The
long training periods combined with a stock of complex techniques for
improving performance are what one would expect from a demanding,
difficult job. Typing made such intense demands on clerical workers
that Taylorites were forced to turn to time-motion study to find compensatory simplifications.

Duplicating machines and addressographs are examples of upgradings that were produced by labor-saving machinery's being introduced
to comparatively unskilled positions. Carbon paper, mimeographs,
and hectographs all replaced hand copyists with other operatives who
were equally unskilled. However, since a mimeograph operator can
turn out multiple copies in a small fraction of the time it takes to
produce individual transcriptions, the demand for copyists became
severely reduced. Addressograph machines eliminated the task of
repetitively hand-addressing envelopes. Once again, a small number
of clerical proletarians replaced what had once been a significantly
larger force.

---

handwriting is generally absent from postal documentation and disappears from the
GWR records in approximately the 1890's. Even in the prime of the Victorian age, some
of the GWR handwriting was quite mundane. Nevertheless, there do seem to have been
talented individuals in the clerical force whose penmanship rose far above the requirements of mere legibility.

Reforms of business correspondence tended to produce upgradings of the clerical force. However, many Taylorite innovations significantly undercut the skill requirements of office workers. One of the most important and least discussed attacks on the stock of clerical knowledge came from the rationalization of filing. Most of the modern equipment used in filing, such as file cabinets, loose-leaf binders, rolodexes, and card indices, were developed by the Taylorites in the early twentieth century. Before loose-leaf filing, business transactions were recorded in bound ledgers, while loose documents were tied together in large bundles and stored separately. Bound ledgers were incredibly inefficient. When a new account was opened, a given amount of space was allocated in a book. If the account outgrew its space, or if part of the account required different treatment, a new section of a book would have to be allocated. The result was that related materials became strung out in a series of isolated, unrelated volumes. Filing was also impeded by poorly designed classification systems for loose documents. It was not uncommon for Victorian firms to file their business correspondence by date of arrival, rather than by client or subject matter. The result was that lost documents were common. Long searches for missing material and random research expeditions looking for information were a standard component of a clerk's working day. The only convenient way information could be found was if someone had a deep personal acquaintance with the files. An experienced clerk who could remember transactions that had occurred years before was an invaluable asset in producing current business analyses.

The Taylorites developed alternatives to the tradition of bound volumes and loose piles of pinned papers. The introduction of loose-leaf records that could be recombined represented a breakthrough in providing file categories that made substantive sense. Files could be adjusted to reflect current business conditions, and mutually relevant materials could be kept together. With the new filing systems, data collection was transformed into a routine activity. This resulted in a significant de-skilling of file clerks, since it eliminated the need to rely on clerks who could remember where everything was recorded. Offices now could be run with inexperienced workers, and it was less important that clerks learn to remember key transactions.

A more well-known innovation that caused de-skilling was the creation of an elaborate division of labor within the office. One of the most common Taylorite recommendations was that managers develop "routines" for most complex tasks; such routines would involve sending work to particular clerks for the execution of single steps within the process. These divisions of labor probably preceded scientific management. On the Great Western Railway, formal descriptions of job duties can be found in the late nineteenth century. At any rate, the fragmentation of the clerical labor process would have reduced a worker's exposure to a large number of clerical tasks and would have contributed to reducing the clerk's intellectual command of office procedures.

Another source of de-skilling was the development of standardized pre-printed forms and letters. Printed forms removed the responsibility of the clerk for designing the layout of a given account and ensured that all the necessary information would be included on the document. The development of a rational system of forms occupied a high percentage of an office manager's attention. The Great Western Railway had an in-house committee of Taylorites who were active from World War I to the 1930's. Their official assignment was to consider all aspects of clerical functioning, making concrete recommendations of sources of economies. It is highly significant that in the first fourteen years of this committee's existence it did not execute a single time-motion study. One such study was attempted in 1930 and abandoned because it did not produce any significant savings (Labour Report 1931). The Great Western Clerical Work Committee spent the bulk of its time on the review of printed forms. The overwhelming majority of the minutes in its records refer to the elimination of forms or the alteration of the format of various GWR documents (Clerical Work Committee 1916–28).

It is not hard to justify such a single-minded focus. A printed form was implicitly a rule book that laid out in elaborate detail how any given clerk was to spend his or her time. The printed form spelled out precisely what information was to be collected, what office was responsible for collecting it, and what other information must be obtained at the same time. The development of such forms did not start with the Taylorites, since even the earliest offices have elaborate specifications for the formats of returns and accounts. However, many unspecified data collections can occur in the form of letters and memos, where the writer can report on phenomena in any manner he or she chooses. The proliferation of forms would have reduced the right of workers to compose their own memos and would have greatly reduced clerical skill and autonomy.

Many of the items that have been discussed in the previous pages have been sources of significant downgrading that were produced by clerical mechanization and rationalization. There is an important countervailing factor that would have upgraded the labor force: the increasing importance of repairs and mechanical maintenance. The early Victorian office was unmechanized. Because of this there was very little that could break down or go wrong. Ink wells had to be filled, and pencils had to be sharpened, but there was very little that could not be fixed instantly or, at worst, replaced. The maintenance problem became far more serious when office functioning became dependent on a large number of complex, expensive machines with multiple moving parts. There was a larger number of units that could go down unexpectedly, each one putting a clerk or a roomful of clerks out of work. These problems could be handled by outside repairmen. If the pace of work was to be maintained, however, it was important for workers to be able to do minor repairs themselves. This eliminated the downtime that is always inevitable when workers must wait for an outside technician. The ability to fix equipment on the spot required mechanical skills that had never been part of office work. Most secretaries can fix their own typewriters if they have to. Many can also improvise successfully with a mimeograph or Xerox machine. To some extent, this can be considered a loss of status, since in this respect the new white-collar jobs had blue-collar manual duties. Nevertheless, repair work added a new human capital dimension to office work that made demands on the skills and creativity of the whole labor force. Since this required mechanical aptitude that had no precedent in the Victorian office, this surely must have been an upgrading.[7]

Conclusion

The above analysis shows that office rationalization affected skill levels in a wide variety of different ways. Some innovations produced significant de-skilling, such as the rationalization of filing and the use of adding machines. Others produced an upgrading, such as the intro-

---

7. A non-skill-related aspect of Taylorism, which has been neglected, is their advocacy of clean, warm, well-lighted workplaces. Many early offices were quite substandard, being dark, underheated, underventilated, and provided with dubious sani-

duction of typing and the mechanization of duplicating. From the qualitative analysis, it is impossible to say whether upgrading or downgrading forces predominated in the office. It is not inconceivable that these forces canceled out, producing an overall effect of little net change. Such an interpretation is consistent with the statistical analysis, which showed different outcomes for different departments that averaged out to an average finding of little net change. To the extent that there is a directionality to the movement, the salary and pyramid data suggest that clerical work upgraded rather than deteriorated.

The analysis in this chapter suggests a reformulation of the relation between sex and job status. If women were generally concentrated in low-status jobs, then feminization could be explained in two ways. The first is that the absolute number of low-status jobs increased, allowing for an increase in the number of jobs appropriate to women. The second is that some other transformation occurred that provided women with a greater share of those low-status jobs that already existed. This chapter suggests that the first process did not occur; what happened was that women were taking menial positions that had in an earlier era been given to men. However, this still does not explain why women are concentrated in low-status jobs in the first place. This question cannot be answered with a study of the evolution of skill levels, but must be addressed by explicitly examining the process by which men and women get sorted into particular jobs. The next section relates the subordination of women in the workplace to internal labor markets and the problems of turnover and legitimation that can occur in such settings.

---

tary facilities. Cleanliness was also an issue. Even in the 1920's, the Railway Clerks Association had a benefit fund for phthsis victims; "white lung" was contracted by the inhalation of excessive amounts of loose dust. One can imagine the appearance of an office whose records were capable of giving clerks asthma. The Taylorites scientifically demonstrated that the increased productivity of clerks in decent facilities more than offset the extra cost of housekeeping and fuel. The Taylorite research on the relation between comfort and productivity was an important contribution to the improvement of the physical quality of life in both factories and offices.

4

Synthetic Turnover

One of the most important concerns in the sociology of gender has been to explain why women are concentrated in occupations with low-status and low-wage attainments. Many writers have suggested what shall be referred to here as the "natural turnover hypothesis." The natural turnover hypothesis argues that women's domestic pressures and sex-role socialization lower their commitment to labor force participation. This increases their turnover relative to men, making them less attractive for jobs involving long preparatory tenure. Since highly paid jobs usually require extensive training and experience, conservation of training costs would mandate giving these jobs to men (Caplow 1954; Oppenheimer 1970). There are a large number of arguments relating turnover differences to hiring practices. Writers usually invoke one or the other of them as a general explanation of occupational sex inequality.[1]

---

1. Most writers claim that the mean labor force commitment of women is lower than that of men, although they also admit that there is variance among women such that some have preferred job tenures equal to or longer than those of men. There is disagreement on the specification of which jobs become less likely to be female. One argument states that higher mean female turnover disqualifies women from jobs with large amounts of employer-financed human capital acquisition (National Manpower Council 1957; Oppenheimer 1970; Davies 1975; Lyle and Ross 1973; Thurow 1975; Rotella 1981). A second version argues that women are barred from jobs involving high skill rather than long learning curves per se (Caplow 1954; Baker 1964; Holcombe 1973; Madden 1973, 1975; Grimm 1978). Others have suggested that women are allocated to jobs with flat wage time curves (Zellner 1975), jobs with no power (Wolf and Fligstein 1979a, 1979b), or jobs in the secondary labor market (Piore and Doeringer 1971; Barron and Norris 1976; Blau and Jusenius 1976).

91

This chapter suggests that there may be limits to the applicability of the hypothesis. The most important critique is that the female turnover differential has been overstated. When appropriate controls are applied, sex differences in turnover often disappear (Stoikov and Raimon 1968; Armknecht and Early 1972; Fry 1973; Laws 1976; Viscusi 1980; Begnoche Smith 1979; Blau and Kahn 1981). A few studies do show strong net sex effects (Parnes 1954; Burton and Parker 1969; Pencavel 1970); however, the bulk of the literature casts doubt on the premise that, net of job characteristics and age, gender has an independent effect on quitting.[2]

In the face of such evidence, some critics have attempted to salvage the theory by modifying it. One such variant is the theory of statistical discrimination (Phelps 1972). This claims that the mean labor force commitment of men and women may be similar but that the unexplained variance in female tenures is greater than that of males. Since employers have difficulty predicting female turnover from standard pre-employment indices, they err conservatively by barring females from superior positions. Statistical discrimination models do not provide an alternative to the natural turnover hypothesis. They, in fact, restate it. In the absence of precise information on turnover, statistical discrimination would only be effective in lowering costs if the true female turnover rates were on average higher than the true male rates. This, however, is the questionable premise from which the theory claimed to be independent (Aigner and Cain 1977).[3]

There is a second, more damaging and heretofore unexamined, ground for challenging the natural turnover hypothesis. The natural turnover hypothesis assumes that it is economically rational for employers to minimize turnover within their ranks, especially in jobs involving a great deal of employer-subsidized training. Keeping women out of occupations involving large amounts of firm-specific skill acquisition would protect employers against economic losses should such positions be vacated. Turnover is not always economically

2. See the extensive literature reviews of B. W. Anderson (1974) and Price (1977).
3. Aigner and Cain (1977) have developed a statistical discrimination model that does not depend on unequal mean attributes between majority and minority. They claim that black occupational performance is harder to predict than white performance from measures of educational attainment. However, its relevance to gender is unclear. No one has developed a concrete analogue of such uneven predictability for gender that does not reintroduce the premise of lower mean female job commitment.

unprofitable, however, and can in many circumstances even be economically advantageous. The profitability or unprofitability of turnover is situation-specific, as will be discussed below. In the cases where turnover is economically desirable, employers will cease trying to minimize quit rates of their staff and may, in fact, seek to increase them artificially. Therefore, a job segregation model based on the presumption of turnover avoidance will be valid only when turnover is costly. When turnover is beneficial, a different explanation must be invoked.

This chapter proposes an explanation of job segregation for the case involving beneficial turnover. To distinguish it from previous arguments, it will be called the "synthetic turnover hypothesis." A series of cases are described where the synthetic turnover hypothesis should have predictive power superior to that of the natural turnover hypothesis. Data are then presented that show the goodness of fit of the synthetic turnover model. It is not claimed that the synthetic turnover model is superior in all cases to the classical explanations but rather that it better explains occupational segregation in a particular well-defined domain, though this domain is probably fairly large.

The Economics of Turnover

Most sociologists tend to overestimate the costs of turnover, probably because they consider primarily the costs of replacing human capital. It is true that many job holders in the course of their careers acquire skills not possessed by a new entrant and that, when an employee resigns, his or her employer may lose productivity until the replacement has acquired these skills. Because these human capital losses are never totally recovered, it is often assumed that employers are inevitably averse to turnover.

However, there are compensatory savings associated with turnover that can override these costs. A new employee can be paid an entry-level wage, while the pay of veteran employees may have been augmented with seniority-related increments. Many organizations use tenure-based salary systems to motivate steady performance. Good work is rewarded with regular year-end raises and by promotion to jobs with higher maximum salaries (Thurow 1975; Williamson 1975; Edwards 1979). While time-based rewards may be effective in motivating personnel, they have the drawback of steadily increasing labor costs. A certain amount of salary increase can be tolerated when it is balanced by an increase in employee productivity. In the early part of his or her career, when an employee learns new skills, raises may be economically justifiable. A some point for most jobs, however, the learning curve flattens. Returns to experience are not unlimited, and promotions and raises eventually translate into higher costs for what is an unchanging amount of employee product. Once learning has stopped, in a time-based salary regime, an employer faces a difficult choice. He may continue to give raises, which will produce higher per-unit labor costs. Alternatively, he can eliminate tenure-based raises. This undercuts incentives to perform and reduces employee output. In such a case, it might be advantageous to allow the employee to resign. A replacement could be brought in at a lower rate of pay, with potential salary increases once again compensating high levels of effort.

The desirability of turnover to an employer is a trade-off between the desire to avoid retraining and a preference for recirculating staff into entry-level positions. The relative importance of these factors is situation-specific. When labor markets are tight and replacements hard to find, employers will prefer to conserve manpower and minimize turnover. The same would hold if the savings obtainable from replacement were small, as in the cases where wages are paid at a flat rate or by the piece. Flat-rate wages are independent of tenure lengths while piece rates are directly linked to productivity. Replacement savings would also be low when learning curves are long and steep. A large percentage of the labor force would still be at early stages of their careers when salary increases are economic. In contrast, an employer would seek to maximize turnover when the opposite conditions hold: when replacements are plentiful, the incentive system is tenure-based and learning curves are short with early crests. These predictions are summarized in Figure 4.1.

Synthetic Turnover and Gender

When turnover is profitable, one would expect that employers would act to increase quit rates beyond their natural level. When an employer proactively induces resignations in his staff, this can be considered synthetic turnover. There are a variety of strategies of synthetic turnover, some of them involving gender.

Some employers withhold organizational rewards from individuals as they reach the crest of their productivity. When successful, such withholding demoralizes the job holder and leads to an early quit. However, there are some individuals and some organizations for which this will not be an effective strategy. If a job holder has little opportunity for comparable employment elsewhere, he or she may remain despite diminished organizational incentives. Non-quitters might include employees of firms with relatively high wages, employees who are poor performers, and those with idiosyncratic, non-transferable skills. Particularistic exclusion is not sex-based, but it is not always practical.

A second tactic is selective recruitment. An employer can intentionally hire employees who are likely to quit early voluntarily. Selective recruitment, however, requires good ability to predict voluntary quits. The employer needs to identify a population who will stay long enough to avoid taxing the firm's retraining capacity but not so long as to create stagnation problems. The natural attributes of workers may not fit a business's ideal tenure plans.

A third tactic is to place maximum tenure limits on positions with short learning curves. After a given number of years, the employee is forced to resign. Tenure bars provide effective limitations on career lengths, but they may create fundamental problems of legitimation.

Figure 4.1
Hypothetical Employer's Preference for Turnover
by Cost and Savings Potentials

	Savings potential Pay system and typical firm learning curve		
	Tenure-based salary scales		Flat pay rate, piece rates
Cost potential Labor market	Short flat learning curves	Long steep learning curves	(All learning curves)
Ample supply of replacements	Turnover maximizer $(+++)$	Variable preference $(+)$	Turnover reducer $(-)$
Constrained supply of replacement	Variable preference $(+)$	Turnover reducer $(-)$	Turnover minimizer $(---)$

Most organizational incentive systems would be undercut if employees perceived the ultimate reward of good service as being dismissal. Tenure bars can only work when the moment of forced resignation coincides with the arrival of some exogenously determined plausible excuse for dismissal. Mandatory retirement age is an example of an effective tenure bar because of ideologies associating old age with decreased performance.

The different mechanisms of synthetic turnover vary in their relevance to the sorting of women into low-status jobs. Particularistic sanctioning is irrelevant to sex discrimination. Selective recruitment has a weak and transitory effect. In contrast, tenure bars can create systematic, lasting sex discrimination.

Particularistic sanctioning should have no gender consequences because both hiring and the withholding of organizational rewards are based on objective measures of productivity. Since men and women are likely to be equally productive, they would receive punishments at equal rates, resulting in equal numbers of men and women at all organizational ranks.

A selective recruitment effect would only be noticeable if employers hired women because they expected women to choose short careers voluntarily. Many employers genuinely believe that women are marginal labor force participants (National Manpower Council 1957; A. Hunt 1975). The literature on sex differences in turnover shows that the magnitude of independent sex effects depends on the precise number and identity of the control variables that are applied. Employers' perceived sex differentials will likewise depend on the sophistication of their analysis. With no experience, an employer might staff a new position with women in the hope of obtaining shorter tenures. Experience gathered over the long term would most likely disconfirm this prediction. However, the original sex composition could stay intact if either the employer failed to perceive these non-differentials or bureaucratic inertia or other rigidities did not permit a change in sex type once such non-differentials were discovered. Selective recruitment for short tenures could then produce sex discrimination; however, such discrimination could persist only under a fragile set of extenuating circumstances.

Tenure bars provide the greatest potential for determining sex-type. This is because the most common tenure bar historically has been the marriage bar. In the past, many employers hired young girls on the condition that they retire at marriage. A girl who started working at sixteen and married at twenty-one would have had a career of only five years. Marriage was one of the very few demographic transitions that could ideologically be held to be grounds for dismissal. Traditional sex-role ideology stressed the incompatibility of work and family; dismissal would be accepted and understood by the women themselves. There were few other occasions for imposing a bar that would have been as easy to legitimate.

The consequences of marriage bars for women's status should be clear. In firms where bars were operative, jobs with short learning curves would have been reserved for young single girls. Jobs with long learning curves for which employers wanted longer tenures would have been given to men. This would tend to confine women to low-status jobs because learning curves are shorter for those positions. Turnover differences would have indeed occurred. However, these would have been due not to the female labor supply but rather to the proactive policies of management.

Several types of data are available to support these claims. First, an examination of the marital policies of a number of firms will show the extent of marriage bars historically. Second, an in-depth analysis of the Great Western Railway and the General Post Office, which had explicit marriage bars, will show the inapplicability of natural turnover models to these settings. Third, data will be presented to show the special relevance of synthetic turnover to clerical work.

The Extent of Discrimination against Married Women

There have been a number of systematic attempts to measure the degree to which employers have explicitly restricted female career lengths with marriage bars. One of the most important studies was done in England by the British government in 1946. The Whitley Council *Report on Marriage Bars* investigated the marriage policies of several large clerical employers (National Whitley Council 1946). Their sample consisted of a set of private firms, some British governmental agencies, and the civil services of a number of foreign countries.

The study found a remarkably high level of discrimination against married women. Virtually every British private employer interviewed had a marriage bar (see Figure 4.2). Marriage bars were also universal among British public employers. Lower levels of discrimination were found overseas, with only half of the foreign civil services having marriage bars. The sampling of organizations in this study was idiosyncratic: the sample size was small and biased towards highly visible bureaucracies. Nevertheless, the findings were probably fairly accurate. Nowhere in the records of the commission is there any indication that any of the members disputed the empirical accuracy of the presented findings. This is significant because the commissioners were

Figure 4.2

Hiring Policies of Major British Clerical Employers
and the Civil Services of Various Governments

Private British firms	Non-civil service British public employers	Civil services
Maintained both marriage bar and dowry		
Bank of England	British Broadcasting Co.	Australia
Boots Pure Drugs	Birmingham City Council	Canada
British Overseas Airways	Lancashire County Council	New Zealand
Cadbury	Liverpool City Council	United Kingdom
Great Western Railway*	London City Council	
Imperial Chemical	Middlesex County Council	
London Midland and Scottish Railway*		
London and North-eastern Railway*		
Rowntree and Co.		
Southern Railway*		
Unilever		
Maintained neither marriage bar nor dowry		
(none found)	(none found)	Denmark†
		Finland
		Sweden†
		U.S.
		U.S.S.R.

*Maintained dowry up through 1921. No Dowry subsequently.
†Had dowry program.
Source: National Whitley Council (1946).

selected for their expertise in current personnel management practices and for their divergent views on marriage bars.

Marriage bars also existed in the United States and were especially prominent in elementary school teaching. The National Education Association monitored the use of marriage bars in the public school systems of cities of 2,500 or more from 1928 to 1956. Before World War II, it was the general practice neither to hire married women as teachers nor to permit them to continue teaching after marriage. In 1928, over 60 percent of all urban school districts did not hire married women and over 50 percent required resignation soon after marriage. In 1941, the comparable figures were 87 percent and 61 percent (Oppenheimer 1970).

Studies of marriage bars have also been conducted using a wider range of industries. In 1936, Purdue University surveyed 250 American firms on their policies concerning married women (see Table 4.1). The survey found that 50 percent of the factories and 61 percent of the offices had some sort of restriction on the hiring of married women.

Table 4.1

Percentage of Firms Practicing Discrimination against Married Women, 1936

Response	Factories (%)	Offices (%)
Do you forbid the hiring of married women?		
Yes, absolute bar	13.7	26.6
Yes, in some cases*	24.9	24.8
Supervisor's discretion	11.4	12.0
No bar	50.0	38.6
Do you require the resignation of single female employees who marry?		
Yes, absolute bar†	7.5	19.8
Yes, in some cases‡	10.0	10.4
Supervisor's discretion	2.5	3.7
No bar	80.0	66.6

*Includes only using married women for temporary posts, applying special needs tests, not hiring wives of employed men, or not hiring company wives, companies with recent policy changes, and other.

†Includes demanding immediate resignation, demoting newly married women to temporary status, and providing grace periods before requiring resignation.

‡Includes retention only in cases of extraordinary service or irreplaceability, applying special needs tests and others.

Note: $N = 250$. Results do not add up to 100 percent due to rounding error.

Source: Best (1938, pp. 212–220), using the Purdue University sample.

Forced resignation was somewhat rarer. Twenty percent of the factories and 33 percent of the offices had forcible marriage bars (Best
1938). A comparable survey was performed by the National Federa-
tion of Business and Professional Women's Clubs in 1940. The study
found that 43 percent of public utilities, 29 percent of large manufacturing concerns, 23 percent of small private businesses, and 13 percent
of department stores had some sort of restriction on the employment
of married women (Shallcross 1940; Oppenheimer 1970). The methodology of these studies is not reported. If these surveys are similar to
others of this period, they probably contain serious methodological
errors. Taken at face value, however, they suggest that marriage bars
were not uncommon among American employers. Bars seem to have
been confined to a minority of employers, and the extent of bar use
varied by industry and occupation. Nevertheless, the absolute number
of employers practicing discrimination would have been very large.

In the early 1960's, the International Labor Office commissioned an
extensive study of discrimination against married women. Labor experts from all over the world submitted reports on the use of marriage
bars in their home countries. No attempts at quantitative verification
were made. Instead, the ILO relied upon the impressionistic accounts
of the local observers. The ILO report is striking, however, in the
breadth of discrimination that was suggested. Reporters from Japan,
the Netherlands, Italy, and Ireland noted that, in their countries, it
was standard practice in most industries for employers to hire young
women with the explicit provision that they resign upon marriage.
Such practices were also found in other countries, although the corre-
spondents only referred to specific industries. Married women were
not employed as nurses in Australia and Belgium. They were barred
from working as bank clerks in England, Belgium, Greece, Australia,
and South Africa. There were comparable restrictions in the textile
factories in Portugal, metallurgical factories in Italy, and chemical
factories in both Italy and Belgium. A very wide range of countries
reported marriage bars for both teachers and airline stewardesses. The
United States was comparatively infrequently mentioned in these
discussions, suggesting a low level of bar usage. Nevertheless, it would
seem that marriage bars were a phenomenon of worldwide importance
(International Labor Office 1962).

The above evidence is based on historical data. However, marriage
bars can also be found in more contemporary settings. Robert Cole
notes that in the 1970's married women are generally expected to

resign from employment in Japan. This policy is not explicitly written into the employment contract, in fact, explicit discrimination against married women was made illegal in the 1970's. The practice persisted, however, despite the legal strictures, by unwritten informal understandings (Hanami 1965; Cole 1979; Cook and Hayashi 1980). The Japanese case also suggests that the extent of discrimination against married women is poorly measured by the presence of formal restrictions. As such, much of the survey evidence given above is likely to underestimate the amount of discrimination.

Turnover and Job Allocation in the Great Western Railway and the General Post Office

In this section we look in depth at the turnover and job allocation dynamics of the two main firms of this study provide further support for the model. Both of these firms used synthetic turnover, because they both had severe over-annuation problems with their white-collar staff. The stagnation problems were so severe as to require sustained attempts to augment employee quit rates artificially. Both firms had incentive systems involving time-based salary increments. Employees were paid on graduated salary scales. All promotion was internal, and employees could expect several major promotions over the course of their careers (GPO Establishment Books 1857–1937). The firms' problems were exacerbated by a policy of guaranteeing continuous employment up through retirement age. Both firms hired employees only at the age of sixteen. Once hired, an employee had lifetime job security and only extreme malfeasance would warrant dismissal (Gladden 1967; Kingsford 1970). Postal jobs were protected by civil service regulations. Railway jobs were safeguarded by past company promises, made in an era of labor scarcity. The time-based salary-promotion system produced rising labor costs that could outstrip worker productivity. Once the stagnation point occurred, however, the only source of relief was voluntary employee exits.

Particularistic sanctions were incapable of raising the level of employee turnover. This was because postal and railway employees had limited employment opportunities in the outside world. Postal skills tended to be non-transferable. The Post Office had a monopoly on mail delivery and telephone and telegraph service. Workers with training in mail-sorting or telecommunications had no other employer to turn to. The clerical force had some salable skills. However, the civil service paid at well above market rates. An accounts clerk was unlikely to duplicate his salary in the private sector (Gladden 1967; Klingender 1935).

Railway immobility was created by the rigidity of railway employers. These employers only hired sixteen-year-olds. Even exceptional performers had difficulty transferring after the age of twenty (Staff Statistics 1870; Clerical Appointments Committee 1924). Much of their work was railway-specific and had few analogues in other firms. Some skills, such as basic bookkeeping, would have been transferrable. However, the idiosyncratic nature of railway accounting and paperwork would have induced other private sector employers to have limited interest in former railway clerks (Jenkinson 1914). As a result, marginal civil servants and railway clerks tended to persist, even when deprived of raises and promotions. The firms needed stronger devices to ensure turnover in the lower ranks.

Both firms had absolute marriage bars. Women were hired at the age of sixteen and allowed to work until they married, at which point they were contractually obligated to surrender their positions. Neither willingness to continue work nor superior performance of duty could be invoked to waive this requirement. However, the danger remained that women might delay marriage to continue working. The bar could be avoided by the willing celibate. To counter this, both firms instituted the payment of marriage dowries. After six years of employment, the firm would pay a woman a substantial cash bonus on the occasion of her marriage. The size of the dowry varied, but it was often the equivalent of a month and a half's salary. In present-day terms, this meant a payment of between $1,300 and $1,800. The firms paid these dowries to most female employees, indicating an enormous financial commitment to creating short female careers.

It should be noted that the employers were not absolute turnover maximizers. A woman had to remain at least six years in order to qualify for her dowry. This is consistent with the hypothesis that employers sought to keep women during the early stages of their careers, during which the salary system is financed by increased employee productivity. The dowry insured against overly short tenures, but it also kept those tenures from becoming too long.

There was a second, more minor, mechanism of exclusion. Many firms used long-term incentives such as pension plans to create loyalty among their employees (Edwards 1979). Women generally had less access to these programs. In both firms there was a substantial period of time during which men were offered superannuation systems and women were not. When pensions were finally offered to women, they were given at lower retirement ages. The male retirement age was sixty-five, while the female age was fifty-five. This is actuarially inappropriate since females generally have lower mortality rates than males. This too suggests that employers were willing to see women's jobs vacated, even if it meant paying early benefits.

There is evidence that the employers actually perceived the problem this way themselves. Many contemporary discussions of the advantages of female labor laid heavy emphasis on the need to keep stagnation low and the promotion process fluid. Consider the following testimony given by Francis Scudamore, controller of the Postal Telegraph Services, to a committee of Parliament in defense of women's employment:

> Permanently established civil servants invariably expect their remuneration to increase with their years of service . . . even in the cases necessarily very numerous in which from the nature of their employment, they can be of no more use or value in the twentieth than in the fifth year of service. There must always be in the Post Office an immense number of duties which can be just as well performed by a lad of eighteen as a man of forty; but when the same person continues to perform the same duty from his eighteenth to his fortieth year, it is impossible to permanently resist his claim for additional remuneration, and when he continues to perform to his sixtieth year, it becomes equally impossible to resist his claim for a retiring allowance.
>
> Nor would it be possible to maintain a rule under which persons employed on certain duties should perforce retire after a short time say five to seven years.
>
> Women however will solve these difficulties for the Department by retiring for the purpose of getting married when they get the chance. If we place an equal number of women on the same ascending scale of pay, the aggregate pay to the females will always be less than the aggregate pay to the males . . . and further there will always be fewer females than males on the pension list [Scudamore 1871, p. 78].

Scudamore's observations closely parallel the theoretical basis of the synthetic turnover model. He points to the gap between tenure-based pay increases and observed productivity curves and notes the difficulty of imposing unlegitimated tenure bars. His hope was that, by hiring women, he would have a workforce that would leave voluntarily. Scudamore was speaking at the date of the very inception of female hiring, at which time the Post Office still had no marriage bar.

The marriage bar was instituted in the late 1870's. The timing, seven or eight years after the introduction of hiring women, suggests that women were not voluntarily leaving in large numbers upon marriage and thus required additional exit incentives. The similarity between the timing of the introduction of the marriage bar and the desired six-year length of female careers consistent with a marriage bar policy is interesting although possibly coincidental.

After the introduction of the bar, managers continued to defend its use in terms consistent with the synthetic turnover theory. In 1945, over sixty years later, the British civil service authorized a commission of government administrators, labor representatives, and community leaders to consider the future of the marriage bar. The committee's role was advisory, and it was specifically prohibited from making any concrete policy recommendation. Nevertheless, there was one argument the commission found so compelling that it was given special emphasis in the body of the report and was reiterated forcefully in the conclusion:

> Where there is a large amount of routine work to be done it is a real advantage to employ women who stay only a few years and retire on marriage. The amount of routine work is so great that the Service can not provide adequate careers for all the young persons recruited to the lower grades. It is essential to have fairly rapid turnover, and marriage wastage is a highly important factor in this [National Whitley Council 1945–46, p. 12, item xi].

And further on:

> The amount of routine work is so great . . . that the Civil Service Staff pyramid is bound to have a very broad base, and promotion to the higher ranks can not come to many.
>   . . . [The retention of women after marriage] would be bound to slow down the rate of promotion. . . . This would not be welcomed by their colleagues whose prospects thereby would be worsened (National Whitely Council, 1945–46, p. 15, item xxxix].

These statements are clearly quite similar to those made by the telegraph controller in 1870. Thus it would seem that, for the entire late nineteenth and early twentieth centuries, the Post Office was formally committed to working towards short female careers. This policy had a visible impact in reducing the opportunities for promotion and advancement that were open to female employees.

Women tended to be concentrated in those jobs for which short tenures were advantageous to the firm. As predicted by both the natural and synthetic turnover models, these were jobs with flat learning curves and short promotion chains. One index of such placement is the extent to which women are placed in non-entry-level jobs.

Table 4.2 clearly shows that women were less likely to hold non-entry-level positions. At the minimum, men had a 3 to 2 advantage in these jobs. At the extreme, on the Great Western Railway, men were nearly nine times as likely to be in jobs with long learning curves. This is consistent with the sorting by sex expected if job allocations were made on the basis of anticipated tenure.

The confinement of women to low-status jobs in these settings cannot be explained by the natural turnover hypothesis. The natural turnover hypothesis is inconsistent with the patterns of quit rates associated with these firms. The standard argument is that women leave employment before they can remunerate their employers for the cost of advanced training. Women either quit during the training period or leave so soon afterwards that the employer loses the anticipated benefits of his investment in human capital. However, if women's job tenures were shown considerably to exceed the period of

Table 4.2

Ratios of Non-Entry-Level to Total Jobs by Sex for the General Post Office and the Great Western Railway, Selected Dates

Firm	Date	Proportion male jobs, non-entry-level	Proportion female jobs, non-entry-level
GPO	1876	.155	.060
GPO	1896	.145	.100
GPO	1914	.151	.100
GPO	1931	.116	.077
GWR	1933	.435	.047

Source: GPO Establishment Books and GWR Staff Census (1933). Metric runs from 0 to 1.

skill acquisition, this would be inconsistent with the natural turnover premise of high absolute female instability.

To test this proposition, one must compare female job tenure with the learning curves of both male and female jobs. Information on job tenures can be found in actuarial records that employers used to calculate the details of their pension plans. Pensions require accurate yearly turnover figures for the adjustment of premiums and benefits. Both organizations therefore endeavored to collect accurate data on career lengths.

The data consist of several series of age- and sex-specific exit rates. Using these rates, one can perform a standard life-table analysis using the period rates to simulate the experiences of a synthetic cohort. This analysis assumes that the entering radix of sixteen-year-olds are subject to the sixteen-year-old rates. Those who survive to age seventeen were subjected to the seventeen-year-old rates. Each year the cohort was reduced by the next sequential rate. The median career length is calculated by finding the age at which 50 percent of the cohort had disappeared. A prospective recruit has a 50 percent chance of surviving up through the year at which half of his or her cohort has disappeared.[4]

There are further analytic possibilities for these data. The female exit rates are divided into marital and non-marital exits. These allow simulation of the effects on turnover of manipulations of the marriage bar policy. Since the bar and dowry affected only maritally based exits, the marital exit rate can be altered in various ways to reflect possible outcomes of eliminating the marriage bar. The precise results of an imaginary bar removal are conjectural. However, estimates of the maximum and minimum effects can help define the range of possibilities. The minimum result would occur if the bar was actually irrelevant to the determination of career lengths; in this case eliminating it would

---

4. The analysis is subject to the methodological dangers inherent in estimating cohort parameters from period statistics. The younger rates are based on the experience of a set of younger workers. The older rates are based on the experience of a different set of older workers. If there are cohort-specific differences, then the younger group will not replicate the older rates when they age. Thus the synthesized career will not reflect the experience of any particular historical cohort (Shyrock and Siegel 1975). Despite these problems, these tables are still useful. Management used these data in actual policy-making. At a minimum, they represent prevailing managerial perceptions of gender differences. If the cohort differences are minor, they also reflect real worldly experience.

have no effect. The minimum effect of bar removal is adequately represented by the observed career lengths. The maximum effect would occur if, in the absence of the bar, no one would have left for marital reasons. In this case, the female quits would be totally represented by the non-marital rates. To simulate this, the tenure lengths are recalculated assuming the marital exit rates to be zero. An intermediate simulation is also included, one that assumes that, in the absence of the bar, the marital exit rate would have been halved.

The analysis indicates that female careers were indeed shorter than male careers (Table 4.3). The observed rates show that men worked about forty years to women's ten to thirteen, a very substantial difference. Furthermore, this gap was not wholly a function of the marriage bar. Even under the most generous assumption of bar removal, that in which female marital exits are eliminated entirely, women worked only thirty-one years. This is a long time, but is nevertheless nine years shorter than the average male rates.

However, the significance of this differential is diminished by the other major finding in the table. Women's careers in absolute terms were quite long. Observed women's careers averaged about thirteen years. One could qualify for a dowry after six years of service. Female career lengths substantially exceeded this. The median age of marriage

Table 4.3
Twenty-Fifth Percentile, Median, and Seventy-Fifth Percentile Career Lengths in Years as Estimated from Observed and Modified Exit Rates for the Post Office and the Great Western Railway

Firm	Sex	Assumed marriage exit rate	Career length* 25%	Median	75%
GWR	male	observed	8.3	40.5	42.9
GWR	female	observed	5.8	9.8	†
GPO	male	observed	18.3	39.9	45.3
GPO	female	observed	8.2	13.2	26.1
GPO	female	1/2	9.2	18.0	38.3
GPO	female	0	11.7	31.0	42.0

*Career lengths are given in years. Careers are assumed to begin at age sixteen.
†Unknown figure for the GWR reflects inadequate data on older women.
Source: The postal rates are from War Cabinet (1919). The GWR data is from Male Pension (1925) and Female Pension (1927). Male data is for 1921–25. Female is for 1923–27.

for English women in this period was twenty-six, which would allow a ten-year career (Wrigley 1969). The careers shown here are longer than those typical of British women of the period. Both the Post Office and the GWR provided unusually high-paying, attractive careers for women. This suggests that when offered better-than-average employment, women were willing to defy both organizational incentives and social convention in order to keep it. Career lengths of thirteen years are inconsistent with the prevailing stereotype of women as transitory employees.

These career lengths are substantially longer than the training times for clerical positions in these firms. Data on contemporary human capital requirements are availible from the Hobhouse Commission on Postal Labor that sat in the House of Parliament in 1906. Both management representatives and union activists testified before this committee on the equities and inequities in civil service pay scales, with both sides providing extensive data on the training required to perform various duties in order to substantiate their pay claims. Not surprisingly, the human capital estimates vary depending on which side is testifying and are often only sketchily supported with empirical data. Nevertheless, by averaging the conflicting claims and identifying consistencies between the rival accounts, some general conclusions may be drawn. The longest learning curves were those for telegraph signalling supervisors and engineers. These were all trained in-house. Telegraph overseers required six to eight years of training, and engineers required even more time (Hobhouse 1906). At the opposite extreme were mail-sorting overseers. A filing supervisor could be trained in two years. A very common intermediate case was the accounting supervisor. Their skills were comparable to those of the modern certified public accountant, who can be trained in about five years (Montagna 1975). Training times were thus distributed from two to eight years, with a peak at the five-year mark.

Observed female careers were over twice as long as these estimates. Removing the marriage bar would only increase this discrepancy. Female careers could theoretically have been extended further by judicious promotion. During apprenticeship, an employer would have been able to identify women with particularly high levels of labor force commitment and, instead of promoting at random from all women, he could promote from the top half of the anticipated tenures. An employer promoting a woman at the seventy-fifth percentile of anticipated longevity could have obtained an expected career length of over twenty-six years, the equivalent of twenty-one years of service after the completion of training. This is inconsistent with the expectations of short female job tenures expected from natural turnover theory. However, long tenures are precisely the problem that necessitates synthetic turnover. Given forty-year male careers, women with low propensities to quit, and a tenure-based salary system, these employers had a strong incentive to increase employee quit rates. The policies of marriage bars and the confinement of women to entry-level positions helped to achieve this end.

The Location of Synthetic Turnover

Synthetic turnover offers an important alternative to natural turnover explanations of low female occupational status. However, it cannot provide a general explanation of this phenomenon. A major objection is that overt discrimination against older or married women has not been a universal aspect of female employment. Marriage bars are virtually non-existent in the United States today. Surveys of American employers before World War II found such overt discrimination only in a subset of employers. The Purdue sample found that 40 to 50 percent of all employers did not formally bar the hiring of married women. Since the theory only applies to particular employers in particular periods, it is necessary to specify the precise circumstances under which a synthetic turnover regime can appear.

As argued above, synthetic turnover regimes are most likely to appear when all of the following are present: renumeration based on tenure-based salary scales; learning curves that peak early; a substantial supply of replacement labor; and a normative climate that will tolerate overt sex discrimination. This last condition rules out the likelihood of synthetic turnover regimes existing in contemporary America. The presence of vigorously enforced equal opportunity legislation makes implementing such a regime unfeasible today. However, overt discrimination would have been consistent with the sex-role ideologies of earlier periods. In those periods, the presence of marriage bars would have been determined largely by the first three economic considerations.

The first factor helps to explain why discrimination against married women is so prevalent in Japan. Japanese employment has long been characterized by tenure-based salary scales, even among blue-collar workers. A common system is one in which a substantial percentage of pay is determined by the age and seniority of the worker. This system, called "nenko," is associated with the extremely well-developed internal labor markets that are typical of Japanese firms. Age-based payment systems are particularly prone to automatic inflation. In Japan, they have been financed by continuing organizational growth and economic profitability. In the 1970's, as Japanese economic growth began to stagnate, the cost burden of the nenko system became particularly intense (Cole 1979). The pervasive use of seniority pay in Japan would have been a strong incentive to introduce synthetic turnover. The 1962 International Labour Office report characterized Japan as an economy-wide user of marriage bars.[5] In the 1970's the need for such a system would have increased. Japan may be one of the only countries in the developed world that still uses bars extensively.

Among occupations, the combination of tenure-based salary scales and short learning curves is most likely to appear in clerical work. Unfortunately, no satisfactory data exist on the precise distribution of systems of remuneration or training requirements in the labor force; this is especially true for historical discussions. The following argument is put forward as a conjecture only; the data used in its support are illustrative, but not necessarily conclusive.

White-collar work—professional, managerial, clerical, and to a lesser degree sales—is particularly likely to pay employees on tenure-based salary scales, while blue-collar workers are more like to be paid with flat rates or piece rates. One indicator of this is the relationship between earnings and age. White-collar workers have pay profiles that increase with age over the entire course of the life cycle, whereas blue-collar profiles are relatively flat, with a slight increase in early youth and a decline in old age (Phelps Brown 1977).

Human capital theorists might argue that the steep white-collar pay profile reflects a long period of learning on the job, because in the human capital model, pay is related to productivity (Mincer and Polachek 1974). However, there is evidence that the increased remuneration of white-collar workers over time is due less to productivity increase than to automatic tenure-based pay raises. James Medoff and Katherine Abraham examined the relationship between tenure, pro-

5. The other three society-wide users of marriage bars, according to the ILO, were the Netherlands, Italy, and Ireland. Further research is needed to identify the factors facilitating discrimination in these countries.

ductivity, and salary among three samples of executives. They found that for these executives salaries routinely increased over time. These raises were only partially related to productivity. Productivity did correlate with pay raises due to promotion. However, non-promoted employees also received substantial pay increases. The correlation between these within-grade pay increases and productivity was close to zero. The fact that salaries increased over time with no clear relation to performance strongly suggests the presence of automatic, tenure-based scales (Medoff and Abraham 1980, 1981).

Managers and clerks tend to be paid under similar regimes. In the Great Western Railway and the General Post Office, both managers and clerks were paid using salary systems that incorporated automatic raises. The only feature that distinguished the two groups was the mean level of remuneration (GPO Establishment Books 1857–1937; GWR Staff Census 1933). However, clerks and managers do differ on one critical aspect; clerks are much less skilled than managers. Most clerical workers enter employment pre-trained. They learn typing, dictation, and bookkeeping in secretarial courses, offered privately or in high school (Oppenheimer 1970; Rotella 1981). Clerical learning curves should flatten out before managerial curves do. If both workers are paid on the same system, clerical work will create much more severe problems of overannuation.

Manual occupations with flat salary scales have no relation to tenure. Levels of remuneration are often set by collective bargaining, with the resulting rates applied to particular jobs, irrespective of the individual attributes of the job holder. Futhermore, manual work is often paid at piece rates. Since piecework relates remuneration to actual output, the contradictions of tenure-based systems are thus avoided. Therefore, in manual occupations there is no need to engage in synthetic turnover.

The service occupations and sales work are intermediate cases. Service occupations are too heterogeneous to allow for simple characterization. Sales work does utilize time-based salary scales. However, in many circumstances these scales are augmented by commissions. These commissions are productivity-based and reduce the threat of superannuation.[6] If these considerations are valid, clerical work

6. Department store clerks provide a significant exception to this discussion. They are usually paid on straight tenure-based salary. Failure to perform, however, is often accompanied by dismissal. By firing non-performers, management keeps salaries and

should be more likely than other occupations to use synthetic turnover because of its combination of tenure-based salary scales and short learning curves.

Of all the surveys of employer behavior reviewed in this study, that which found the highest extent of discrimination against married women was the British National Whitley Council Study of 1946. This survey found that every private employer in its sample used marriage bars. The Whitley Council sample was the only one that consisted entirely of large bureaucratic clerical employers. Large bureaucracies should be especially prone among clerical employers to use synthetic turnover because they are especially likely to utilize internal labor markets (Edwards 1979). The Whitley sample thus had a very high propensity to use tenure-based salary scales.

Studies of marriage bars in multiple industries tend to support the correlation between clerical work and discrimination. The Purdue study found that offices were more likely than factories to restrict the employment of married women. Sixty-one percent of the offices had some form of bar on the hiring of married women, as opposed to 50 percent of the factories. Thirty-three percent of the offices required resignation upon marriage, while only 20 percent of the factories did so. The Internal Labor Office reporters also noted a predisposition of clerical employers towards discrimination. The ILO accounts were largely impressionistic. No systematic attempts were made to compare industries; rather when an observer found a particularly striking example of the use of bars, it was included in his nation's report. Nevertheless, there are systematic tendencies as to which industries are cited and which are not. The reporters from western Australia, Belgium, Colombia, El Salvador, and Italy all explicitly noted that discrimination against married women was more common among salaried employees than among wage workers; no one reported the opposite trend (International Labor Office 1962).

A more systematic measure of discrimination against older women is available: the actual age structure of occupations. Very few older

---

productivity mutually consistent. Productivity in sales work is easily measurable by sales. Productivity in clerical work is harder to measure. Furthermore, individual sales are likely to fluctuate from period to period. Clerical productivity is likely to be fairly constant over time. The lack of readily observable short-term slumps in productivity may have kept clerical employers from using particularistic firing to keep costs in line.

women will show up in an occupation having a marriage bar in effect. Young age distributions are also a product of selective hiring in favor of juveniles. A preference for female juveniles is a preference for women who may self-select out of employment on the occasion of marriage. Table 4.4 comes from a survey of American employers in seven cities in 1955.[7] It shows the age structure of female employment in the eight-code census category occupations. In most occupations 36 percent to 40 percent of the women were older than forty-five. A marked exception was clerical work. Clerical work had by far the youngest age distribution among women, with only 22.8 percent of its employees being older than forty-five.

Table 4.4

Percentage of All Female Employees Who Were Forty-Five or Older, by Occupation, 1955

Occupation	%
Clerical	22.8
Skilled manual	37.4
Semi-skilled manual	34.5
Unskilled	28.5
Service (primarily domestics)	37.3
Professional/managerial	40.6
Sales	39.1

Note: N = approx. 10,500.
Source: U.S. Bureau of Employment Security Sample, 1955. From U.S. Department of Labor, Bureau of Employment Security (1956).

There are several alternative explanations of why clerical work might have a young female age structure. It could be that an absence of older women represents a high female propensity to quit because of domestic obligations. But it is hard to see why women in clerical professions would feel more domestic than those in other occupations. Women may leave in reaction to the monotony and low pay of clerical work; unskilled labor, which is also poorly paid, has the second youngest age distribution in the table. However, consider the service occupations, which are made up in large part of private domestic

7. The seven cities are Detroit, Los Angeles, Miami, Seattle, Philadelphia, Minneapolis-Saint Paul, and Worcester.

workers, waitresses, and the like. These are unremunerative, dead-end jobs with an age distribution that is relatively old.

A young age structure could alternatively be the result of employers' preferences for young, attractive employees. Certainly such a case could be made for clerical work, where receptionists and secretaries are often hired to work with the public. However, other occupations requiring female contact with male customers do not have particularly young age structures. Service occupations are in the middle of the female age distribution, and female sales workers are the second oldest in the table. The previous arguments suggest that neither high natural female turnover, low pay per se, nor bias towards physical attractiveness adequately explains the unusually young age distribution of female clerks. Such a unique position is completely consistent with the synthetic turnover model.[8]

Labor scarcity also has an impact on synthetic turnover. When replacement workers are difficult to obtain, increasing turnover is no longer rational. Marriage bars were fairly common during the Great Depression, but they became much less common during the labor scarcity of the 1950's. Valerie Oppenheimer presents data on the extent of discrimination against married women as school teachers in American urban school districts. In 1928, nearly 60 percent of all school districts discriminated against married women. This figure rose to 77 percent in 1930 and 87 percent by 1941. After the war, the figure dropped to 18 percent and has declined to negligible levels since then (Oppenheimer 1970). What is true for American schoolteachers may

---

8. The relative rankings of age distributions by occupation for men are roughly similar. The percentage of all male employees who were forty-five or over for the various occupations was as follows: clerical, 32.1; unskilled, 33.2; semi-skilled, 30.4; service, 54.1; skilled, 40.3; sales, 35.4; professional-managerial, 36.5. For both sexes, clerical, unskilled, and semi-skilled work were the youngest occupations, while sales, professional, skilled, and services were much older. The correlation between an occupation's percentage over forty-five for men and women is .41. The relatively young age of male clerks undoubtedly was not caused by marriage bars. Here the primary mechanism was the selective recruitment of juveniles. Upward mobility could also play a role; male clerks, for example, may move into managerial occupations.

Male clerical workers are only the second youngest occupation in the table because the male clerical workers tended to be older than the female clerical workers. Male clerical workers might be expected to hold more skilled positions than female clerks. If this is the case, male clerical workers are not obvious examples of salaried workers with short learning curves. Tenure-based salaries with medium learning curves have effects similar to low skills with flat rates and produce a male clerical age structure similar to that of unskilled workers.

have been true universally. The 1962 ILO study still found substantial evidence of discrimination. Nevertheless, most reporters remarked that the extent of such discrimination was decreasing. Many referred to particular discriminatory industries as isolated cases of policies that were steadily disappearing from general practice.

Conclusion

This study has shown that there is a clear domain of employment in which the natural turnover theory is inappropriate. These are the firms with explicit policies of synthetic turnover, fims that confine women to low-status positions as a strategy to reduce the need for incentive wages. While this practice has never been universally followed, it was implemented by a relatively large percentage of employers in earlier times, particularly for salaried positions. Where such practices can be clearly documented, the natural turnover hypothesis must be rejected as an explanation of low female status.

Women's confinement to subordinate economic positions has been a general phenomenon. Synthetic turnover regimes have been much more restricted in their application. The question arises as to how one could explain women's low status in these industries that have no apparent marriage bars in operation.

It is plausible that policies of synthetic turnover that have existed in the past could have a lagged effect on sex-typing, even if the actual discriminatory policies themselves have been abolished. Many occupations may have had marriage bars at the time of their inception. Sex types are remarkably stable: most occupations do not change sex composition by as much as 5 percent per decade (Snyder et al. 1978). Norms prohibiting women from access to certain positions could have been created in the era of marriage bars. A marriage bar is likely to be buttressed by the creation of an elaborate ideology "explaining" why women cannot be considered for certain superior jobs. After the marriage bar disappears, this ideology could remain, creating a lasting barrier to female advancement.

The natural turnover hypothesis remains questionable. Its major premise, the intrinsically higher turnover of women as compared to men, has never been convincingly demonstrated. Synthetic turnover is probably only part of the explanation of the overall occupational subordination of women. New strategies of explanation are clearly required if we wish to understand the phenomenon in economic terms.

5

The Legitimation of Exclusion

One of the most important factors contributing to the limitation of women's opportunities in the General Post Office and the Great Western Railway was the sexism of male managers. Employers' belief in innate female inferiority and their preference for interacting with male employees led to women's exclusion from offices that were non-clerical-labor-intense. Sexism may have contributed as well to the confinement of women to low-status jobs. Excluding women from jobs with long learning curves was consistent with synthetic turnover and the economic need to create circulation among the staff. However, such a policy was also consistent with the interest of male managers in patriarchy and, in particular, the preferential allocation of promotions to men.[1]

However important this concern with sex privilege may have been, it was a dubious basis on which to justify a business decision. All major personnel policies at some point had to be defended before the superior. Department heads had to submit staff budgets to the Secretary's Office. The Secretary had to report to the board of trustees, if the firm was private, or to the Treasury Department, if it was public. Even decisions that were made on the most personal, idiosyncratic grounds had to be rationalized with arguments that used good business sense or

1. Note that the data in the Chapter 4 chapter cannot be wholly explained by simple sexism, with no reference to the underlying economics. It would be difficult using patriarchy alone to explain why discrimination against older women was less pronounced in blue-collar jobs than in white-collar jobs. If anything, the machismo environment of the factory should have intensified rather than reduced such discrimination.

incorporated sound public policy. In private firms, the former rather than the latter were especially important. Given that men are more expensive than women, the exclusion of women always had to legitimated to local referees in terms of a larger organizational policy.

The significance of such ideologies has to be placed in proper perspective. A good explanation was neither necessary nor sufficient to exclude women from the job. People are intellectually very capable of bending the terms of a given set of beliefs to justify the policy they want to pursue. Max Weber was able to take the anti-materialism of early protestantism and twist it into a justification for capitalism (Weber 1958). "Equal pay for equal work," which sounds like a reasonably feminist position, has been used by male unionists to legitimate paying women less than men (Kessler-Harris 1982).

Nevertheless, a manager could significantly contribute to the maintenance of an all-male labor force by developing an ideological defense of such a policy that could withstand the scrutiny of his immediate superiors. A sexist manager whose covering explanation was weak could expect constant challenge from budgetary watchdogs. The use of males would require extended confrontations with his colleagues and the expenditure of a substantial amount of time and energy. A well-accepted justification could be the basis of permanent organizational policy; once the principle was established, a precedent could be set that would allow for the easy exclusion of women from comparable positions in the future.

Not all such arguments are intellectually interesting. In the setting of the sex-type of any particular job, managers are likely to make a fairly large number of arguments, each of which may contribute in some way to the final decision that gets made. Those ideological statements that are particularistic and case-specific will have little predictive power in a general discussion of sex-typing. Within the Great Western Railway and the General Post Office, however, there were a number of principles that became important general guides to policy. These principles became accepted because they were consistent with the objective economic requirements of each firm; once instituted, however, they attained a life of their own. They introduced minor rigidities that kept women out of job assignments for which they would have been economically appropriate. They also provided a cover with which managers could obscure large-scale de-feminizations and rationalize the preferential allocation of rewards to men. The economic considerations motivating the original policies by themselves would have justified the exclusion of women from some attractive forms of employment. However, these programs were implemented in a fashion that was blatantly discriminatory against women. Furthermore, management justified these policies both with economic considerations and with bald, forthright discussions of the inferiority of women. Thus, for many managers the appeal of these policies was that they provided a legitimate, defensible cover for the extension of male privilege.

Women and Nightwork

One of the most important of these policies was the prohibition of women from working at night. In both the Great Western Railway and the General Post Office, women were generally only permitted to work shifts that started no earlier than seven in the morning and ended no later than nine at night. Related to this ban on nightwork was the rule that only men were allowed to work on Sundays. Thus, all positions that required irregular attendances were given by default to male employees.

The importance of the nightwork ban in limiting female employment cannot be overestimated. Most of the work in sorting mail occurred between three and seven in the morning, when sorters prepared mailbags for morning trains. Depot clerks often had to work at comparable hours preparing the invoicing and accounts for early departures. These early-morning duties were one of the fundamental reasons that women were barred from sorting offices and railway depots. Nightwork was also important in telegraph work. A substantial proportion of telegraph transmission was done at night. News stories would be transmitted late at night for use in the morning papers; non-urgent messages were also sent at this time, when the lower volume of traffic on the wires justified charging a lower rate. Women were traditionally given the daytime duties in signalling offices, while night duties were given exclusively to men.

Sorting offices, depots, and telegraph offices were the most important cases of women's employment being limited by paternalistic restrictions on hours. Most other offices worked on a nine-to-five schedule and had limited requirements for their staff to stay late. It was true that during annual peaks, or when offices were understaffed, overtime could be required. In these cases, men had to remain at work while women went home. However, most clerical offices never generated enough overtime to require a night staff, thus preventing the rise of a set of positions from which women would be prohibited.

To some extent, the banning of women from nightwork was voluntary on the part of the firms. They were not forced to adopt their hours policy because women were unwilling to accept night positions, nor were they under legal compulsion to make such restrictions. Women themselves would have been entirely willing to accept clerical employment at night or on weekends. This was actually demonstrated during World War I, when the shortage of male labor forced the Post Office to use women for all duties, including those at night. The Post Office had been reluctant to have women sort at all. After it became necessary to bring in women temporary sorters, they still attempted to give men the night duties. However, complaints from the men and the growing labor shortage finally required that women be placed on non-daylight shifts. Originally, women were put on a three P.M. to midnight duty. This proved to be extremely unpopular with the women because they were forced to go home in the middle of the night on dark, unsafe streets. As an alternative, the women were put on a shift from nine P.M. to six A.M. This solved the transit problem, since women could now take the late trams to work every evening and return home during daylight on the early-morning trains. The commuting was made more pleasant by their going in the opposite direction from rush-hour traffic on both halves of their daily route. Furthermore, the new shift was compatible with the women's family responsibilities. The three-to-midnight shift kept women away from home during the dinner hour. The nine-to-six shift allowed women to be home during the day, prepare dinner for their families, and see that the children were in bed before reporting to work. This new shift was acceptable to the women and was generally adopted during the war whenever female nightwork was required (WWI Nightwork 1918).

Many employers were legally forbidden to use women at night. Britain had an extensive body of protectionist legislation that put limits on the situations in which an employer could hire women or juveniles. There were restrictions on the kinds of industries in which women could be employed and there were limits on the hours that women could work. Nevertheless, none of these laws applied to clerical positions on the Great Western Railway, and they had no relevance whatsoever to the General Post Office. Office employment was exempt from most protectionist legislation. Whatever laws did exist applied to factories, and specifically to those parts of the factory where manufacturing actually took place. An office within a factory would have been exempt both from the hours limitations of the Factory Acts and from the health and sanitary provisions as well. The Railway Clerks Association lobbied in the 1920's to extend the Factory Acts to railway offices, but never received even modest support (Walkden 1928). The Post Office would have been exempt from protectionist legislation in any case, because they were an agency of the crown. Factory laws were limited in their application to the private sector.[2]

However, this said, it should be noted that the Post Office often voluntarily followed policies that were mandated by law for other industries. In order to facilitate the enforcement of labor legislation, the civil service usually attempted to run the government by the same laws that it was advocating to industry as sound public policy. Thus, when the government began to encourage the use of industry-wide collective bargaining, it set up formal negotiating machinery for its own employees. When, at the turn of the century, national employment policy consisted of discouraging employers from hiring boys to dead-end positions that could create later unemployment problems, the government voluntarily reduced its own reliance on juvenile labor, even though this entailed substantial costs. The Post Office's tendency to act as a model employer may have carried over into its nightwork policies. Although there may have been external political pressures for the Post Office to abstain from nightwork, there would have been few formal legal barriers. However, the Post Office's willingness to cooperate with national policy was probably facilitated by some internal considerations. Not only did the nightwork ban appeal to the local patriarchical concerns of Post Office management, but it had economic advantages as well.

The restriction was made economically viable by the side benefits that came from imposing large amounts of nightwork on men. Late shifts were generally unpopular among the men. Most night shifts were staffed with men who had been assigned to such rotations against their will, since the Post Office could rarely find men who would take such hours voluntarily (Telegraph Substitution 1880; Hobhouse 1906).

2. I am very grateful to W. B. Creighton for a personal written communication that provided the legal analysis in this section. Creighton is the author of *Working Women and the Law* (1979), the definitive published work on the evolution of protectionist legislation in England.

Duncan Gallie has a perceptive discussion of why in general workers do not like working late shifts. Nightwork seriously disrupts people's personal lives. Early evening is when most people have their social lives. Nightwork not only restricts workers' ability to see their friends, but keeps them from attending meetings or cultural events. Late shifts also provided a source of tension for family life. Late hours keep the worker from interacting with his or her family; futhermore, the presence of a day sleeper inhibits the patterns of living of those family members who are home during the day and have to remain quiet. Most important, the irregularity of sleep and meals that come from an off-cycle schedule can be seriously detrimental to a worker's health. The change in eating habits can have as much of an impact as sleep loss in producing physical problems, exhaustion, and psychological distress (Gallie 1978). In the GWR and GPO, both men and women avoided late hours whenever possible; there are few cases of women's volunteering to work evening hours. Women were no more incapable of working late than men were, but both sexes preferred daytime employment.

Because of the unpopularity of nightwork, it was against Post Office policy to assign anyone to such a position permanently. The Telegraph Department explicitly kept a set of permanent day positions open as promotions for those workers who had worked disproportionately at night. The special reserve of day jobs was the linchpin of the economic strategy that made the scheduling of nightwork a tool for sex discrimination. If only men could do nightwork, and there was a reserve of day jobs left over for nightworkers, then this day reserve would also be all-male. The same logic applied for the supervisory force. Nightworkers would need superintendents. However, the night supervisory positions were the least attractive of the better positions. Thus, there would have to be a reserve of supervisory day positions left open to provide relief for the night supervisors (Hobhouse 1906).

The night reserve system had important economic advantages as well. The Post Office incentive system was based on annual salary increases coupled with the prospects of promotion. However, the number of superior positions was limited by economic constraints; not every male worker could expect regular promotion throughout his career. Since the supply of both annual pay increments and promotions was financially limited, the telegraph service needed a scarce resource that could be distributed preferentially and that would not cost the Post Office any money. Daytime positions were such a resource, so the Post Office began to use the night/day distinction as an inexpensive way to provide mobility for the men.

By 1880, the outlines of the shift incentive system were in place. There was no permanent night shift per se. Instead, all entering workers were subject to irregular mandatory night duty. The night jobs would be first filled by volunteers; then, after that, the supervisor would assign workers temporarily to the late shift until all posts were filled. All workers were subject to being tapped for late-night duty until they could get promoted or transferred to an all-day position. Some skilled jobs were only performed by day, making promotion to such a position a double benefit. Likewise, some offices were only open by day, making a transfer to such a site automatic protection. If a worker could not get one of these positions, he had to wait until a job in the day reserve opened up and then he would be guaranteed freedom from the night draft. Note that both the lateral transfers and the day reserve represented prizes that a worker could compete for, which cost the Post Office nothing to distribute.

This explains why women were barred from nightwork in the telegraph department. The development of long-term incentives was only an issue for permanent staff. Women were temporary staff who were expected to leave upon marriage. The Post Office wanted to restrict the improvements a woman would receive in her career so that as many "promotions" as possible would be concentrated among the men. There are two regimes that would have been consistent with such a strategy. All women could have been put permanently on nightwork, along with a minority of men. The minority of men would have then competed for a daylight assignment. The Post Office chose the other alternative, putting all women on daylight assignments and making all men work to obtain a daytime job. Because women's hours were constant, they received no improvements over their career, excluding them from the Post Office's incentive system.[3] Not only was the entire population of men thus put into a competitive situation, but the value of a daytime job became inflated. Removing women from the draft pool meant that the odds of any individual man's having to do nightwork were increased, just as the supply of daytime jobs was artificially restricted. This increased the pressure felt by men to compete for a daytime slot and thus further bound the men to the postal incentive

3. This is one form of "exclusion" of which most women approved.

system. Thus the linking of nightwork to gender was intrinsically related to the policy of synthetic turnover that divided workers by the need to provide them with long-term incentives.

There were other points of convergence between the nightwork ban and the operation of the postal internal labor market. In the Telegraph Service, the confinement of women to low-status jobs, which was an essential component of the synthetic turnover regime, was originally instituted as a by-product of the creation of the male day-shift reserve. The vigorous implementation of the nightwork ban was facilitated by the fact that it provided a second justification for the artificial encouragement of early female retirement and the elimination of women from complex, highly paid positions.

In the early days of feminization of telegraphs, women were given a number of duties that were far more responsible and complex than those they would receive in later periods. This was due to the idiosyncrasies of the market for telegraph operators in the early 1870's, when women were first introduced to telegraph work. The management of the Post Office committed itself early to the principle of a female signalling force. There were many factors that contributed to heavy early feminization, such as a concern with reducing labor militancy and an overall need to economize on personnel due to the high labor intensity of hand-transmitting messages. Once the telegraph force had been made primarily female, however, it was difficult for the Post Office to confine women strictly to the low-status positions. In the late 1860's and early 1870's, competent Morse code operators were extremely scarce. Telegraph signalling is a highly skilled occupation that requires years of training. A signaller needs at least a year to learn the rudiments of Morse code and then several years after that to become proficient. The Post Office could not train its labor force gradually because, at the time of nationalization, the telegraph service was rapidly expanding, creating an enormous number of vacancies. This created a very large number of jobs that had to be filled by whomever was available to fill them. Under these circumstances, the Post Office could not afford to be too particular about which jobs were open or closed to women. Women made up 60 percent of the learners in any given year (GPO Establishment Books 1876). There were so few operators of any sex that could proficiently work the more difficult lines that the Post Office assigned these positions to anyone who could do the job.

One important implication of this was that many women found

themselves operating long-distance inter-city lines. In general, the difficulty of operating a telegraph line correlated with its length. Local lines within a city were relatively easy to operate, because the connections on these wires usually produced a clear signal and the transmitters used for local messages were not particularly complex. Inter-city connections were both weaker and more prone to breaking down, requiring subtlety in one's fingering technique and the ability to do quick repairs. The long-distance transmitters were substantially more complex than a simple Morse device and varied significantly between one manufacturer and another. In the 1870's, women worked long-distance lines alongside the men and handled these duties with great proficiency. In 1876, in the Central Telegraph Station, the men raced the women sending out the Queen's opening speech to Parliament. The detailed results of the test are not known, but in the aggregate the women significantly outscored the men. According to the Controller of the Telegraph Service, in normal service, under non-competitive conditions, the performance of male and female signallers was roughly equal (Telegraph Report 1876).

This came to an end in the late 1870's. By the 1880's, the telegraph service was strictly segregated into male offices and female offices. Local branch offices were worked by individuals of a single sex. In the Central Telegraph Station, women were removed from the inter-city galleries and forced to work in an all-female Metropolitan gallery that only did local signalling. The primary reason for this transformation of telegraph work was the introduction of the reserved male day shift. Women had been excluded from night duty since the beginning of feminization. By 1875, however, the ban on women's doing nightwork was creating real difficulties for the staffing of the late shifts. The ratio of women to men at the Central Telegraph Station was at an all-time high, possibly due to an overcommitment by management to female labor. The late duties were falling on an ever-decreasing supply of men. Since the same individuals were consistently being selected for involuntary late shifts, morale became extremely bad. Telegraph management realized that in order to create an acceptably large pool of candidates for nightwork, the sex ratio of the telegraph service would have to become more male. The need for males became intensified by the creation of the male day-shift reserve, which was first developed and implemented during this period.

The Post Office was then faced with the problem of how to adjust the ratio of males to females to comply with the new nightwork-related requirements. Some of the adjustment in the sex ratio could be accomplished through the natural growth of the Post Office. The new vacancies created by expansion could be given to men, producing a painless strategy of de-feminization. The Post Office took the maximum advantage of this kind of tactic by closing its training program to women telegraphists and refusing to make any more female hires. However, the supply of male entrants was insufficient to produce a proportion of men that would be large enough to support both the night shift and the day reserve. Some of the change in the sex ratio would have to come from established female employees leaving the service. So in the mid-1870's the Telegraph Service began a campaign to encourage women signallers to resign from postal employment (Telegraph Substitution 1880).

The first step was the imposition of a marriage bar. The Telegraph Service had not used a marriage bar in the early 1870's, since the general shortage of qualified operators motivated management to encourage women to remain on the job (Scudamore 1871). By 1876, however, a bar was in place to encourage a high rate of female exits. Postal officials noted, however, that even with a marriage bar, women were not resigning fast enough to bring in the required number of men. To further stimulate the quit rate, the Post Office froze all promotions of female staff. It was decided that until the sex ratio of the service was brought to an acceptable level, all supervisory vacancies were to be filled with men. In the same spirit, the women were taken out of the Provincial Gallery, where the work was complex and technically stimulating, and put in the Metropolitan Gallery, where they could operate the simpler machines. Women were also taken out of branch offices where nightwork was performed and put in all-female branch offices that only operated by day.

Given the enormous scope and scale of the personnel readjustments that were being made, it is unlikely that the nightwork ban alone can totally account for these changes. The need to reduce the percentage of women in the Telegraph Service was relatively short term; however, the redistribution of women that resulted was a permanent transformation of Post Office practice. Additional support for these policies may have come from particularly sexist male managers who would approve of the limitation of female opportunity purely for patriarchical reason. However, what made these transitions economically viable was the fact that those policies that in the short term would help to produce an all-male reserve day shift would in the long term help contribute to the synthetic turnover regime. By the time that the staff adjustments required by nightwork were complete, the Post Office could reasonably expect to be suffering from the problem of an overly mature labor force on tenure-based salary scales. The solution to both the nightwork and salary-scale problems were the same: encourage women to leave, and allocate women to low-status positions to minimize the human capital loss entailed with these organizationally induced exits. The complementarity of nightwork policy with other important organizational concerns contributed both to the implementation of the staff adjustments of the 1870's and to the long-term viability of nightwork itself as an accepted organizational principle.[4]

Segregation by Sex

There was a second process equally important to the limitation of female employment, the sex segregation of offices. Both the Great Western Railway and the General Post Office maintained separate promotion chains and salary schedules for their male and female employees. The General Post Office went one step further and wherever possible kept men and women in different rooms or buildings. Local London telegraph offices were either all male or all female; if an office was worked by both sexes, the women worked by day and the men worked by night. Money order work was arbitrarily divided into two sections, money order and postal order. The processing of the two orders was virtually identical, except money orders had a lower limit on the size of a transaction. Throughout the nineteenth century,

---

4. It is ironic that a policy designed to promote male employment, provide supervisory openings for men, and shorten female careers resulted in the immiseration of the lives of entry-level male clerks. There was a parallel situation in World War I, when the Sorters Union was attempting to forestall the use of female temporary sorters. The union leaders offered to have their men work double shifts if this would guarantee that the Post Office would not introduce women (WWI Sorters 1915). Both the sorters case and the telegraph case seem to illustrate Michael Reich's contention that competition between majority and minority workers can lead to a worsening of conditions for both parties (Reich 1981).

money orders were processed by an all-male staff, and postal orders were processed by an all-female staff. The postal order women were further isolated by being placed with other women in the Receiver and Accountant General's Office. The sections were merged in 1906, although this was combined with staff changes that made the new division over 90 percent female. The Receiver and Accountant General's Office was further divided into two divisions, the main section and the telegraph accounts section. The first was all-male and the second was all female, although this distinction was relaxed after World War I. The segregation of the sexes even applied to temporary workers. During World War I, when temporary women sorters were introduced to the London sorting office, they were confined to an all-female floor, while men were restricted to the rest of the building. Sex segregation was also practiced by the Great Western Railway, but in a far more limited fashion. The need for isolation of the sexes dominated the early discussions of feminizing, and sex segregation was implemented up through World War I. After World War I, however, the practice was abandoned, and male and female employees were mixed freely.

Sex segregation had a mixed impact on women's economic opportunities; it reduced the absolute number of jobs for women, but it upgraded the quality of those positions that remained. Sex segregation produced rigidities in the determination of occupational sex-typing by making the sex-type of a job dependent on the aggregate properties of an office rather than on the particular qualities of the job itself. The operation of segregation can be seen most clearly with a simplifying example. Assume that the only determinant of occupational sex-typing was the status of the position. If there were no sex segregation of offices, all high-status jobs would go to men and all low-status jobs would go to women. Under a regime of sex segregation, however, the sex composition of the office will be determined by the average properties of all jobs within the office. Thus, departments with a high proportion of supervisory positions will be male, and those with a low proportion of such positions will be female. However, jobs with atypical status will be misallocated in both kinds of departments; high-status jobs in the low-status offices will go to women, and low-status jobs in the high-status offices will go to men. Most offices have more unskilled positions than skilled ones. Therefore, a trade of skilled for unskilled positions leaves the side receiving the unskilled positions with a larger number of jobs. Segregation ends up defeminizing a large number of female jobs and feminizing a small number of formerly male jobs. This reduces the total amount of female employment, but improves the quality of those jobs that remain.[5]

Sex segregation was by itself substantially less important than many of the other factors affecting sex-typing. It involved the misallocation of a minority of jobs in departments whose majority was correctly sex-typed in terms of its economic attributes. Furthermore, serious misallocations could be corrected by the physical relocation of personnel. In the male Money Order Department, much of the filing and sorting was done by women. Since technically they were not supposed to be part of the Money Order Department, which was by definition male, they were hired as part of the female staff of the Savings Bank. Part of the explicit job duties of female sorters in the Savings Bank was to do sorting and filing in other departments, sparing these departments from having to hire their own female staff (GPO Establishment Books 1901).

Sex segregation was a comparatively transitory device for the exclusion of women. Sex segregation had been originally justifiable because Victorian managers feared that the mingling of the sexes would lead to a weakening of work discipline, as normally productive male workers gave in to the temptation of flirting, courting, and making casual conversation. Such fears seem groundless now and were probably groundless then. Workers in all-male environments lose time in stag conversations; introducing women would have changed the content but not the amount of the non-work-related fraternizing. Thus, to the extent that sex segregation represented a sincere concern by management with the deleterious effects of mixing, such concerns were likely to be allayed by actual experience with a coed labor force.

Furthermore, managers who attempted rigid sex segregation found this led to a wide variety of practical difficulties. The isolation of one sex from the other was often allowed to lapse through benign neglect.

5. Unfortunately, it is difficult to test these propositions quantitatively. There is no meaningful data on within-firm variance in office sex segregation, ruling out large-sample analyses such as those in Chapter 2. Differences between the GPO and the GWR are more likely to be due to clerical labor intensity or to differences in the status structures of the firms.

A particularly short-lived case of sex segregation occurred in the Foreign Office of the British civil service. The Foreign Office hired a small number of female typists, whom they sought to isolate from the male clerical staff, fearing that, if men began to socialize with the new typists, there would be an uncontrollable disruption of normal work activities. Therefore, they placed the women in an isolated room in the attic, far from the normal flow of Foreign Office activities. Male clerks were strictly forbidden from entering the attic, and the women's presence was never officially announced except for an arrow on the attic staircase that said "To the Typewriters." Obviously, under such circumstances, the female typists could not be kept a secret for long. Matters came to a head the first time that the women were to be paid. It was strictly inappropriate for men and women to fraternize in the corridors. However, it was equally inappropriate to give a worker's check to anyone other than the worker himself. Thus, if the women were to be paid, they would have to report during working hours to the Cashier's Office, which was located on the ground floor. Somehow, the women were going to have to get from the attic to the ground floor and back again without anyone either seeing them or having a chance to talk with them. So on payday, when the women's turn came to receive their checks, all the corridors of the building were evacuated. The doors of all the offices were shut. Then the women were sent running down the stairs as fast as possible to get their checks and sent running back up to the attic again. As soon as they were safely concealed, the corridors were reopened and business was allowed to continue as before. Obviously, such a disruptive and cumbersome procedure could not have been made part of the weekly routine; management quickly perceived the difficulty of maintaining total segregation and moved the typists downstairs with the rest of the staff (Martindale 1938).

A comparable situation occurred in the Secretary's office of the Great Western Railway. Most of the Great Western Railway was unsegregated. However, the supervisor of the Registration section of the Secretary's office preferred a segregated staff. The Registration Office was responsible for servicing the GWR's obligations to its stockholders; it sent out dividend checks every quarter and kept records of the ownership of individual shares. The office occupied three rooms, two of which were all male and the third of which was all female. To justify this physical division of labor, all women were given the job title "addressograph and duplicating machine operator."[6] The men were given a wide variety of job titles reflecting the diversity of tasks within the office. Thus, the women could be relegated to the room with the addressograph machine and kept apart from the male employees.

However, the separation of the sexes quickly broke down. First, for the women to make addressograph plates, they needed to know the addresses of the stockholders; these addresses were kept in the main files located in the mens' offices. The regular passage of women to and from the files provided ample opportunities for conversation. Second, it was impractical to confine women merely to addressograph work. Every three months, dividend checks had to be distributed, producing regular peaks in the workload of the office. During these peak periods, it was necessary to assign women to check preparation in order to relieve some of the pressure on the men. Since both men and women were working on the same tasks, it was impossible to coordinate the work without a substantial amount of interaction between the sexes. Thus, in practice, there was neither a rigorous isolation of the sexes nor an ironclad division of labor between men and women. It is easy to see how as a practical matter sex segregation would make a poor basis for the legitimation of all-male offices (GWR Women 1906).

The Great Western Railway followed the practice of most modern corporations in freely intermingling the sexes. The Registration Office maintained the fiction of hiring only men for two rooms and only women for the third, but in this regard it was an idiosyncratic exception. However, the Post Office maintained fairly rigid sex segregation up through World War II. The persistence of sex segregation in the Post Office is not easy to explain, but several factors may have contributed to it.

The first consideration is that the Post Office grew by the steady creation of new departments and divisions, as opposed to simple growth in numbers or growth from the absorption of pre-existing units. The creation of new units meant that there were always a large number of vacancies that could be arbitrarily filled with members of either sex; in the case of simple growth or growth through absorption, although vacancies are created, the units in which these new positions occur are

6. This job title only applied within the office. For salary purposes, the women were either grade 1 or grade 2 women clerks.

already partially filled with pre-existing job holders. The presence of this earlier cohort of workers produces a pre-existing set of occupational sex-types that may not be consistent with an economic sex-segregated regime. It may be theoretically possible, given a particular distribution of jobs in a department, to create an arbitrary division of some offices as male and others as female that would produce an optimal overall sex ratio for the entire department. If a given department should be 40 percent male, it might be possible to arrange a set of single-sex offices so that 40 percent of the total staff is male, with no individual offices suffering from a grossly incorrect sex-type. However, the number of possible administrative solutions to such a problem will be small. Pre-existing staff in the wrong locations can add to the cost of setting up a segregated regime, as personnel have to be reallocated and retrained in new positions. The continual creation of new organizational units in the Post Office, such as the Telegraph Accounts Branch, the Postal Order section, the Telephone sections, and an immense number of local telegraph offices, provided the staffing flexibility to create a viable segregated regime.

Second, because the Post Office had been feminized during the nineteenth century, the labor shortages of World War I had a negligible impact on local patterns of occupational sex-typing. World War I had a far more disruptive impact on offices that in 1914 were predominantly male. Military enlistments created large numbers of vacancies that were randomly distributed throughout the male clerical ranks. Female replacements were required in virtually every office of most firms; since women were being brought in as short-term temporary help, they were assigned to the simpler jobs within each office. Thus, in a firm like the GWR, where World War I produced the first large-scale feminization of clerical work, women would have been distributed among low-status positions within every office and department within the organization. The widespread dispersion of women among departments would have eliminated any immediate prospects of creating segregation. The crisis atmosphere of maintaining smooth operations during the war would have reduced the prospects of developing a long-term segregation plan before 1919; after 1919, the post-war adjustments to the new economic environment would have pushed segregation far down the list of managerial priorities. In the years between 1919 and 1921, the Great Western Railway management was dealing with a series of crippling strikes by their manual laborers and an impending nationalization threat from the government. Many

other industries were dealing with comparable changes in labor relations and government regulation. By 1923, when the business climate
stabilized, the post-war gender regime would have been established
for four years, making segregation an expensive and time-consuming
reorganization.

In contrast, the Post Office introduced women through a series of
planned innovations in which individual offices and departments were
feminized one at a time. The staffing decisions were not made in a
period of general organizational crisis, but instead under conditions in
which the staffing of each individual department could be made the
single preoccupying concern of management. Furthermore, there was
no exogenous force scattering women throughout the organization,
but instead the limited introduction of female clerks into those positions that were designated as being suitable for women by management. By feminizing in a gradual fashion, postal management was able
to plan its sex-typing. By not having war, or past policy, predetermine
various job allocations, the Post Office had the flexibility to develop an
economic segregated regime. Thus, by being an early feminizer experiencing growth through diversification, management could custom-
tailor their sex decisions to fit their own patriarchical needs.

However, it is one thing to explain how it was that the Post Office
had the ability to create segregation; it is another to explain why they
bothered to maintain such a system. In the early years, segregation
seems to have been motivated by a genuine concern with work discipline and propriety. Nevertheless, given the impracticalities of maintaining segregated systems, it is hard to see why the Post Office
persisted in its policies. It would have been administratively simpler
and more cost-efficient to let supervisors in every office hire both male
and female employees and put each sex in those positions that were
appropriate for each sex.

The persistence of segregation may have been due to the unwillingness of postal management to handle the administrative difficulties
that would have been associated with mixing pre-existing single-sex
office staffs. Dorothy Evans, a civil service administrator of the 1930's,
compared the segregation policies of older and newer divisions of the
British civil service. She found the older departments to be much more
rigidly segregated, with the oldest department, the Post Office, being
the most divided of all. To some extent, this might be explainable by
older departments' being run by older and more conservative administrators. However, Evans noted that there was a second problem; those

departments that had been founded early had tended to feminize early and developed several cohorts of mature, experienced women. Some of these women had been promoted to supervisory positions and within the women's sections exercised considerable authority and responsibility. The integration of these women into a male-dominated middle management force would not have been easy. The fairest solution would have been to integrate the male and female promotion chains completely and let the most senior supervisors take the combined responsibilities. In this case, however, many women would have outranked their male competition, which would have been intolerable to both middle and top postal management. A second alternative would have been to let men supplant the women supervisors, de facto demoting these women back to common workers. This would have been an extremely awkward situation, because these men would have had no experience in the work of the women's divisions. The men would have had to have been trained by the very women whose jobs and status they were usurping. This would not have been an insurmountable organizational problem, since firms often depose supervisors when a change of leadership is needed. Given that the women were probably perfectly adequate supervisors, however, one can see how the Post Office might have been loath to engage in the large-scale disruption that would have been required to transfer the superior female positions back to men (Evans 1934).

For whatever reasons segregation survived, it nevertheless produced a small but real impact on women's economic opportunities. It created a microscopic number of advanced positions for women that would not have existed otherwise. In 1931, 7.7 percent of women in the Post Office held non-entry-level jobs. This figure was only 4.7 percent in the unsegregated Great Western Railway. These figures have to be treated with caution. There may have been technical differences between the two firms in the quality of work that could account for these status differentials. The differences could also be due to the different metrics used by the organizations to measure entry level. There is a suggestion, however, although not by any means a strong confirmation, that segregation benefited women by opening up some positions of autonomy.

The study of particular patriarchical constraints on female employment can provide some interesting insights into the process of ocupational sex-typing. Nevertheless, the observer should be wary of assigning any particular mechanism a central role in the overall explanation of the use of women. Nightwork and segregation played a part, but their impact was small relative to such purely economic factors as clerical labor intensity or the dynamics of synthetic turnover. The impact of the nightwork ban was quantitatively tested by including a dummy variable representing the presence of nightwork in the postal equations that were estimated in Chapter 2. There was the expected zero-order relation between nightwork and sex type; women were more likely to appear in those offices that only operated by day. However, when clerical labor intensity, the percentage of non-political jobs, and the percentage of non-entry-level jobs were controlled, the coefficient for nightwork invariably became insignificant. Such a statistical finding is not surprising given the actual distribution of women in the Post Office. Although women were excluded from the sorting offices, which were often open twenty-four hours a day, the telegraph offices contained the heaviest concentrations of women in the Post Office. Telegraph signalling was clerical-labor-intense, and the telegraph offices had no carry-over employees from the pre-1871 era. Both economic factors caused the Telegraph Service to hire massive numbers of women in the 1870's. The adjustments to allow for the demands of nightwork were trivial in comparison.[7]

Predicting occupational sex type from particular cultural or patri-archical ideologies of management is not easy. This is because it is fairly hard to specify a priori precisely what non-economic utilities a management will attempt to maximize in developing its gender policies. Male managers like an all-male labor force, if they have one already. They are usually in favor of confining economic opportunities to men, a value that is partially economic but partially cultural. However, individual managers can often differ dramatically in what other gender-related goals they would like to attain. Postal managers were very concerned about restricting conversation between the sexes; this has hardly been a universal concern of capitalists.

An example of the diversity of non-economic sex utilities can be found in the case of sexual harassment. Some employers have taken sexual advantage of their position, either by discriminating on the basis of physical attractiveness or by actually making personal de-

---

7. Unfortunately, a parallel test can not be done for the GWR, since nightwork is perfectly collinear with depot status. The most that can be said is that some caution should be used in interpreting the meaning of the depot coefficient.

mands on their female workers. Other employers would find such behavior morally indefensible, even as they discriminate against women in other ways. Managers make a free choice between abusive privilege and conformity with accepted principles of proper behavior. Both companies and individuals vary dramatically in which of these two selections they are likely to make.

Cultural considerations can have general predictive power when they are imposed by an external force on the labor market as a whole. The legal prohibition against women's working at night in blue-collar occupations is an example of a cultural restriction that has been given universal applicability by the power of the state. In the absence of such environmental restrictions, however, cultural limitations on women's employment come from the imaginations of managers themselves. There may be universal trends in the preferences of these managers; the general exclusion of women was quite common at one time. However, more particular preferences are likely to random out, losing their ability to affect more than a fraction of the labor force.

Even the most important cultural considerations are likely to be subordinated to economic considerations. In the GWR and the GPO, nightwork and sex segregation were only maintained when they could be conveniently integrated into the economic functioning of the firm. Even the preference for a male labor force was overruled when such a policy was counterbalanced by a pressing need to economize on labor. Legitimating ideologies are important in understanding the history of particular workplaces, but they operate within a very limited domain. The major parameters of sex-typing are determined by technology, labor markets, and cost structure; the minor details are then affected by local managerial preferences.

6

Exclusion by Organized Labor

One of the most fundamental issues in the area of occupational sex-typing is assessing the role of organized male labor in reducing economic opportunities for women. Male workers have often been vociferous opponents of equal opportunity in employment.Men have barred women from union membership when such membership was needed for access to employment. Unions have agitated for protectionist legislation excluding women from various "dangerous" occupations. They have gone on strike to protest the introduction of female co-workers. Besides these formal mechanisms, there have been informal actions such as the harassment within the workplace of new female employees. Opposition to women workers has not been universal, but it has been quite common. In the American case, Alice Kessler-Harris has documented the existence of anti-feminization campaigns among printers, iron workers, cotton spinners, and subway conductors, among others (Kessler-Harris 1982).

In most cases, these actions can be explained in terms of the traditional union tactic of raising wages by restricting the labor supply. Organized labor has attempted to create an artificial scarcity of workers by invoking a large number of criteria that might disqualify new entrants to employment. There have been explicit limits on the number of apprentices; these have been accompanied by restrictive definitions of who can qualify for apprenticeship. Excluding female workers from employment can effectively cut the labor pool in half. It can be plausibly argued that such a strategy can be counterproductive. Exclusionary campaigns have often resulted in the creation of hostile pools of scab labor. Women and blacks have been quite willing historically to cross the picket lines of sexist or racist white male unions. Nevertheless, most male workers have not conceived the issues in these terms. When men have dropped their opposition to female employment, it has usually only been in the face of an inevitable feminization against which opposition would have been futile.[1]

For the student of sex-typing, the question of what causes worker resistance to feminization is only of secondary interest. The fundamental question is whether such campaigns have an effect on the percentage of women in an occupation. There are two primary positions on this issue. The first is that organized labor can exert a significant influence on management in determining occupational sex-type. No one would say that labor determines occupational sex-type unilaterally. However, sustained and militant opposition to female workers might induce management not to use female workers in settings that otherwise would have been feminized.

The opposite position is that sex-typing is determined unilaterally by management. This is the assumption that intrinsically exists in any mode of feminization based purely on "economic" (in this case managerial) utilities. Thus, the clerical labor intensity theory and turnover theories in general all assume a process of determining sex type that gives no role to the sentiments of employees.

It seems likely that, if organized labor has an impact on gender-related matters at all, this impact is confined to a relatively limited number of industrial settings. Male workers can only ban women where they have the labor strength to control entry into their trade effectively. This represents a fairly high level of worker control. Historically, most workers have faced real challenges in maintaining unions against the resistance of employers. Many have not been able even to obtain union recognition. Others have obtained meaningful wage concessions, but have not been able to restrict management's right to make decisions concerning the labor process unilaterally. Only a small elite of workers consisting largely of traditional crafts workers such as printers or construction workers, have obtained significant control over the labor process. These workers have been only occasionally able to control entry into employment. Thus, if strong workers

1. An example of such concession to the inevitable is the change in the policy of male cigar-makers. Initially vehemently opposed to women workers, they became quite conciliatory to women after feminization had become a fait accompli (Kessler-Harris 1982).

will be more successful than weak workers in controlling entry, the empirical question of interest is where on the continuum of organized labor strength workers obtain the ability to influence sex-typing.

The logic of inquiry can be more easily understood by considering two extreme findings. Imagine that one studied an incredibly powerful set of workers and found that these workers were incapable of having any impact on feminization. Such an example would strongly suggest that workers in general have little imput into sex-typing decisions. At the other extreme, imagine one studied a completely weak and unorganized occupation. If one found that these workers made a significant contribution to managerial decisions concerning sex-typing, one could conclude that probably all workers exert such an independent influence. Neither of these scenarios is likely to occur in real life. In the absence of such pre-emptory case studies, an appropriate research strategy would be to do a series of studies of occupations with varying degrees of labor power, seeking a cutting point between effective and ineffective exclusionists. By finding precisely how much organizational strength is required for a role in sex-type determination, one can discover what percentage of the labor force could reasonably be expected to possess such resources.

The present research is a first step in the execution of this grander design. The Great Western Railway and the General Post Office allow for a strong test of whether male clerical workers had any input into determining the rate of feminization.

Clerical work represents a case of weak unionization and unmobilized labor power. Only slightly over 10 percent of all private sector clerks were unionized by 1975, despite a renaissance in white-collar organizing (Freeman and Medoff 1979). Those clerical unions that have existed have generally not been particularly militant. Few of them ever strike. The successful unions rarely achieve more than union security and wage concessions. If male clerical workers were able to pose significant obstacles to feminization, this would suggest that a very large percentage of the labor force would be capable of winning such victories. If male resistance to feminization were ineffective, it would leave open the possibility that better-organized workers might yet have a meaningful impact. Considering clerical work thus represents a test of the role of labor strength that is biased towards finding no effect.

Within clerical work, however, the General Post Office and the Great Western Railway represent the cases most likely to generate a significant labor effect. These two organizations represented the vanguard of clerical organizing. Before World War II, the civil service unions and the Railway Clerks Association were two out of the three clerical unions in Britain that had ever obtained any concessions from management (Lockwood 1958). The density of clerical union membership in the Post Office and in the railways was the highest among all industries in Great Britain. The Post Office had been continuously organized from the 1870's; the GWR had been organized from the turn of the century. Both sets of unions had been involved in major strikes, and had engaged in successful parliamentary agitation. On the minus side, it must be noted that the independent economic power of these organizations was questionable; they lost every strike they engaged in. Nevertheless, the presence of actual walkouts, long campaigns of workplace agitation, the successful use of political tools, and the maintenance of consistently high levels of union membership put these unions far in the forefront of worker organization and militancy. If the postal and rail clerks could not slow down the flow of feminization, it is unlikely that other clerks would have had more impact.

Clerical-Industrial Conflict within the Post Office and the Railways

In order to understand the evidence and interpretations provided below, it is helpful to consider first the overall histories of labor relations in these two firms. The railway situation was substantially simpler, so it will be considered first.

Labor Relations in the Railways

In the nineteenth century, the clerical force of the railways was wholly non-unionized. Labor relations worked in a fashion similar to that described by David Lockwood in *The Blackcoated Worker* (1958). Office supervisors exercised personal control over their subordinates. Standardized pay rates and job descriptions did not exist. Remuneration was determined largely by the department head based on the individual characteristics of the worker. The absence of any organized counterforce to managerial autonomy forced employees to get ahead solely through obedience, loyalty, and the development of personal ties with their employers.

The Railway Clerks Association (RCA) was formed in 1897 as an industry-wide union. In its early days, if two railways served the same city, unionists from both companies were in the same local. The Great Western Railway lagged slightly behind the other companies in the early recruitment drives. Bristol and South Wales had a strong chapter from the beginning, and Paddington later became very important. However, Paddington was one of the last major London stations to open its own local branch (RCA Annual Reports 1903–28; Walkden 1928).

In the early stages, the RCA largely confined itself to political tactics. It affiliated with the Trades Union Congress Political Committee, and early on successfully sponsored a small number of parliamentary candidates. This allowed the RCA to win significant concessions by strategically delaying important railway legislation. The most important of these victories was the winning of a government inquest into railway pension funds that resulted in the payment of substantial compensatory damages by management. This tactic was also used to prevent the harassement of local RCA organizers (Walkden 1928).

The first economic concessions were won in 1911. Traditionally, railway clerks worked six days a week. However, supervisors could routinely demand an extra day on Sunday, which was unpaid. In 1908, the RCA petitioned the GWR to provide payment for Sunday labor. Indirect negotiations on the issue lasted for three years, with the railway finally granting remuneration to all clerks who worked at least six hours on Sunday. The victory, however, turned out to be largely symbolic. When the railway implemented the policy, the Sunday shifts were all made five and one-half hours long, allowing very few clerks to qualify for the supplemental payments (GWR Petitions 1914).

The next concessions, however, were substantial. In 1912, after extensive petitioning, the RCA won an upgrading of entry-level pay. This was followed in the same year by amelioration of the other workers' salaries. The RCA was only partially responsible for these improvements. The Great Western Railway for some time had been suffering from difficulties in recruiting junior staff. One problem had been that starting salaries had been allowed to slip to levels uncompetitive with those of other employers. Thus, it is not insignificant that entry-level pay was increased first and senior pay was raised subsequently. Nevertheless, the RCA probably played an instrumental role in accelerating the pay raise and seeing that it was generalized (Salaried Recruitment 1912).

World War I produced major gains for the RCA. Due to the fact that railways played a vital role in the defense effort, the government semi-nationalized the industry. The railway companies were guaranteed a high fixed level of profit in return for providing uninterrupted service, eliminating any financial incentive on the part of the companies to conserve on costs. In return, the government put pressure on management to avoid strike-related shutdowns in an economy in which labor was generally scarce (Pratt 1921; Aldcroft 1968). The companies were thus strongly motivated to grant the railway unions whatever they wanted, and the unions took immediate advantage of this leniency. Wages were raised no less than eight times during this period. Although inflation absorbed much of this improvement, railway employees made substantial gains (GWR Petitions 1914; Colours 1920; Pratt 1921).

After World War I, the government rescinded control of the railways and began forcibly to amalgamate many private lines. During the amalgamation period, labor relations on the railroad were completely reorganized and formalized. The British government had developed a plan for the overall reduction of industrial conflict. Every industry in the British economy was to adopt industry-wide collective bargaining between employer confederations and trade unions in forums known as Whitley councils. Disputes not resolvable by mutual consent were to be submitted to public arbitration. The British political elite believed that union recognition and open collective bargaining were in the public interest (Phelps Brown 1983). During the amalgamation period, all aspects of railroad organization were reconstituted with an active participation by the government. Railway labor relations incorporated many of the institutions of the Whitley Council movement (Bagwell 1963; Aldcroft 1968). Thus the Railway Clerks Association along with the blue-collar unions participated in industry-wide collective bargaining. Salary scales were standardized across the major railways using a uniform job classification scheme (Grand Classification 1920). In the first formally negotiated pay settlement, a substantial portion of the wartime temporary increases was incorporated into permanent wages (Contract Talks 1919–20; Bagwell 1963).

The RCA's role in obtaining these benefits was mixed. The union was directly responsible for its own inclusion in the railway negotiating machinery. The original plans had called for collective bargaining only with the blue-collar unions. The RCA threatened a strike if they did not receive comparable treatment. The railways could not tolerate a major union recognition strike during the sensitive amalgamation proceedings, particularly when public policy militated for union recognition, so management conceded the RCA procedural demands just before the strike deadline (Lockwood 1958).

Once bargaining rights were granted, however, management proved to be unyielding on other issues. The first collectively negotiated wage agreement provided few new benefits for the clerks. Some of the "temporary" war bonus payments were incorporated into regular salaries, a fact that merely reflected the inflation of British currency during the war. However, the union had little impact in determining the amount and form of these concessions. The pay package that was put into the final contract was virtually identical to management's initial offer, while none of the RCA negotiating planks appeared in the final settlement, even in diluted form (Contract Talks 1919–20; RCA Contract 1925). In later years, the pay issue remained deadlocked. The union made several attempts to increase wages, while management made several attempts to reduce them. Both types of demands were repeatedly rejected in arbitration (Railway Clerk 1907–37; Walkden 1928).

The early post-war period shows some ability by the RCA to at least maintain a defensive strength against hostile managerial initiatives, but the balance of power swung decidedly in managments' favor in 1926. The RCA joined the blue-collar railway unions in supporting the General Strike of 1926. The railway clerks stayed out for the duration of the strike. When the strike collapsed, labor power on the railways was effectively crushed. The strike leaders were suspended and punitively transferred. Pay for all railway employees was dramatically reduced, and it was cut several times more in the following years (General Strike 1926; Labor Report 1930–33).

Thus, despite the bargaining privileges that the RCA enjoyed, labor control was very uneven. The RCA won major benefits in 1912 and during the war. It was able to prevent management attempts to reduce wages in the 1920's. However, its ability to obtain wage increases on its own was very weak after World War I, and after 1926 its power was negligible.

Labor Relations in the Post Office

The labor relations in the Post Office were somewhat more complex. The Post Office workers were represented in a wide variety of single-occupation associations. The identities of these unions changed over time as varying organizations underwent mergers. However, the distinctive character of postal industrial relations existed largely apart from the reorganizations of the unions themselves.

The lead sector of postal unionism was the telegraph force, who were the earliest group to organize. In the mid-nineteenth century, postmen had engaged in ad hoc organization, and clerks throughout the civil service had lobbied in the 1850's for the right to vote (Swift 1900). However, the telegraph clerks were the only workers with a visible and commanding strike threat. Most of the work in the Post Office was either semi-skilled or involved little demand for timely performance: delivering mail was simple manual labor; sorting mail required low levels of training; most of the bookkeeping in the GPO was not done under pressing deadlines. Substitute labor could be obtained from elsewhere in the civil service or the private sector. The telegraphists, however, were irreplaceable. Telegraphy was a skilled occupation requiring long training. Merely learning the rudiments of using Morse code took a full year. It took years of practice before a telegraphist could work at high speed. The use of untrained scab labor to operate the telegraphs would have resulted in a significant deterioration of the quality of service. Furthermore, the telegraph system was indispensible to the functioning of British business. The financial community would have been unlikely to tolerate a telegraph strike that produced delays and inaccuracies in stock market reports or impeded the transmission of urgent commercial news. The Post Office was thus under strong pressure to avoid a protracted stoppage of telegraph service, and the signalling force was quite willing to exploit this vulnerability.

The second most militant workers after the telegraphists were the sorters and postmen. These workers were not particularly skilled, but they were employed in sufficient numbers to provide a modestly visible strike threat. Any particular postman on strike was easily replaceable, but replacing every postman on strike even in a small city would have made extraordinary demands on the local labor market.

The postal clerks were the third largest category of unions. In many cases their participation in industrial conflict was nominal. The postal clerks had some firm-specific skills, but in many respects their labor resembled tasks being done by other financial clerks. In the event of a strike, they could have easily been replaced with workers from the temporary clerical market. Clerks were rarely employed in large numbers except in London, and in London the clerks were divided among a multiplicity of offices scattered among many buildings. It would have been extremely difficult to organize a clerical strike that would have been sufficiently large to challenge management's ability to use scab labor.

The postal unions did not rely exclusively on the strike in pressing their demands. They made extensive use of political tactics and vigorously pursued their claims in Parliament. They monitored the votes of Members of Parliament on bills germane to postal workers and rewarded those members who sought to raise civil service salaries with electoral support from a large bloc of single-issue voters. Most civil service employees were concentrated in London. Because of this, only the London representatives needed to pay attention to the clerical constituency. However, telegraphists, postmen, and sorters were distributed throughout England. There was not a seat in Parliament that could not be affected by the "postal bloc." This political threat bolstered the claims of the unionists and gave the postal workers power far beyond what one would expect from their economic position.

Postal voting power should not be overestimated. Postal unionists commanded respect but not obedience. They were but one of many interest groups within a politician's district. Many politicians chose to seek support from more conservative sources, openly resisting postal union claims. Still others temporized by making concessions to the unions that were purely symbolic. Many parliamentarians would pay off their debts to the postal workers by delaying the postal budget appropriations in committee, making long speechs deploring the postman's conditions but rarely putting forward any resolutions or making amendments to the budget. Despite the show, most postal bills passed in their original form. By the twentieth century, the postal unions finally learned how to press their sponsors for more concrete forms of political assistance, but then the Whitley Council movement neutralized many of their legislative victories. Lobbying posed great potential as a tactic for agitation; nevertheless, the returns from this activity were often disappointing.

In the late 1860's and early 1870's, labor relations within the Post Office were undergoing a fundamental transformation, due to two changes. The first was the enfranchisement of government employees in 1868. The second was the nationalization of the telegraphs and the subsequent absorption of the signallers. The enfranchisement of the civil service gave birth to the strong stream of labor-related political organizing that would characterize the postal unions. The precise reason why Parliament gave government employees the vote is unknown. The civil service had lobbied for their electoral rights and may have attracted help from sympathetic democratic allies. Enfranchisement may have also been related to the civil service reform movement of the late 1860's. The original rationale for denying government workers the vote was that, under a patronage regime, politicians might improperly reward supporters with jobs. As patronage declined, the threat of machine politics faded and the need for disenfranchising government employees was reduced. Whatever the reasons for the change, the result was the creation of a new actor in the national political arena.

The incorporation of the telegraphists into the Post Office meant the introduction of a well-organized set of artisanal laborers. Before incorporation, there had been occasional public meetings by postmen protesting wages and conditions, but these meetings had generally been ineffectual; there had never been a strike or any labor-induced pay increase (Swift 1900; Hall 1902). The telegraphists posed a much more severe labor relations problem. They had been formally organized under the private companies and had actually had a small strike in the 1860's. In 1871, soon after absorption, they organized the first strike in postal history, when the telegraphists of several northern English, Scottish, and Irish offices went out on a one-week stoppage. The Post Office had never dealt with such a situation before, but managment was able to obtain a short-term victory. By firing six of the union leaders, management precipitated the strike before the union was ready. The defensive strike that followed was largely confined to a minority of urban stations. Management then imported replacements from non-striking districts and broke the workers' resistance. The strikers returned, receiving no immediate concessions, and the leaders were punitively transferred (Telegraph Strike 1872). However, management's success was dependent on the partial support the strike had received; a more complete shutdown would have had more devastating consequences.

In 1873, the Post Office raised the telegraphists' wages. A wage increase had been promised back in 1868; nevertheless, the amount of the increase was non-trivial. When the telegraph increase was finally granted, this spurred a parallel movement among the sorters, who supported their wage demands by calling what was to be a much-imitated tactic, a no-overtime strike. Management traditionally had had the right to demand unpaid overtime from the men. The sorters refused to work more than seven hours a day. The 1873 strike was foiled completely, however; six men were suspended, and no concessions were made (Swift 1900).

The sorters then turned to political agitation. In defiance of postal regulations, they held two large public meetings to portray their plight. Public meetings were usually demonstrations of political strength. They were chaired by Members of Parliament sympathetic to the postal workers, and they often received favorable attention from the press. Such meetings were good devices for obtaining public action. This time the results were dramatic. The Queen called for an investigation into the sorters' conditions. The tribunal found in favor of the sorters, and pay rates were raised dramatically.

The sorters attempted to follow up on their victory the next year, in 1874. They put out an memorial requesting further increases over the 1873 increase. However, this time they met with substantially less success. Five men were dismissed merely for delivering the memorial, and the request was rejected out of hand. The sorters did get a debate in Parliament to discuss their claims, but their advocates made no formal motions. Nothing concrete emerged from the hearing (Swift 1900).

After this setback, the postal workers temporarily concentrated on obtaining new parliamentary forums for their grievances. The late 1870's were characterized by a long campaign to obtain the right to testify at a major inquest into the overall operation of the civil service. Despite an extensive lobbying campaign, the workers were denied access.

In 1881, the postal unions won another major wage increase. This drive was spearheaded by the telegraphists and supported by the sorters and postmen. The early states of the campaign consisted of collecting memorials from postal workers all over Britain. An earlier set of petitions in 1880 had been turned down. The new memorials were to be supported by a two-pronged offensive. Pro-union MP's were to voice support of the proposal during the debate on the postal budget. At the same time as the debate, the London telegraphists were to go on a no-overtime strike. The Post Office capitulated before the double threat. A new telegraph pay scheme was announced just before the no-overtime strike and the debates were to have occurred.

The central role of the telegraphists in this activity should not be underestimated. Most of the parliamentary speeches protesting low levels of postal pay focused primarily on the telegraphists. It was the telegraphists who threatened the no-overtime strike, so when the original postal revisions were announced, only the pay of the telegraphists was raised. Other employees did receive some improvements but only much later. Although participation in the 1880–81 campaign was general, placating the telegraphists seems to have been the prime concern of both parliament and management (Swift 1900; Hall 1902).

The events of 1889 and 1890 paralleled those of 1880 and 1881. The postal unions pressed to participate in another other civil service commission. This time, too, they were denied. This was followed by a general pay increase, won by the combination of a London telegraphists' no-overtime strike threat and political support in Parliament. As before, a pay increase for the telegraphers was announced just before the no-overtime strike was to be instituted and immediately before a pro-union parliamentary debate (Swift 1900).

In 1888 there had been a petition by sorters and postmen for higher pay. This memorial had been denied, but subsequentially the Postmaster General had agreed to an inquiry by postal management into sorters' and postmen's wages. In 1890, the in-house review concluded that no adjustments in wages were necessary. This decision provoked great discontent among the staff. The independent agitation by the telegraphists was diminishing the postmaster's ability to quell this second wave of discontent, and he agreed to reconsider the commission's findings.

While this reconsideration was pending, the sorters and postmen suffered a few blows. The postmen decided to threaten a strike, and held a large rally before the event to articulate their claims. Several postmen who attended this rally were dismissed. Four sorters publicly offered support to a potential postmen's strike. These workers too were dismissed. The unions then took defensive actions protesting the harassment of the militants. After achieving no results in this agitation, the postmen finally called a strike. The results of the strike were dismal. Fewer than 600 postmen supported the strike, most of these from a single district of London. The strike was crushed in one day, resulting in the suspension of 435 men (Swift 1900).

Similar tactics of harassment began to be used on the telegraphists. During 1889, in the initial periods of the telegraph campaign, several Cardiff telegraphists published some protest telegrams in the local newspaper. They were punitively transferred. Several meetings were held in sympathy for the "Cardiff martyrs" but no restitution was ever made.

In 1890, on Jubilee Day, the head of the Central Telegraph Station assembled the signallers and gave a customary patriotic speech. After finishing his presentation he called for three cheers for Queen Victoria, which were given. He then requested three cheers for the Postmaster General. The Postmaster General received three groans.

Most modern managers would dismiss such a display as a joke. The Post Office took the incident very seriously. Management circulated a formal disclaimer among the staff to sign. While some employees signed it, most did not. Management then called each of the union leaders and gave them a choice: sign a formal apology with a vow of future obedience or face immediate dismissal. The union leaders had to undergo the humiliating ritual of applying to their supervisors for pardon. These setbacks were obviously less dramatic than those suffered by the sorters and postmen, but they do show that even the most powerful postal workers faced some risk in engaging in union activity (Swift 1900; Hall 1902).

The only incident of a strike among the clerical staff took place in 1891. The second division clerks in the savings banks went on a no-overtime strike a few months after their general pay revisions were announced. This was a gender-related strike. The issues involved will be discussed in greater detail below; for present purposes it is enough to say that the strike collapsed after one day. No concessions were made, and 250 male clerks were suspended (Swift 1900; Hall 1902).

Between 1890 and 1914, the strategy of the postal workers changed. The unions continued to seek inquests into their wages. However, the 1889 sorters' pay inquest had shown that, when management was allowed to run these inquests internally, the investigations would turn into nothing but an elaborate stalling device. The unions began to press for inquests that would be staffed by sympathetic referees. Since the workers had more leverage on members of parliament than on any other group, the overall stategy became one of seeking a parliamentary wage investigation. Over the course of this twenty-five-year period, the unions won a series of different investigations into wages. The composition of each committee became closer and closer to the union ideal; finally in 1906 and 1914 they obtained two all-parliamentary commissions (Humphreys 1958).

In 1895, the postal unions obtained a wage commission staffed by representatives of management throughout the civil service. This represented an improvement over 1889, when the commissioners had been drawn exclusively from the upper levels of the Post Office.

Nevertheless, this new committee not surprisingly showed little sympathy to the postal workers' claims. After three years of investigation, they wrote a final report recommending negligible increases in overall wage levels.

The events of 1890 repeated themselves. The London telegraphists threatened a no-overtime strike, demanding higher increases. Parliamentary allies of the postal unions negotiated a postponement of the strike pending the working out of a superior arrangment. After some parliamentary debates and a second impromptu inquiry made by the postmaster himself, postal wages were raised by a generous amount (Swift 1900).

Agitation for an all-MP commission continued. In 1898, the unions polled every candidate for a parliamentary seat in Britain, asking if they would explicitly endorse an all-MP commission. Nearly every candidate promised future support. Circulating to such a survey by civil servants was technically illegal, however, and the newly elected Parliament refused to pass a bill legalizing the practice. In 1899, a resolution pressing for an an all-MP commission was defeated. Nevertheless, the postal union pressure continued to be intense. From the late 1880's up through 1906, every single vote on a postal budget had been delayed pending a forced debate on postal worker wages and conditions. Amendments were added to the postal budget moving the impounding of £100 from the Postmaster General's salary if postal wages were not improved. (Such amendments usually got withdrawn before the final reading). Nearly thirty questions a year were being put on the floor of the House to the Postmaster General demanding written explanation of why postal conditions should not be improved. There clearly was a small minority of parliamentarians such as Albert Rollins from Islington who vigorously supported the union's position. The mainstream was also having trouble resisting the union's appeals (Swift 1900).

In 1903, the Postmaster General noted that several MP's had come to him seeking some buffer from the persistant lobbying of postal unionists. To alleviate the pressure, he nominated a new commission. This time the committee was made up of businessmen in the private sector (Humphreys 1958). The 1903 Bradford Commission surprised everyone by reporting in favor of a major across-the-board pay raise. The Postmaster General refused to implement the report. For two years there were parliamentary attempts to force compliance with the Bradford recommendations. Some wage adjustments were made, but the arbitrators' recommendations were generally ignored (Hobhouse 1906).

In 1906, the postal unionists finally triumphed. As a device for resolving the dispute over the Bradford Commission, Parliament agreed to a full parliamentary investigation into wages. The investigation was a slow process, taking over three years. The results of the Hobhouse Commission were mixed. Provincial workers received a wage increase that pushed them towards parity with their better-paid London counterparts. The rest of the postal claims were denied (Hobhouse 1906). The Post Office delayed the implementation of the plan so that it was not until after 1910 that the postal workers received the benefits of the inquest begun in 1906. Nevertheless, the majority of employees received real wage benefits from the endeavor.

The next move was to press for a second parliamentary commission to benefit the workers left unsatisfied. In 1914, the Holt Commission was established with a composition similar to that of the Hobhouse panel. World War I prevented the Holt Commission from issuing their report. It also marked the close of an era of parliamentary influence by civil servants.

The government took action after the war to insulate the legislature from postal union interference by the establishment of Whitley Councils. The Whitley Council movement was the same movement that helped bring about collective bargaining for the railway clerks: the attempt by the British government to institute industry-wide collective bargaining throughout the nation as a whole. Since the government was expending considerable resources in attempting to persuade private industrialists to adopt the system, the state was under moral pressure to use Whitley Councils to take care of its own labor relations problems. Thus, throughout the civil service, an elaborate machinery of grievance committees and consultation boards was set up to deal collectively with all manner of disputes concerning personnel policy (Humphreys 1958; Wigham 1980).

The effect of permanent dispute machinery on civil service negotiating strength was mixed. The postal workers no longer had to fight a major political battle every time they wanted their wages reconsidered. At the same time, however, they lost the ability to staff such commissions with referees of their own choosing. In fact, their political organization was effectively neutralized. Parliamentarians with mixed sympathies could now argue that the postal workers had a valid channel for expressing their grievances and that parliamentary intervention was not only superfluous but inappropriate. The amount of postal parliamentary agitation dropped dramatically after 1920. While the success rate of such tactics had always been mixed, even in the best of times, after 1920 the unions won no major parliamentary victories.

At the same time, the economic bargaining strength of the telegraphists took a major downturn. This was brought on by the introduction of the telephone and the telex. The telephone had been around since the beginning of the twentieth century. However, only after World War I did it achieve fundamental penetration into routine patterns of business communication. As the telegraph system lost its monopoly on the transmission of urgent commercial information, the national ability to withstand a telegraph strike was significantly increased.

The telex allowed for the significant de-skilling of the signalling labor force. The scarcity of telegraphists had centered around the long training times required to be able to transmit quickly in Morse code. One not only had to learn the code itself but had to develop high levels of dexterity and accuracy in the physical tapping out of the signals. Furthermore, the instruments were unreliable and often required continual adjustment and maintenance by the operator.

The telex eliminated the need for most of these skills. Telegraph messages could now be sent out on a keyboard resembling a typewriter, with the coding being done by machine. Since the physical skills of typing at a keyboard were well distributed throughout the female labor force, most telex operators were fully trained at the time of their recruitment. The machines were reliable and did not require continual maintenance between transmissions. The result was that the number of replacements to striking telegraphists was limited only by the number of available telex devices (Telegraph 1927). This produced a quiet period in postal industrial relations. Wages stagnated for sorters and postmen. They declined for telegraphists. For some reason, clerical wages increased in the late 1920's, although this was accompanied neither by parliamentary agitation nor by a strike threat (GPO Establishment Book 1918–36; Humphreys 1958).

These clerical union histories should make one point reasonably clear. The bargaining strength of these unions was always problematic. The Railway Clerks Association achieved a few successes in the 1910's and 1920's. Its strength, however, was somewhat dependent on the patronage of the railwaymen's union; even with this asset there were many periods, such as after 1926, when the union suffered from complete powerlessness. The telegraphists had a consistent record of winning pay advances, but even they suffered from frustrations in Parliament, a failed strike, and the final undermining of their bargaining power. The independent power of the other postal workers was even more modest. Thus, in wage negotiations, the issue of central concern to these unions, the winning of concessions was difficult and subject to failure. On matters of gender, the ability of these unions to enforce their will was substantially more tenuous.

The Efficacy of Gender-Related Union Campaigns

Neither the RCA nor the postal unions were neutral to the sex issue. The postal unions aggressively sought to limit clerical feminization. The Railway Clerks were mixed in their sex demands. The male rank and file was anti-feminist. The leadership favored equal opportunity for women. Thus, the official goals of the Railway Clerks Association was to increase employment for women clerks. However, very few of these campaigns, whether for or against women, could be said to have had any success. In the short term, the unions were able to stall or to accelerate a variety of reforms. However, ultimately the occupational sex type of most disputed jobs became that which was preferred by management.

The sex-related campaign that would have seemed to have had a high prospect for success was the Postal Telegraph Clerks' campaign of 1910–14. This was an attempt to forestall the feminization of London branch telegraph offices. As London gained in size and population, the demand for mail and telegraph service increased. The London Postal Service was thus required to open a large number of new branch offices. Very little sorting was done at these offices, this function being performed at large centralized sorting depots. The primary functions of the branch post offices were to provide window service and to serve as a local base for the transmission and receipt of telegrams. These offices when opened were usually sex-segregated. They were all male, all female, or occasionally female by day and male by night.

At the turn of the century, the London Postal Service committed itself to a policy of feminizing these branch offices. In order to minimize disruption, the Post Office arranged to leave all pre-existing offices with their sex composition intact. However, all new offices were to be all female. The policy was kept secret, but the demographic trend soon became clear to the rank and file. (An exception was made for exceptionally busy offices, such as that at Charing Cross, and those in rough or unsavory neighborhoods, such as Bethnal Green or Crystal Palace.)

In 1910, the Postal Telegraph Clerks Association began to memorialize management about the transition. The male telegraphists' concern was based on substantive economic considerations. The opening of each office created a series of new supervisory positions. Single men were supervised by men, and women were supervised by women, the new offices represented opportunities for promotion. The men were thus attempting to reserve for themselves a share of the new supply of superior jobs. The PCTA demands were two-fold. First, they wanted some of the branches to be reserved to men. Second, in redress for the new feminization, they wanted offices that were female by day and male by night to be made all male. By sending an old female staff to a new office, the telegraphists could have ensured that the newly created supervisorship at the old office would be a male position (London Branches 1914).

At the time, the Postal Telegraph Clerks had a very reasonable bargaining threat. Their parliamentary influence was at a maximum. The market monopoly the telegraphists had on Morse signalling was still intact. Nevertheless, the telegraphists were unable to extract any meaningful concessions from management. Every new office opened from the inception of the program until World War I was staffed by women. Between 1901 and 1911, the percentage of females in the district signalling offices had gone up 9 percent. In the years between 1911 and 1914, it went up another 7 percent. In the three main years of the protest, as many women had come in as had been introduced in the previous ten years (GPO Establishment Books 1901–14).

In compensation, the Post Office did eliminate some of the mixed-sex branch offices. However, this proved to be a nominal rather than a substantive improvement. Management did a cost-efficiency study of the split offices and discovered a wide variety of practical problems. The transfer of keys and work instructions between shifts was inefficient and error-prone. The night male staff often had to do day duties at other offices, resulting in inefficient between-shift shuttles. Postal management decided to eliminate the split-sex offices, but in a way that would incur no extra expense to the department. Single-sex offices were created by shuffling pre-existing personnel. The final plan did not result in a single new male hire or promotion. Technically the union's demands were met, but in a form that violated the basic intentions of the campaign (London Branches 1914).

Following World War I, the development of the teletype induced a further feminization of telegraphy. The telegraphists (now merged with the sorters and postmen to make the Union of Post Office Workers, or UPOW) attempted to block this feminization. Although they failed in their ultimate goal, they were able to delay the introduction of teletyping. The rules of the new Whitley procedure required that management consult with the unions before implementing such a change. Feminization was supposed to occur under a set of guidelines jointly agreed upon by union and management, with these guidelines being expected to include compensation to the unions for whatever damage might be suffered by them in the process of the transition. The UPOW simply refused to accept any of the proposed guidelines or compensations. Their position was that nothing could reasonably buffer them from the harm that they would suffer by a major wave of feminization. The conciliation process allowed for the operation of multiple levels of grievance machinery. By fully exploiting these, the UPOW was able to tie up negotiations for four years.

In 1927, the conciliation process was brought to a close with no significant concessions having been made by either side. Management then implemented a policy of hiring two women for every three new hires. The postal unions resorted to their traditional tactics, memorializing and political pressure. Several deputations were sent to top management, both by the UPOW and by various supervisory unions. Sympathetic MP's took their legal prerogative of demanding formal written responses from governmental officials to questions from the floor. At one point, the Postmaster General had to demonstrate to the house that increasing the proposition of female telegraphists would not jeopardize the nation's signalling capacities in the event of war. Such harassment tactics had only a symbolic impact. A one-sentence response was considered a legal and acceptable answer to a parliamentary question. The efficacy of the UPOW campaign can be measured by its objective results. Between 1926 and 1931, the percentage of females in the Central Telegraph Station went from 47 percent to 61 percent. This was the fastest rate of feminization since 1870 (GPO Establishment Books 1926–31; Telegraph 1927).

The sorters rarely had to make any explicit gender claims due to the all-male composition of their labor force. However, in World War I, it became necessary to introduce female substitutes for men who had left for military service. The Fawcett Association, the major sorter's union, vehemently protested this temporary labor. The union feared that the use of female temporary sorters might create a precedent whereby sorting might become feminized after the war. To resist this threat, union leadership actually offered to exchange extension of the normal workday in return for the preservation of an all-male force. Negotiations over the sex of temporary substitutes occurred several times during the war, re-emerging every time the use of temporaries was extended. In no case was the union able to prevent or even delay the use of women substitutes. They were not even able to obtain a trade-off benefit (WWI Sorters 1915).

The Savings Bank clerks were the only workers driven to striking over gender issues. The militancy of their tactics is remarkable in the light of their modest degree of bargaining power. Their numbers were too small to allow for a meaningful voting threat. Their skills were common to a wide variety of private clerks and were nearly duplicated by the staff of the Postal Accountant General's Office and the Money Order Department. A post office-wide coalition of financial clerks might have had some strike power. A financial office acting on its own account had nearly none.

The Savings Bank no-overtime strike occurred in the aftermath of the 1890 salary revision. The Savings Bank reacted to the general increase in pay rates by increasing the rate of feminization. The management announced that all future vacancies were to be filled exclusively by women. This produced widespread protest among the male staff of the bank. As in the case of the telegraphists, one issue was the loss of male supervisory positions. However, there was an additional issue concerning the distribution of nightwork. Women were not expected to work overtime. The Savings Bank was perpetually understaffed and required substantial inputs of evening labor in order to handle peaks in demand. The declining proportion of male employees ensured that the night duties would desolve upon an increasingly smaller percentage of the labor force. The male clerks naturally resisted this substantial increase in their hours of labor.

The Savings Bank clerks circulated two memorials, held a public meeting, and lobbied for letters of public support in newspapers. In 1891, they decided to imitate the London telegraphists and threaten a no-overtime strike. Management refused to concede, forcing the clerks to implement their walkout. The strike was an immediate disaster, collapsing after one day with over 240 clerks being suspended.

Feminization continued at a brisk rate, and the financial clerks never struck again (Swift 1900; Hall 1902).

The Railway Clerks were equally incapable of exerting an independent influence on gender hiring decisions. This assessment, however, becomes complex when one considers the conflicting goals of the organization. The Railway Clerks Association was characterized by an anti-feminist rank and file dominated by a pro-feminist leadership. The Executive Committee of the RCA considered that the feminization of clerical work was inevitable in the long run. Short-term opposition to female employment was only likely to create a body of female workers outside the union who could effectively serve management as scabs. By 1914, the Executive Committee was explicitly telling local unionists not to resist the extension of women's employment. The official strategy was to work towards the amelioration of both men's and women's conditions by actively working to organize and support female clerks (Bevan Letter 1914).

This policy was not well accepted by the rank and file. The majority of local union activists probably favored an aggressive policy of anti-feminism. Such a claim can be validated by a reading of the union newspaper. Local columnists repeatedly inveighed against the dangers of female employment. The Bristol and South Wales correspondent wrote several stories a year noting how female employment led to favoritism among employers and overwork among the men required to make up for female deficiencies. Satirical poems appeared, attacking the suffragetting and slow work that the authors associated with women clerks. The editors usually balanced these with feminist comments or with centrally written counterpoems urging solidarity among the sexes. During World War I, the newspaper attempted to balance the male commentary by hiring a female clerk to write a column on women's issues. After World War I the editors moved to eliminate the flow of hostile commentary. They closed down the offending regional columns, but still felt pressure from the rank and file to discuss the problem of women clerks. In 1920, the editors permitted the publication of a one-time forum on sex equality on the railways. Views on both sides of the issue were published, with the editors adding favorable comments on the feminist letters and unfavorable comments on the sexist letters. Subsequently, the newspaper declared the issue closed and forbade any further letters or communications on gender (Railway Clerk 1907–37).

The conflict between the rank and file and the executive became particularly pointed at annual conventions. At the conventions it was customary to vote on a number of planks representing the next years' union program. The Executive Committee usually sponsored a plank supporting equal pay for equal work. This plank was a sanitized expression of the board's feminist sentiments. If challenged, such a position could be defended to exclusionists as protective of male privilege. Since women were "inherently less productive" than men, equal wages would cause employers to prefer efficient male labor.

The Executive Committee, however, was often seriously embarrassed by male local representatives who wanted the supposed exclusionist goals of the policy explicitly stated in a formal motion. In 1914, 1915, and 1916, against Executive Committee recommendations, hostile amendments were moved to the equal pay plank that specified female labor as being by definition two-thirds that of labor performed by men. In 1914, the amendment passed. In 1915 and 1916, the amendment was only defeated after extended debate. In 1917, the Executive Committee solved its problem. Amendments to convention resolutions were explicitly forbidden. Subsequently, the equal pay platform in its feminist version was passed without problems. Thus, the egalitarian policy of the RCA was only achieved by the centralization of power by the Executive Committee, requiring the censoring of dissent and the brokering of union conventions. These policies silenced but did not eliminate mass exclusionist sentiment. In 1946, twenty-five years after the final censoring of public anti-feminist complaints, the Executive Committee at an annual convention put forward a plank condemning discrimination against married women. The convention rejected the plank overwhelmingly (Railway Clerk 1907–37; Convention 1946).

The split had a predictable impact on the efficacy of union gender policy. It was very difficult for exclusionists to implement any campaign of opposition to female employment. In the entire period from 1900 to 1940, the RCA only made one demand for the restriction of female employment, a request that women be barred from all-night employment. Since these jobs were very few and were traditionally all male anyway, the impact of this demand was slight. Exclusionists were thus forced to rely on informal wildcat tactics if they wished to press any claims upon management independently. The ability of the union to obtain benefits was problematic even when it made use of its full range of organizational resources. The impact of a small, resourceless, faction would have been much less. This is particularly true when one considers that the dissidents involved would merely have memorialized, rather than struck. Thus the rank-and-file members of the railway clerical force would have had little impact on the hiring policies of the Great Western Railway.

Ironically, it would seem that the leadership was equally ineffective at increasing opportunities for women. The Executive Committee only put forward two sex-related negotiating claims during the 1900–1940 period. Both were made during the 1920 contract negotiations. The first demand was for equal pay for men and women. This was rejected by management in the first day of bargaining on women's salaries and was never raised by the union again. The second was for the protection of women's jobs during the return of male workers after World War I. During World War I, the GWR had hired a large number of temporary women to replace clerks who had joined the military. After the war, the RCA wanted the railways to keep the temporary women on as permanent employees. They, however, also wanted the returning men to be allowed to resume their jobs with no loss of benefits. The union plan for achieving this seemingly contradictory program was to put the women on short time for the indefinite future. Some vacancies had already been created by former clerks who would not be returning. Others would be created over the long run by natural attrition. The RCA hoped to avoid the mass dismissal of women by having the railway overstaff for a few years. In this way the temporary women could be integrated into permanent staff as vacancies arose. The railway did not explicitly reject this demand. However, they postponed discussion of the issue until the rest of the 1920 contract details were negotiated. In the meantime, they dismissed most of the temporary women. The mass firings made the RCA request academic. At the end of negotiations, the subject was dropped by mutual agreement (Contract Talks 1919–20).[2]

---

2. The dismissals severely weakened overall RCA negotiating strengths. The RCA had a benefit program that provided substantial relief to any railway clerk who was involuntarily dismissed. Before World War I, this has been a gratuity, since forced resignation was extremely exceptional on the railways. During World War I, the Executive Committee extended this benefit to female temporary employees (over the substantial protest of many local activists). At the end of the war, the RCA had to pay benefits to an enormous number of departing women. In 1919 alone, the RCA paid out over one quarter of its entire assets in unemployment compensation (RCA Annual Reports 1918–20).

The anecdotal evidence presented above suggests that unions played a negligible role in determining sex type. Consistently, management stonewalled union sex demands, denied them outright, or granted them in a form that deprived the concession of substantive meaning. In some cases, this can be explained by union weakness, as was the case with the telegraphists of 1926. Even relatively strong unions, however, like the telegraphists of 1910, were unable to obtain significant concessions. The resources of these unions were exhausted in the struggles over wages and salaries, leaving them with little capital with which to pursue auxiliary demands.

Quantitative Tests of the Role of Informal Exclusion

Although this discussion thus far has emphasized formal mobilizations against women, informal resistance may have been equally important. Many males when confronted with the introduction of a set of unwanted women have acted on an individual level, rather than working through their unions. By complaining to their supervisors, sexually harassing the women, and not cooperating with or training the new employees, men can create a deterioration of productivity and office climate that is so severe that employers will remove the offending women and restore the pre-existing order. Most of the opposition to women clerks in the Great Western Railway probably took this form; the feminist tendencies of RCA leadership would have deprived sexist railway clerks of any formal union channels for acting on exclusionary demands. Such informal mobilizations could have occurred in the Post Office as well, where anti-feminist campaigns were stalled or ineffectual. Thus, to consider fully the impact of resistance by male workers to feminization, it is necessary to measure the impact of such clandestine exclusionary campaigns.

There are obvious methodological problems involved with estimating the effects of informal campaigns. Such activity tends to be lost to the historical record, with both management and workers denying that such a process occurred. Even when such activities are acknowledged, one can not be sure that the absence of a record implies an absence of resistance. Thus, it is impossible to correlate direct measures of the amount of informal opposition to female employment with measures of the subsequent use of women.

If one wishes to study clandestine exclusions, there is a second strategy available. One can study the distribution of worker militancy and union power and observe whether this correlates with the sex composition of offices. If work settings with well-organized, powerful men had few women, while settings with unorganized, marginal men were heavily feminized, a plausible interpretation might be that the strong workers were excluding women. The finding of no relation between levels of worker power and the use of women would suggest that sex-typing is determined entirely by managerial discretion. In general, the data overwhelmingly support the low union influence hypothesis. There is a very poor correlation between changes in sex type and changes in worker bargaining strength.

Data from the Great Western Railway will be considered first. Table 6.1 shows the ratio of female to total clerical employment for the Great Western Railway for several dates. It also shows comparable figures for the Chief Mechanical Engineer's Office, a major department within the GWR that will be used in subsequent analyses. The critical contrast implicit in the table is the sex type before and after 1926, the date of the General Strike. Before the strike, the Railway Clerks Association was relatively strong; afterwards, its bargaining power was completely undercut. If worker resistance had any impact on the percentage of women hired, then feminization should have

Table 6.1

Ratio of Female to Total Clerical Employment in the Great Western Railway and in the Chief Mechanical Engineer's Department, Selected Dates

Date	GWR	CME*
1923	—	.258
1924	.157	—
1925	.155	.263
1926	.154	.254
1927	.162	.268
1928	.160	.268
1929	.158	—
1930	.160	—
1931	.159	—
1932	.157	—
1933	.162	—
1937	—	.288

*CME figures include only non-shop offices.
Source: Staff Charts (1923–37); GWR Staff Census (1933).

increased after 1926. No such pattern emerges in the data. Both the Great Western Railway and the Chief Mechanical Engineer's Office show little change in sex from 1923 to the mid-1930's. The years around 1926 show changes in occupational sex-type of less than a percentage point.

The departments with a high level of labor organization were not particularly prone to be less female. The most rigorous support of this claim comes from an internal analysis of the Chief Mechanical Engineer's Department. Sketchy, but nevertheless suggestive, data are available for the GWR as a whole. Ideally one would like to correlate departmental sex ratios with an explicit measure of union activity. Union membership would be an acceptable measure. Participation in the 1926 General Strike would be equally valid. None of these data is available in systematic form for departmental comparisons.

An indirect measure of labor strength is the level of wages. Raw wages per se are a poor measure of organized labor strength. The impact of union activity is confounded with skill, status, and age. The effect of some of these exogenous considerations can be neutralized if one contrasts pay in two periods in which the rate of change of pay would have been particularly subject to the effects of union agitation. Not all of the noise is eliminated by this method, but the impact of such factors is considerably reduced.

In 1920, the first industry-wide clerical pay contract was negotiated. This entailed the widespread standardization of wages throughout the railways. Before 1920, clerks were paid on a series of local-specific scales. Pay rosters of this early era show that a given department could have an enormous number of maximum salaries for differing types of work (Staff Statistics 1870; Salaried Recruitment 1912; GWR Petitions 1914). The RCA contract had but seven grades of male salaries. This meant a necessary assimilation of the old grades into the new.

This transformation had obvious implications for the advancement and maximum salaries of the clerks in question. These individuals had a substantial interest in pressing for the best classification possible. Probably most of these decisions were made by managerial fiat. However, there was a neutral appeals process for the correction of unfavorable classifications and clerks could make informal complaints to their immediate supervisors. The extent and distribution of such activity are, of course, unknown. Nevertheless, such individual complaints are the precise informal mechanism one would wish to analyze for its impact on female employment. One can thus analyze wages before and after the 1920 contract negotiations. The offices where there was substantial wage inflation are likely to be those where employees had some impact on the classification procedure.

The following regression should be interpreted cautiously. The best estimates of departmental wages before and after the contract negotiations come from observations in 1919 and 1933. The 1933 figures were affected by wage changes that occurred after the contract negotiation. Some of these wage changes reflect subsequent informal bargaining and thus measure latent worker strengths. Other influences include changes in the labor market and the working of seniority, which would not have been affected by the internal labor relations of the railway. Thus 1919–33 salary differentials are an imperfect measure of clerical bargaining strength, although they represent the best data that are available at a departmental level for the GWR as a whole.

Table 6.2 regresses the percentage of females within departments in 1933 with the male wage change from 1919 to 1933. A second equation includes clerical labor intensity and past sex composition as controls. The small N reflects missing data due to the non-comparability of some departments between the two dates.

The bivariate equation shows almost no zero-order relation between sex composition and wage change. This persists when the control variables are included in the equation. The coefficient of the wage variable is negative, which is consistent with an exclusionary model. However, the overall effect is both small and statistically insignificant.

The above analysis is flawed by the indirectness of the measure of

Table 6.2

Regression of the Ratio of Female to Total Clerks in 1933
on Male Salary Change between 1919 and 1933
among Departments of the Great Western Railway

Male salary change (1919–33)	% female (1919)	% clerical (1933)	Adjusted R^2
−62.8 (.674)	—	—	.01
−1.31 (.235)	.660 (.013)	.108 (.098)	.64

Note: $N = 14$. The top figure is the unstandardized regression coefficient. The lower figure is the significance level.
Source: GWR Staff Census (1919, 1933).

male labor strength. More direct measures are available for offices within the Chief Mechanical Engineer's Office. The Chief Mechanical Engineer's Office was located in the west of England in a company town called Swindon. The GWR built all of its own locomotives and rolling stock, as well as rolling a substantial proportion of its rails, and all of these factory operations were concentrated in Swindon and supervised by the Chief Mechanical Engineer. Furthermore, the department functioned as a central accounts station for the western branch of the railway.

Not surprisingly, the CME encompassed a wide variety of work situations. There were factory offices, where clerks worked in close proximity to workers on the shop floor. There were technical offices, where clerks worked in laboratories next to technicians. There were purely administrative offices. Some of these involved secretaries working as personal assistants to teams of managers. Some were large concentrations of clerical proletariats doing semi-mechanical data entry and processing. The shop-floor and technical offices tended to be all male. The purely administrative offices varied from nearly all male to all female. Thus within the CME one could find examples of virtually every kind of clerical work organization imaginable.

Data exist for each of these offices on the percentage of clerks who joined the General Strike of 1926. These rates are available separately for men and for women. The male strike rate is a good indicator of the degree of commitment of male clerks to the Railway Clerks Association. The strike rate represents the extent to which clerks were willing to defy management in order to show their concrete support for labor. The data were compiled from non-attendance records kept by management and are available for each of the 101 offices the CME maintained in Swindon.

Table 6.3 shows the bivariate relationship between male militancy and sex composition. The equation provides modest support for an exclusionist interpretation. The male strike rate is negatively correlated with the percentage of female clerks. The coefficient is close to but not quite significant at the .05 level. The equation only predicts 3 percent of the variance, which is an unimpressive performance. Nevertheless, the correlation could be interpreted as supporting a hypothesis of a weak but real relationship between male militancy and sex-type.

However, the bivariate relation very much overstates the role of male exclusionism. This is because male radicalism was coincidently associated with clerical labor intensity. The primary centers of strike

Table 6.3
Bivariate Regression of the Ratio of Female to Total Clerks
on the Male Strike Rate within Offices of the
Chief Mechanical Engineer's Department, 1926

Male strike rate	R^2
−.103	.03
(.074)	

Note: $N = 101$. The top figure is the unstandardized regression coefficient. The lower figure is the significance level.
Source: Staff Charts (1914–37); General Strike (1926).

support were the shop-floor offices. The major organizers of the General Strike were the blue-collar unionists; the shop-floor clerks would have been swept up in the militant struggles typical of the railway manual labor force. The "office" clerks would have been less exposed to class conflict, their only mobilizing agent being the somewhat more staid Railway Clerks Association.

A second feature of the shop-floor offices is that they were decidedly less clerical-labor-intensive than the administrative offices. The shop-floor clerks were part of work units that were truly non-clerical. They were not on the standard clerical job classification scheme, which effectively meant they could not be promoted into the mainstream clerical hierarchy. They were supervised by blue-collar foremen and superintendents. These foremen would have been primarily responsible for the effective management of the shops as a whole and thus have been primarily concerned with technological issues and the control of the blue-collar labor force. Reducing clerical costs would have been a lower priority. The bivariate relation between militancy and sex composition thus could have been the spurious result of clerical labor intensity.

Informal support for this assertion can be found by considering the technical offices. These are offices whose functions and personnel were primarily scientific. Among them are drafting offices, material inspection sections, and laboratories. The ratio of clericals to scientific personnel in these offices was very small, usually under 10 percent. However, the militancy of these offices closely resembled that of the administrative offices. In the average technical offices, 37.1 percent of the male clerks struck. The comparable figure for the administrative office was 35.1 percent.

The clerks in these offices thus resemble the shop clerks in clerical labor intensity, but resemble the administrative clerks in labor strength. If an employee discrimination model is correct, then the administrative and technical offices should have comparable sex distributions. If a clerical-labor-intensity model is correct, the technical offices should resemble the shops. Table 6.4, which gives the mean percentage of females of the various types of office in the CME, shows that the technical offices were far more similar to the shops than they were to the administrative offices. Both the labs and the shops had clerical forces that were 99 percent male. This is consistent with a clerical-labor-intensity model, but not a union-exclusion model, for there was little exlusionary pressure from the clerks in the labs.

Table 6.5 shows the result of including clerical labor intensity as a control in the bivariate equation in Table 6.3. Actual clerk/staff ratios are not available at this low level of aggregation. Administrative status is used as a proxy for clerical labor intensity. An office is considered to be administrative if it was not technical and was not located on the shop floor.

Including clerical labor intensity diminishes the effect of the strike rate to insignificance. The coefficient shrinks to one-tenth of its former size, representing a negligible impact in absolute terms. Administrative status, however, is highly significant. Overall, the two variables explain nearly half the variance in clerical sex type within the CME, with clerical labor intensity carrying by far the brunt of the explanatory power.

The overall sex ratios of the Chief Mechanical Engineer's Department did not generally respond to changes in the power of organized labor. Table 6.1 shows that, like the GWR, the sex ratio of the CME

Table 6.4

Characteristics of Office Types within the
Chief Mechanical Engineer's Department, 1926

Office type	N	Male militancy	Clerical labor intensity	Mean % female
Administrative	35	low	high	29.2
Technical	9	low	low	1.2
Shop	57	high	low	0.9

Source: Staff Charts (1914–37); General Strike (1926).

Table 6.5
Regression of the Ratio of Female to Total Clerks on
Administrative Status and the Male Strike Rate within the
Offices of the Chief Mechanical Engineer's Department, 1926

Administrative status	Male strike rate	R^2
281.3	$-.010$	.49
(.000)	(.810)	

Note: $N = 101$. The top figure is the unstandardized regression coefficient. The lower figure is the significance level.
Source: Staff Charts (1914–37); General Strike (1926).

was generally fairly constant over time. The decline of RCA strength that came with the collapse of the 1926 General Strike did not significantly change the patterns of sex preference in hiring. Thus, both longitudinally and cross-sectionally, in both the CME and on the Great Western Railway as a whole, variations in the bargaining strength of male workers do not significantly explain variations in the use of women.

A similar pattern emerges when one considers data from the Post Office. If employees with labor power successfully excluded women from employment, then telegraph offices should have been less female than the rest of the Post Office. The signallers' position as a labor vanguard should have given them superior capacity to restrict entry into employment. Table 6.6 shows the average percentage of women in telegraph and non-telegraph offices at four critical dates in postal labor history: 1881, the year after the telegraphists won their first retroactive pay demand, the Fawcett revision; 1891, the period of the Raikes revision, when the telegraphists obtained a Post Office-wide wage increase; 1906, the date of the Hobhouse Commission, the highwater mark of postal parliamentary agitation; and 1926, a low point in signalling labor strength, the period of the transfer to telex and telephone communications.

The findings in Table 6.6 are precisely the opposite of those one would expect from a labor exclusion model. In each of the three periods of telegraph labor strength—1881, 1891, and 1906—there were more women in telegraph offices than in the less well-organized sectors. The one date in which telegraph offices had fewer women relative to other offices was when their strength was vitiated.

These counterintuitive findings can be explained. As shall be seen in the next chapter, management feminized the telegraphs service very heavily in the early years. Part of this policy was due to a scarcity of skilled labor, requiring the training of new labor sources. Part of it was also due to a misconceived strategy of labor control through gender segmentation. For whatever reasons, the telegraph offices started with substantial complements of women. This presented labor with a fait accompli that was very difficult to reverse.

The increase in the percentage of females in non-telegraph offices is due both to general feminization and to compositional changes in the Post Office. Most offices feminized between 1870 and 1926. Another contributory factor was that the Post Office continued to absorb new functions that were staffed by women. The high percentage of females in 1926 is partly due to the addition of several new telephone offices that had large staffs of women operators.

Changes in labor strength within the telegraph service seems to have very modest explanatory power in accounting for changes in telegraphic sex types over time. The figures on the left side of Table

Table 6.6

Percentage of Female Clerks in Telegraph and Non-telegraph Offices of the General Post Office, Selected Dates

Date	Telegraph*		Non-telegraph (%)
	All (%)	Non-elite only (%)	
1881	39.0 (6)	46.7 (5)	7.4 (18)
1891	37.6 (4)	50.1 (3)	11.0 (11)
1906	28.3 (8)	45.5 (5)	21.8 (17)
1926	35.5 (5)	59.2 (3)	42.0 (15)

*Non-elite signal offices are the signalling galleries at the Central Telegraph Station, the London EC Signalling Station, the London district telegraph stations, Dublin Telegraph and Edinburgh Telegraph. The elite offices are the Central Telegraph Control Room, the Intelligence Division and the Cable Room, which are all male.

Notes: Figures in parentheses are N's.

Source: GPO Establishment Books (1881, 1891, 1906, 1926).

6.6 could be used to construct a labor-exclusion argument. The percentage of females declines during the years of labor strength and increases during the years of labor weakness. However, this seeming trend is somewhat misleading; the figures are heavily influenced by several very small offices within the sample. There were several elite telegraph offices that were reserved for male workers. This includes Central Telegraph Control, the International Cable Office, and the Intelligence Office, which transmitted news and race results. These offices were filled with lucrative jobs for workers who were at the apex of their careers. They were non-entry-level; they were well-paying; and the actual number of men involved was very small. Most of these offices employed fewer than twenty clerks, while the main offices each employed over a thousand. The elite offices would have been all male regardless of their union policies simply because they contained no entry-level positions. The critical question for a employee-discrimination theory is whether unions were capable of excluding women from mainstream jobs that employers might have been interested in feminizing. Thus, the cases of interest in the telegraph example are the large, centralized, urban signalling stations with their high percentage of entry-level positions. The middle row of Table 6.6 shows the percentage of females in the non-elite telegraph offices: the Central Telegraph signalling galleries, the London East Central Telegraph section, the London District Telegraph offices, and the telegraph departments of Dublin and Edinburgh. Note that when these offices are considered, the weakness of a labor-exclusion model becomes even more apparent. During the years of telegraph union strength, the telegraph offices were more female than their counterparts; during the years of union weakness they were less female than their counterparts. Furthermore, during the years of union strength, they were unable to secure any lasting trend towards de-feminization. Sex-typing was virtually constant during the 1881–1906 period, and whatever minor fluctuations occurred were feminizations just as often as de-feminizations. Although the percentage of women did increase when union strength became weakened, it is not clear which was cause and which was effect. It was the very introduction of female typists in the first place that undercut the monopoly power of the Morse signallers. Thus the mainstream telegraph workers seem to have been unable to control entry into their profession in periods either of strength or of weakness; the only areas that remained all male were offices in which management had little economic incentive to feminize.

Another test of the role of labor power is available. One can estimate the correlation between union activity and sex-typing for a large sample of departments of different types, controlling for exogenous factors that could be obscuring a relation between male militancy and the exclusion of women. No sophisticated measures of union membership or strike participation exist at the department level. Thus, the best available measure of union activity is a simple dummy variable with 1 representing activity and 0 representing passivity. The dummy was coded in such a way as to recreate the historical account given in the earlier section. In addition, organizational histories of postal unions such as B. V. Humphreys' history of civil service labor relations (1958) were used to find the dates of origin of various early unions. In most cases, postal unions once founded never became inactive. Thus, once some form of organizing activity had been located within an office, it is assumed that such activity continued at later dates.

The N for this analysis is smaller than that presented for other postal equations. This is for two reasons. First, in some cases, such as the Edinburgh offices, the historical record is very thin. It thus becomes impossible to distinguish between a true absence of unionization and gaps in the survival of archival material. Provincial activity where known is included in the sample, but passive provincial cases must be treated as missing data. London, however, is sufficiently well studied to allow for the confident coding of some offices as quiet. Second, after World War I all civil servants came under the coverage of the Whitley Councils. Inter-departmental variance in formal participation in collective grievance machinery virtually disappeared. Thus, inter-departmental tests of the role of union activity are only meaningful up through 1914.

Table 6.7 shows the bivariate regression of sex-typing on union activity by year. Overall, the performance of union activity is very poor. In none of the cases did the regression coefficient attain statistical significance, and in only one year was male militancy capable of explaining as much as 10 percent of the variance. Furthermore, in that year, the sign of the coefficient is in the wrong direction.

Table 6.8 shows regressions of the percentage of females on union activity and the three control variables from the core postal model of Chapter 2. The performance of militancy is as weak here as it was in the bivariate equations. In most of the equations, the coefficient is in the wrong direction, and in no case is the variable statistically

Table 6.7

Bivariate Regressions of the Ratio of Female to Total Clerks on Levels of Male
Militancy for Departments within the Post Office, Selected Dates

Date	Militancy	Adjusted R^2	N
1876	−.238 (.135)	.10	15
1881	.059 (.624)	0	17
1886	−.019 (.899)	0	17
1891	.009 (.961)	0	12
1896	−.072 (.583)	0	18
1901	−.106 (.476)	0	18
1906	−.123 (.424)	0	19
1911	−.189 (.218)	.03	19
1914	−.220 (.170)	.06	19

Note: The top figure is the unstandardized regression coefficient. The lower figure is
the significance level. All negative adjusted R^2 values have been reported as zero.
Source: See text.

significant.[3] Longitudinal analyses of these data also fail to uncover a
meaningful labor effect. Thus, overall, one would have to conclude
from the Post Office materials that cost structure and synthetic turn-

3. It should be noted that clerical labor intensity does not fare much better in these
equations. To some extent, this is an artifact of the reduced sample; on an N of 18 it is
difficult for four variables to be statistically significant simultaneously. However, even
the zero-order relation between clerical labor intensity and sex type is weak in these
instances. Because the cases for which information on union activity is available is only a
subset of the total population of offices, it is thus possible that union militancy might
have shown more of an effect in a more complete database.

Table 6.8

Regressions of the Ratio of Female to Total Clerks on Levels of Male Militancy and Other Control Variables for Departments within the Post Office, Selected Dates

Date	Militancy	% non-entry	% clerical	% non-political	Adjusted R^2	N
1876	−.235 (.325)	−.747 (.007)	−.234 (.472)	.373 (.137)	.56	15
1881	.116 (.384)	−.475 (.041)	.255 (.413)	.353 (.045)	.33	17
1886	.052 (.702)	−.670 (.014)	.131 (.687)	.693 (.687)	.46	17
1891	.010 (.497)	−.595 (.042)	−.203 (.574)	.979 (.024)	.39	12
1896	.048 (.694)	−.575 (.020)	.053 (.867)	.576 (.049)	.33	18
1901	.060 (.687)	−.632 (.035)	.127 (.739)	.630 (.080)	.27	18
1906	.083 (.583)	−.609 (.015)	.011 (.969)	.762 (.043)	.34	19
1911	.014 (.898)	−.652 (.006)	−.012 (.969)	.857 (.017)	.48	19
1914	.022 (.867)	−.695 (.005)	.096 (.790)	.812 (.027)	.50	19

Note: The top figure is the unstandardized regression coefficient. The lower figure is the significance level. All negative adjusted R^2 values have been reported as zero.
Source: See text.

over exerted a far more important influence on sex-typing than either formal or informal campaigns of union exclusion.

Conclusion

Overall, neither the anecdotal or the quantitative evidence support a strong impact of employee discrimination on workplace sex composition. It would seem that managerial responsibility was primarily responsible for the exclusion of women from all-male environments. This is consistent with the anecdotal evidence given in Chapter 2 and with the general good fit of the earlier statistical model.

These findings imply that the attitudes of male co-workers probably had little to do with the determination of sex type in clerical work. These firms represent an unusual high point in clerical union-organizing and sophistication. If these clerks could not make an impact on sex-typing, it is hard to imagine what office workers would have had a better chance.

However, such a finding does not rule out the role of unions in influencing sex issues in the workplace. Many blue-collar workers, particularly those in craft occupations, have had much more control over the labor process than did the unions discussed here. The present findings, in fact, suggest a plausible labor-related explanation that clerical work feminized because of the absence of a body of male workers capable of putting forth effective resistance. Women's concentration in white-collar occupations is due to the prevailing weakness of labor organization in this sector. The present research can not parse between this explanation and one based purely on managerial utilities. The degree to which blue-collar managers are frustrated feminizers can only be determined by direct study of manual work settings.

This discussion does not exhaust the possible links between class conflict and sex. It is also conceivable that women can be used to reduce class conflict. Sex-based hiring may be determined by the dynamics of the segmentation of the labor force and by managerial reaction to labor's offensives. The next chapter considers the role of industrial-conflict models that are not based on the assumption of employees' determining hiring policies.

7

Women as Labor Control

In discussing employers' motivations for hiring women, women are customarily referred to as a "cheap docile labor force." That women work for low wages is well known. However, whether women inhibit labor conflict is a complex and more subtle question. It is well documented that women are less likely to join labor unions (Antos et al. 1980; P. Hunt 1981). There are suggestions that women are less likely to strike. However, the interpretation of these differentials is controversial.

There are three ways to conceptualize gender differences in labor militancy. The effect of gender could be direct, indirect, or spurious. A direct effect would be one due to differential behavior by women themselves. Women for whatever reason would be inherently less militant in any conceivable work setting. An indirect effect is one created by the presence of women, not necessarily involving any distinctive action on their part. If male co-workers were to change their behavior on account of women, this would be an indirect effect. A spurious effect has no basis in gender per se. Such differences are created by women's being disproportionately distributed into occupations or work settings that induce passivity. Any worker recruited into such positions would replicate the behavior observed in women. The fundamental question of the interrelation of gender to class conflict is the decomposition of the observed gender gap in militancy into these three components. One could then empirically determine the comparative importance of female behavior, male non-cooperation, and occupational distribution.

Most of the direct effects that have been suggested explain women's non-participation in unions by invoking conflicts arising from tradi-

173

tional sex roles. Some authors have viewed women as marginal and temporary labor force paticipants. Women could escape the deprivations of the workplace by retreating into full-time family life. Furthermore, women's short anticipated careers lowered their interest in the long-term prospects of their occupation (Bliss and Andrews 1911; Barkin 1961; Blackburn 1967; Blum 1971; Moore and Newman 1975; Hirsch 1980). Alternatively, in some industries, female employment has been restricted to juvenile labor. The young age distribution of female employees is sometimes held to produce this "short-horizon" passivity (Tilly 1981). Traditional sex roles are also seen as inhibiting the union participation of married women as well. Union activities make time demands that are often inconsistent with domestic obligations or child care (Wertheimer and Nelson 1975; P. Hunt 1981).

Changing sex roles have reduced the saliency of these arguments. Rising labor force participation has decreased the supply of passive future housewives. Housework may be playing a smaller role in determining women's use of time. Yet the present liberation of women has not made debates about direct effects moot. Most advocates of strong direct effects would argue that changing women's societal roles is a necessary pre-condition to militancy. Raising gender consciousness is an important pre-condition for raising class consciousness. An opponent of the direct effect thesis would claim that changing sex roles has little impact on creating female labor militancy. The only way to increase female militancy would be for them to move into jobs with more intrinsic bargaining power.

Indirect effects stem from male workers' unwillingness to cooperate with female workers to obtain common benefits. Established male unions have in general been quite slow about organizing female workers. Those attempts that have occurred have often foundered on the simultaneous campaigns by these workers to win sexist demands such as restrictions on female labor. The result has been either the neglect or the alienation of otherwise willing female unionists (Wertheimer and Nelson 1975; Kessler-Harris 1979; Feldberg 1980; Milkman 1980). The advocates of indirect effects have not fully explained why, in the absence of male organization, rival all-female unions do not develop. The experience of the CIO shows that the absence of established union sanction does not stifle worker militancy when other pre-conditions of organization are met. However, labor force segmentation still remains an important theoretical possibility in explaining female docility.

Spurious effects are those created solely by the occupational or industrial distribution of women. Female non-participation is a surrogate for the behavior of people in weak labor market positions. Such arguments are usually difficult to disconfirm. Since men and women rarely hold jobs with identical skills or prospects, it is hard to parametricize these completely and examine pure residuals. This notwithstanding, occupational effects appear to be quite potent. Joseph Antos et al. found in an analysis of current population survey data that 57 percent of the gap between men and women in union membership could be explained by a simple decomposition into crude occupational and industrial categories using only eight industries and seven occupations. How much more would have been explained by a full decomposition into more sophisticated occupational categories can only be imagined (Antos et al. 1980). George Bain has shown that among British white-collar workers sex differences in union membership disappear with the simple introduction of firm size (Bain 1970).

Determining the causes of low female union activity is especially important to the study of white-collar labor. The relative docility of white-collar workers has sometimes been explained by the high percentage of women in these occupations (Blum 1971). Furthermore, increasing female labor force participation has been offered as a partial explanation of the decline of union membership in the United States as a whole (Barkin 1961). Finding low direct and indirect effects would weaken the case for both of these propositions.

This chapter considers the effect of sex on the activity of white-collar unions of the General Post Office and the Great Western Railway. There are two measures of worker militancy that can be considered, union membership and participation in strikes. The former measures the willingness of workers to make long-term commitments to their union, although the costs of such involvement are often low. Strike participation is more short term but represents a more explicit demonstration of opposition to an employer. Both are valid, complementary measures of militancy; in general, studies of white-collar organization have emphasized union membership rather than strike participation, due to the relatively small number of white-collar strikes that can be analyzed.

The two firms in this study allow a test of the effect of sex on both measures of union activity. Union membership data exist both for the civil service and for the clerical force of railways as a whole. Detailed strike rates are available for the two most important strikes of the period, the 1871 postal telegraph strike and the participation of the

Great Western Railway Railway Clerks Association in the General Strike of 1926. These two actions were probably the largest and most important white-collar strikes in Britain before 1945.

The reader who is primarily interested in contemporary occupational sex-typing may question whether strike rates from the early twentieth century are at all germane to a test of women's role in reducing labor militancy today. Actually, the early date of these strikes is a very attractive methodological asset. Strikes before World War II provide a strong test of the direct effects of sex in inhibiting participation in unions. In the Victorian era and the early twentieth century, traditional sex roles were very strong. If repressive female socialization and limited labor force participation has any effect on strike activity, such an effect should be particularly manifest in early data. If no direct effects are found in these data, it is even less likely that direct effects would be found in modern data, where the impact of traditional female roles would be far less pronounced. Thus, these cases allow for a test of the effect of sex on industrial conflict that is biased towards a finding of strong non-spurious effects.

The analysis suggests that after occupational barriers to organization are taken into account, the differences in militancy between men and women were not very pronounced. In the case of union membership, there were simply no differences between men and women. David Lockwood has analyzed the union membership data in his book *The Blackcoated Worker*. He found that, in both the RCA and the civil service unions, the ratio of female to male membership in the unions was exactly proportional to the ratio of females to males in the relevant occupations (Lockwood 1958). Lockwood's analysis of these materials is entirely reasonable, and there is little reason to belabor these findings here.

For strike data, the situation is more complex, but the general findings are similar to those of Lockwood. In the Post Office, the raw data show men and women striking at similar rates. This is despite substantial sex-specific barriers to mobilization. In the GWR, there were raw differences in the strike rates of men and women. However, controlling for a few sex-neutral occupational characteristics reduces the differential to a very small amount. Furthermore, much of the remaining gap can be attributed to occupational power rather than gender per se. Direct and indirect effects are not explicitly measured here. However, the residual sex differences are so small after simple job-related characteristics are taken into account that the direct and indirect effects are likely to be miniscule.

The General Strike of 1926

The evidence about the behavior of railway clerks during the General Strike of 1926 comes from the Chief Mechanical Engineer's Department in Swindon. For every office we know the sex composition, the job structure, and the extent to which the men and the women in the office went out on strike. Because of the extraordinary diversity of the Chief Mechanical Engineer's Department with its combination of shop offices, secretarial offices, and large concentrations of clerical semi-proletarians, there is a rare opportunity to control for objective differences in the organization of work, to see how the labor process interacts with sex in determining rates of clerical militancy.

Of all clerks, 44.7 percent struck. Of all male clerks 50.6 percent struck, but only 26.9 percent of all female clerks struck. There was, thus, a difference of 23.7 percentage points between men and women in the likelihood of striking. This is not an extreme effect, but the sex difference is fairly substantial. The difference is statistically significant by most normal criteria. However, the sex gap is severely overestimated. Women were disproportionately concentrated in offices that suffered from non-sex-based obstacles to effective organization. When one controls for these organizational impediments, the sex differences decrease dramatically.

To understand the analysis that follows, it is helpful to elaborate the different kinds of work settings that existed in Swindon in some detail. The biggest difference was between workers who worked in the shops and workers who worked in the administrative buildings. The shop clerks were the clerks who worked on the actual premises in which factory work was done. Other clerks worked in office buildings that were purely clerical in function. The shop clerks were divided into three types: administrative, stock-checking, and factory floor. The shop administrative offices did routine clerical work and had no contact with the factory operations themselves. Workers were wholly isolated from both the production process and the blue-collar workers on the floor. The factory floor offices were just the opposite. They were desks located within the factory where clerks recorded output and circulated job orders. These clerks had intimate contact with blue-collar laborers and were integral parts of shop-floor personnel networks. In an intermediate status were the stock checkers. Their work involved record-keeping in the front offices of the factory. However, inventory control required constant trips onto the production floor to examine supplies. They thus had an intermediate amount of blue-collar contact and intimacy.

The shops were also divided into different buildings. Each building had its own level of militancy. There was a carriage and wagon works, a sawmill, and a locomotive works. The sawmill and the locomotive works were quite radical, the carriage and wagon works comparatively conservative.

There were enormous differences, as well, among the non-shop offices. Most of these were located in one central administrative building, which was located in the complex with the rest of the mills. The addressograph operations and the train statistics division were located at some distance from the main complex in an old railway depot nearer town. This isolated subunit consisted largely of unskilled machine operators. They were overwhelmingly female, with a small number of both male and female supervisors who shuttled back and forth between the town station and the main building.

Within the main building there was also a mix of office types. There were some virtually all-male offices, containing no women or having a single female secretary. These usually dealt with technical and engineering matters. There were a variety of larger offices having several work groups, each with a minority of female clerks. These dealt with a variety of administrative matters, with the women doing general clerical work. Finally, there were some large, heavily female offices resembling the town station. These offices employed large numbers of replaceable clerical proletariats and the work usually involved simple statistical calculations. Arithmetic processing may have been more mechanized at the town station; nevertheless, both types of heavily female offices specialized in the more menial aspects of quantitative data-processing (Staff Charts 1926).

Women were not randomly distributed among the offices, but were concentrated in offices that were prone to passivity. First, women were less likely to be employed in offices that allowed close contact with manual workers. Stock clerk posts and factory floor offices provided for blue-collar contact. Only one woman was employed in such a situation. The importance of blue-collar contact for railway clerical organizing can hardly be underestimated. The Railway Clerks Association largely grew as a by-product of the National Union of Railwaymen. The railwaymen's victories lowered management's resistance to collective bargaining for the clerical staff. Furthermore for some grades, such as some blue-collar supervisory positions, the boundary line between NUR and RCA coverage was ambiguous enough to warrant jointly coordinated and conceived bargaining offensives.

Furthermore, the general strike of 1926 was a political strike induced by developments in mining. The NUR was one of the major sponsors of the strike nationwide. The NUR had direct links of cooperation to the craft and industrial unions working in the Swindon shops. Thus the prime momentum for mobilization for the General Strike would have come from the Swindon shop floors (Bagwell 1963; Tucket 1976). Anyone working in such a setting could not have avoided being swept up in the preparations for this major offensive, and shop-floor contact would have been a major stimulant to radical activity.

Second, women were concentrated in buildings with bad organizing climates. The extreme cases were the town station, the locomotive works, and the sawmill. The town station was several miles from the main complex. Any organizing drive by the RCA among the main body of railway clerks would have missed the workers at the town station. Furthermore, the workers at the town station were very unskilled. The women were entirely machine operators. Most women in the main building would have had significantly more market power. The town station thus for both organizational and occupational reasons would have been an infertile source of union activities. Women were disproportionately concentrated in this sector.

In the locomotive works and the sawmill, on the other hand, all the clerks had either direct shop-floor contact or indirect contact through working in close proximity to visitors to the shop floor. Workers in these buildings were very militant, but very few women were employed here. The scarcity of women in these settings helped to reduce levels of overall female militancy.

The main building, where most women were concentrated, had intermediate levels of union activity. These clerks would have been cut off from the blue-collar mobilization on the shop floor but would have been in the mainstream of the RCA's own campaigns. The carriage and wagon mill was also very conservative. The reasons for this are not easy to determine. It could have been due to lower militancy among

Table 7.1
Male Strike Rates in the Chief Mechanical Engineer's Office
by Office Type and Shop-Floor Contact, 1926

Male Clerks Only

Amount of contact	Carriage and wagon works (%)	Town station (%)	Main building (%)	Loco- motive works (%)	Saw- mill (%)	Total (%)
With shop- floor contact	44.7 (141)	—	—	71.6 (141)	85.7 (7)	58.8 (289)
Without shop-floor contact	17.2 (29)	42.9 (7)	45.5 (413)	62.8 (43)	83.3 (6)	45.8 (498)
Total	40.0 (170)	42.9 (7)	45.5 (413)	69.6 (184)	84.6 (13)	50.6 (787)

Source: General Strike (1926).

wood-working locals than among the boilermakers and machinists. It could have been due to differing plant management policies. This was an exception to the pattern of female concentration in passive areas, being a heavily male enclave that happened to be conservative. Thus, both building and shop-floor contact had independent effects on levels of militancy. How these interacted with sex can be seen in Tables 7.1–7.3.

The tables show male, female, and total strike rates for workers in every building both with and without direct shop-floor contact. Workers in stock offices and those actually located on the shop floor are defined as having shop responsibility. Before considering the impact of sex itself, we should note how the sex-specific rates confirm the discussion of the roles of the control variables. Within each building, those workers with direct shop-floor contact are more likely than their counterparts to strike. The size of the differential varies from 2 to 28 percentage points.

Clerks with intermediate amounts of shop-floor contact had intermediate strike rates. Stock clerks spent part of their time on the shop floor. Fifty percent of the stock clerks struck. This figure is

Table 7.2
*Female Strike Rates in the Chief Mechanical Engineer's Office
by Office Type and Shop-Floor Contact, 1926*

Female Clerks Only

Amount of contact	Carriage and wagon works (%)	Town station (%)	Main building (%)	Loco-motive works (%)	Saw-mill (%)	Total (%)
With shop-floor contact	—	—	—	0.0 (1)	—	0.0 (1)
Without shop-floor contact	0.0 (5)	4.0 (75)	35.6 (174)	100.0 (5)	—	27.0 (259)
Total	0.0 (5)	4.0 (75)	35.6 (174)	83.36 (6)	—	26.9 (260)

Source: General Strike (1926).

Table 7.3
*Total Strike Rates in the Chief Mechanical Engineer's Office
by Office Type and Shop-Floor Contact, 1926*

All Clerks

Amount of contact	Carriage and wagon works (%)	Town station (%)	Main building (%)	Loco-motive works (%)	Saw-mill (%)	Total (%)
With shop-floor contact	44.7 (141)	—	—	71.1 (142)	85.7 (7)	58.6 (290)
Without shop-floor contact	14.7 (34)	7.3 (82)	42.6 (587)	66.7 (48)	83.3 (6)	39.4 (757)
Total	38.9 (175)	9.3 (82)	42.6 (587)	70.0 (190)	84.6 (13)	44.7 (1,047)

Source: General Strike (1926).

between the 58.0 percent shop-floor figure and the 45.8 percent non-floor figure.

The buildings also affected militancy. For each sex, carriage and wagon workers were the least radical, town station workers were the next most conservative, main office workers were in the middle, and locomotive and sawmill workers were the most radical. This holds for both sexes and for workers with and without direct shop-floor contact.

None of these controls is a surrogate for gender. If building or shop-floor effects were entirely due to sex composition, then one would find no building or floor effects after controlling for sex. However, these differentials exist within sex categories. This strongly suggests the independent importance of building and shop-floor contact. Since women had no shop-floor contact and were located in non-militant buildings, these factors would have reduced overall female strike rates.

Because of this, there were large raw differences between male and female strike rates. As we saw, 50.6 percent of all male clerks struck, but only 26.9 percent of all female clerks. The 23.7 percent difference is not overwhelming, but it is statistically significant by most criteria. However, after one takes the control variables into account, the difference becomes much smaller. The best estimate of the effect of the sex gap net of building and shop-floor contact is a 7.4 percent difference. This is one-third the size of the originally observed 23.7 percent difference. A 7.4 percent gap is what would be observed if 47.4 percent of the men, but only 40.0 percent of the women, struck. The difference is real and statistically significant, but is, in absolute terms, fairly small.

Before examining the precise derivation of the 7.4 percent estimate, we should consider the differences between male and female workers who had identical building location and shop-floor contact. Large differences between men and women are noticeable in the locomotive works, the carriage and wagon works, and the town station. Of these three contrasts, however, only two show women being more passive. In the locomotive works, in fact, the women were more strike prone than the men. Furthermore, one of the cases of relative female non-striking, the town station, is overstated. In the town station, most of the men shuttled between the town station and the main building. Most of the women were isolated in the town station. There is a 42.9 percent difference between the sexes, but that is because the men's rate resembles that of their counterparts in the main building.

Differential contact with the mainstream of organizing probably accounts for much of this difference.

All three of these contrasts are based on small numbers of either males or females. The main building is the only contrast with large numbers of both. In the main building there was a 9.9 percent difference in strike rates favoring the men. This is one-third the size of the gross differential and is objectively quite small. This estimate is close to that obtained from the combined data.

To obtain an estimate of sex effects net of control variables that uses all of the data, an indirect standardization was performed. Assume that there are no sex differences in strike rates whatsoever after building and sex are controlled. We can then simulate what the overall male and female strike rates would have been. The difference between the sex gap calculated this way and the observed gender gap is the gender gap net of building and shop-floor contact.

To perform the indirect standardization, we assume that men and women in each building-contact category would have struck at the combined sex-blind rate. These sex-blind category-specific rates are listed in Table 7.3. The two sexes differ in the percentage of each that would be subject to each rate. For example, 5.5 percent of the men but only 1.9 percent of the women were located in low-contact locomotive works offices. The indirect standardization involves multiplying every rate in Table 7.3 by the percentage of workers of each sex subject to each rate. Adding up these weighted figures for males and females separately gives an estimate of the strike rates that allows for compositional but not within-category sex effects.

By these calculations, men would have had a strike rate of 48.8 percent and women a rate of 32.5 percent. This represents a gender gap of 16.3 percent that is attributable exclusively to the different distribution of men and women among buildings and differential access to blue-collar workers. Subtracting 16.3 percent from the original gap of 23.7 percent provides the sex differences due to all other causes. This is 7.4 percent.

It should be noted that the 7.4 percent difference, while small, is statistically significant. A logistic regression containing sex and both control variables provides significant coefficients for all variables (Table 7.4). No variable can be removed without a significant loss of overall goodness of fit. This also reconfirms that the control variables act independently of sex.

However, 7.4 percent is an overestimate of the size of the direct and indirect sex effects. This is because some of this difference is due to the difference between sexes in market power. Since menial jobs carry little market power, regardless of which sex holds them, estimates of the true gender effect must be purged of as much of the effect of market power as possible. Even within the control categories already used, occupational power still predicts some unexplained variance in the strike propensity of the women clerks.

The women clerks could be divided into two groups, the secretaries and the single-task operatives. A secretary is a single woman with primary responsibility for providing a variety of clerical services to a small number of individuals. The secretary's most important task usually involves typing reports and correspondence. However, these can expand to include dictation, telephone work, and ultimately participation in the administrative affairs of the office. Single-task operatives are the workers invoked in popular stereotypes of clerical proletariats. These are workers in large, centralized, depersonalized offices doing routinized and repetitive work. Such workers are usually given a single primary task: keypunching, addressographing, tabulating, or making ledger entries. While there is some division of labor,

Table 7.4

*Logistic Regression Model of Individual Probability of Striking
in the Chief Mechanical Engineer's Office, 1926*

Variable	Coefficient	Standard error	Coefficient/ standard error
Sex			
Female	−0.271	−0.089	−3.06
Shop-floor contact			
Present	0.296	0.132	2.24
Building			
Locomotive/sawmill†	1.15	0.188	6.14
Main building	0.499	0.169	2.96
Town station	−0.262	0.208	−1.26
*Constant**	−0.639	0.131	−4.88

*The constant represents the effect of having the values of the omitted categories, i.e., male with no shop-floor contact in carriage and wagon works.
†Locomotive and sawmill locations are merged in this analysis.
Note: N = 1047. Effects coding is in use.
Source: General Strike (1926).

each worker's tasks are essentially similar to those being done by her officemates. Large insurance and accounting offices are major employers of such labor.

Secretaries have substantially more market power than do single-task operatives. This comes from the personalized nature of the relationship between the secretary and her employer and the ambiguous definition of secretarial job duties. Secretaries are expected to handle whatever clerical and minor administrative problems their employers are likely to be faced with. Proficient secretaries, as they gain experience, usually learn to provide a variety of services beyond merely typing dictated letters. This can entail providing information on commonly used files, composing routine statements for frequently sent letters, or making practical arrangements for the solutions of petty problems. Rosabeth Moss Kanter has argued that, in some cases, this can mean the substantial transfer of responsibility from executive to secretary. Examples involve those secretaries who graduate to handling some of the duties of the executive himself and secretaries who collude in the protection of deficiency, such as covering up for an alcoholic.

Kanter argues that such expansion of responsibilities is very person-specific. It depends both on the qualifications of the secretary and on the needs of the employer. Different individuals have their own routines and require different responses from their secretaries. As a result, good working relationships are often difficult to achieve. When these occur, executives work to preserve these ties by taking their secretaries with them from job to job. A good secretary becomes difficult to replace; this gives her a viable exit threat (Kanter 1977).

The situation is different for the single-task operative. Because of the lack of variation among job duties, single-task operatives are interchangeable. This standardization also allows for the easy training of new recruits from the labor market. Because of the easy replaceability of single-task operatives, the threat of withdrawal of their labor poses only minor burdens for the employer. From a position of market power, one would thus expect more resistance to employers from secretaries than from operatives.

The measure of secretarial status used in the following analysis is the sex composition of the office. Women working in offices less than one-third female are considered secretaries. Women working in offices one-third female or more are considered single-task operatives. The measure may seem counterintuitive, but it is supported by the organizational charts of the CME. The task descriptions and spatial organization of women completely differ in the two types of offices. In the heavily female offices, there are usually several work groups. There is usually one or more clusters that are predominantly male, occasionally including one or two females. These are balanced by large clusters that are very heavily female. These clusters have job titles suggesting machine operation, such as "Addressograph" or "Tabulation of Mileage Statistics." While there are some women in these clusters whose status is ambiguous, they are outnumbered by the large pool of women in the machine subgroup.

In male-dominated offices, a different pattern emerges. One sees several clusters of male workers, each with one or two women attached to them. The job description for each cluster is complex and technical. Most involve several different duties. The job titles involve knowledge of railway administrative procedure and are often incomprehensible to outsiders. This suggests jobs requiring firm-specific training. Because of the small number of women in each cluster, and the fact that the clusters did substantively different kinds of work, the women in these groups would have been somewhat less replaceable. This makes sex composition a rough indicator of secretarial status.

Table 7.5 shows the difference in strike rates for each sex in the two kinds of offices. Due to the low variance in sex composition of offices in the town station and mills, the analysis is confined to the main building. The table shows that 41.1 percent of the women in secretarial offices struck. This contrasts with 28.8 percent in those offices where

Table 7.5
Strike Rates in the Main Building of the Chief Mechanical Engineer's Office by Sex and Sex Composition of Office, 1926

	Office sex composition	
Sex of worker	Less than one-third female (%)	One-third or more female (%)
Female	41.1	28.8
	(73)	(101)
Male	44.4	48.3
	(234)	(144)

Note: Offices with no women are excluded.
Source: General Strike (1926); Staff Charts (1926).

women were single-task operatives. This is a 12.3 percent difference. Note that this difference does not apply to the men. The strike rate for men in the two types of offices are practically identical. This suggests that the explanation of the strike difference among women is not to be found in some sex-neutral aspect of the offices involved. These offices had some factor that affected only the women. Variations in female market power is consistent with these differentials.

Secretarial status also enhanced the ability of women to resist opposition from male co-workers. Table 7.6 shows the female strike rates for secretarial and operative workers in offices with and without substantial male support for the strike. An office was coded as having low male strike participation if less than 45.5 percent of the men went out, 45.5 percent being the mean male participation rate in the main building. There are two major findings in the table. The first is that male support dramatically increased female strike participation rates. In secretarial offices, male support raised the female strike rate 14.4 percent. In the operative offices, male support produced a very substantial 31.3 percent difference. These findings have two conceivable interpretations. It could be that some exogenous factor such as organization jointly increased male and female rates in these offices. Or it could be that women used men as role models and imitated their strike behavior. Probably both factors were at work.

The second finding is that secretarial status increased women's ability to strike in the face of indifferent male support. Where male support was high, secretaries were more likely to strike than operatives, but the differences were very minor. Less than 5 percentage points separates the two groups. However, there was a 21.3 percent difference in striking when male support was absent. Over one-third of the unsupported secretaries struck, while fewer than one-sixth of the unsupported operatives did so. It would thus seem that male peer support and female market power were functional equivalents in producing female militancy.

What these findings suggest is that women's occupational characteristics to some extent determine their propensity to strike. Weak market power correlates with conservatism and passivity. We also know from the data on non-entry-level positions that women were disproportionately confined to low-status jobs. Thus, occupational differences in bargaining strength would have explained some of the differences between the sexes in strike rates. A direct test of the effect of status on the militancy of both sexes would be desirable. It is impossible with the data currently available. However, the figures presented here suggest a sensitivity to measures of bargaining strength that were only tangentially tapped by the previous control variables. Thus, the already small 7.4 percent strike difference between the sexes would have to be further reduced should occupational status be taken into account. None of the control variables explicitly measured or implied in the discussion of bargaining power are in any way direct or indirect effects of gender. Thus, the GWR data suggest negligible direct and indirect effects of gender on strike militancy.

The Telegraphists' Strike of 1871

The telegraphists' strike of 1871 also shows negligible direct gender effects. What is especially remarkable about this case is that this is one in which enormous obstacles were placed in the way of female participation. The strike was over issues relevant only to the men. Most of the women had been brought in explicitly as strike breakers. Furthermore, the women were isolated from most of the physical locations where organization occurred. Under such conditions, female inactivity would have been wholly understandable. Instead, the women struck at almost the same rate as men. The women did not stay out as long as the men; however, those that returned systematically frustrated management's attempts to replace striking workers. Thus, the women served both as strikers and as strikers' auxiliaries.

Table 7.6
*Female Strike Rates in the Main Building of the
Chief Mechanical Engineer's Office
by Sex Composition and Male Strike Rate of Office, 1926*

	Office sex composition	
Male strike rate	Less than one-third female (%)	One-third female or more (%)
Less than 45.5%	35.6 (45)	14.3 (42)
45.5% or more	50.0 (28)	45.6 (57)

Note: Offices with no women are excluded.
Source: General Strike (1926); Staff Charts (1926).

In the 1860's the Post Office nationalized the previously private telegraph companies. With nationalization came a long and controversial reorganization of personnel policies (Cohen 1941). In the private era, telegraphists had been paid modest salaries. These, however, had been substantially increased by bonuses and the right to collect fees for certain services. The Post Office, following civil service precedent, sought to incorporate these into a basic salary. The private companies had paid on a variety of different wage scales. The Post Office sought to standardize these. However, the most immediate grievance involved promotions. The private companies had provided regular annual promotions and increases in pay. However, between the announcement of nationalization and the actual transfer of managerial responsibility, a period of two years, the companies had frozen wages. The Post Office thus inherited a labor force that perceived itself as being owed two years' worth of back pay raises.

Postal policy immediately inflamed the situation. Since all payment was to come in salary form, the Post Office canceled all fees and premiums. They did not, however, replace these with a comparable salary. The telegraph service argued that fixing salaries would be a complex affair due to the problems of merging the different salary scales and calculating future staffing requirements. Part of the fees were remanded in the form of salary. However, the missing salary increases and the rest of the fees were to be given only after exhaustive consideration of the matter. Until a policy could be set, all salaries were refrozen.

The Post Office then took no action for two years. During this time, two more raises that the workers would have otherwise received were lost. During this period of both absolute and relative pay loss, the Post Office divulged nothing about what future salary levels would be like and made no guarantees that back pay would be given. Not even regional postmasters were given any information that could be used to comfort the men. Worker morale dropped to very low levels. Union agitation, which had existed to a small scale in the private companies, began to increase in scope and intensity.

The government was fully aware of these developments. The telegraphists communicated with each other over night telegraph lines. After hours, supervision was intense, and telegraphists could carry on private communications over the less heavily used wires. Management had become aware of this and had instituted wiretaps on lines connecting union centers. The authorities thus had perfect knowledge about the union's leaders, centers of militancy, and future plans. Anticipating a strike of national proportion, the government began to prepare large bodies of substitute labor (Telegraph Strike 1872).

The eastern district of the telegraph service was transferred to the Royal Engineers. This was the branch of the army in charge of military signalling. The working of this section by the army was supposed to provide a training for wartime signalling operations. However, the creation of skilled telegraphists under military discipline had obvious civilian functions as well (Telegraph Strike 1872).

The Post Office also began aggressively to recruit female telegraphists. The private companies had made very sparing use of women in a small number of urban offices. The Post Office began to train women on an enormous scale. Large all-female classes were taught in a specially constructed telegraph school. A new central station was constructed in London to coordinate the facilities once handled by separate lines. The new station was staffed with a majority of women. The authorities had great hopes of female docility. When Francis Scudamore, the director of the telegraph service, was justifying this feminization to a parliamentary committee, he explicitly cited low female labor militancy (Scudamore 1871). When the Edinburgh postmaster feared an imminent strike among his men, he wrote to London requesting the implementation of an all-female instrument room (Telegraph Strike 1872).

When the strike came, it was decisively defeated. Management precipitated it by dismissing six of the union leaders. Only a few cities went out in support. Management threatened the strikers with dismissal. Five days afterwards, the workers returned with no concessions in hand. Over two hundred workers were transferred, suspended, or dismissed. However, sex played little role in the defeat. This can be seen in Table 7.7, which shows the strike rates of both male and female offices in major telegraph centers. The unit of analysis is the staff of workers in a particular office. When offices employed both sexes, the male and female staffs are considered as separate units. Thus, the Manchester men, the Dundalk women, the London men, and the London women are considered as four equal and separate cases. To keep small units from swamping the analysis, staffs are only considered if they include at least fifteen workers of a particular sex.

Male staffs and female staffs were equally likely to strike: 23.5 percent of the male offices and 20 percent of the female offices left work at some point during the action. These percentages are virtually identical. The differences in Table 7.7 are not at all statistically significant. To be sure, most women did not support the strike. Four out of five offices continued work as usual. However, this same low level of commitment was also shown by their male counterparts. The loyalty of the women was simply the loyalty typical of the telegraph staff.

One problem in the analysis is the small number of female cases. Only one female office went out: Dublin. Since the analysis rests on the behavior of these Dublin women, some closer inspection is clearly warranted. Dublin was one of the first cities to join the strike. More men went out in Dublin than in any other city in the United Kingdom. When the signal for the strike arrived, both men and women left their posts. In the course of the first day, the postmaster negotiated separately with the men and the women. By mid-day, he was able to convince most of the women to return to their stations. It thus temporarily appeared that strategy of division by sex was likely to succeed.

This proved false when the postmaster brought in Royal Engineers to replace the rest of the striking men. On the arrival of the military, the women summarily ceased work, declaring that it was unbecoming for refined ladies to work side by side with common soldiers. The postmaster was told he could use the women or he could use the

Table 7.7

Strike Support by the Staff of Each Sex within Urban Telegraph Offices during the Postal Telegraph Strike, 1871

Strike activity	Male staffs (%)	Female staffs (%)	Total (%)
Struck	23.5	20.0	23.1
	(8)	(1)	(9)
Did not strike	76.5	80.0	76.9
	(26)	(4)	(30)
Total	100.0	100.0	100.0
	(34)	(5)	(39)

Note: Unlike Tables 7.1–7.6, the unit of analysis is collective staffs rather than individual strikers. The Edinburgh men only joined the strike on the last day before collapse. They are treated here as full strike participants, overstating male activity.

Source: The sex composition of offices is from Telegraph Estimates (1872). Strike activity is based on materials drawn from Telegraph Estimates (1872) and Telegraph Strike (1872). In addition, the following newspapers were consulted for the month of December 1871: *Birmingham Daily Gazette; Bristol Times; Daily Bristol Times and Mirror; Glasgow Evening Citizen; Glasgow Star; Glasgow Weekly Citizen; Liverpool Daily Post; Newcastle Daily Chronicle; North British Daily Mail;* and *Whitby Times.*

Engineers, but he could not use both. An agreement was finally reached by which the military would only work at night, after the women had gone home, and the women returned to their work. The men stayed out for four days. The women had returned early. Nevertheless, it was clear from their early walkout where their sympathies lay. Furthermore, throughout the strike they continued by their non-cooperation to undercut managerial attempts to replace the union men.

There were also significant differences among the women themselves. The staff consisted of four experienced women from the private company era who were highly proficient signallers. The rest of the staff dated from the recent feminization. These girls were just a few months out of telegraph school and were essentially trainees. The trainees were the ones who went back early and created the incident with the soldiers. All four of the older women refused the postmaster's request to return and stayed out until the end with the men. Those women veterans, who had established network links to male co-workers and developed marketable skills, behaved exactly like their male compatriots. The sex differences in willingness to stay out were thus to some degree spurious effects of experience (Telegraph Strike 1872).

It is fairly remarkable that the Dublin trainees supported the strike at all; there were several considerations that should have ensured their apathy and inactivity. First, as recent entrants into the postal service, they had suffered none of the grievances germane to the strike. They had never lost any pay increases; they had never been deprived of fees or pay supplements. The concerns of the private company workers were for the women a mere matter of history. Second, the women had been hired explicitly as future strike breakers. They were visibly expected to remain aloof from combinations. Third, the women had had little time to establish social relationships with male workers. They were newcomers breaking into on-going male social networks. Fourth, the women were isolated from the physical locations where union activity occurred. The major organized activity occurred at night, when the wires permitted clandestine communication. The women were confined to day shifts, when the supervision was more intense. Finally, the women had less market strength than did the men. Labor throughout the system was generally scarce. However, female applicants were readily available while male applicants were harder to find. The expanding telegraph system gave women some job security, but they were less secure than their male counterparts.

Postal management generally viewed the feminization policy as a failure. This can be seen from subsequent gender policies in times of labor agitation. In 1880 and 1890, the Post Office faced parallel crises of strong, well-organized telegraphists pressing for improvements in their wages. Yet the late 1870's saw the introduction of a policy of de-feminization, which continued sporadically throughout the 1880's and 1890's. If management had perceived feminization as being a viable tactic of labor control, it is unlikely that they would have acquiesced to such a policy. Although women's natural docility was used by the controller of the telegraph service as part of his justification for the hiring of women, after the 1871 strike postal management dropped this line of argument from their internal discussions of female hiring.

Conclusion

The findings here support those of other investigations that have found low or insignificant gender effects. These small effects were found using a methodology that was biased towards finding large direct effects. The period chosen was one of popular acceptance of female sex-roles emphasizing docility and obedience. Furthermore, such spurious effects as differential access to promotion remained unmeasured, while occupational market power was measured only partially. Studying the modern data and using a fuller range of control variables would have made the direct effects of gender even smaller.

Two cautions should be put forward, however. One is methodological, the other substantive. The methodological warning is that the case base for this study is necessarily small. A great deal of weight has been put on the evidence from the Dublin post office and from a minority of women in unusual positions in the Great Western Railway. Further replications on other sets of early women strikers would be desirable to generate more confidence in these findings.

Second, it should be noted that the gross effects of gender were sometimes substantial. There was a 24 percent difference in male and female strike rates in the GWR. This was largely due to occupational distribution, but it still existed. The difference between gross effects and total effects has been discussed well by Paula Voos. Voos reviewed the contemporary quantitative literature on the effect of gender on union membership, dividing these studies into two types, those that studied individual predispositions to join unions and those that studied actual membership. In general, women were less likely to join unions than men. However, they were equally likely to approve of unions, to state that they would like to join a union, or to vote for unions in National Labor Relations Board certification drives. Voos suggests that these findings are inconsistent with the hypothesis that women have a low demand for unionism due to their short-term labor force participation and are more consistent with the claim that women are differentially sorted into jobs that inhibit participation in class conflict (Voos 1983). This chapter considered men and women with relatively similar although not identical occupational distributions. It is not surprising that the gross differences in union activity were small. If, however, the analysis consisted of a diverse group of workers where men were in core occupations with solid bargaining strength and women were in marginal occupations with little skill or power, then one would expect that, due to these compositional differences, the traditional gap between men's and women's union activities would reappear.

8

Alternative Sources of Secondary Labor

The analysis thus far has presupposed an extremely simple labor market. There are only two forms of labor: adult men, who are relatively expensive, and women, who are relatively cheap. If the labor force is to be bifurcated, or treated differentially, this split will occur along sex lines. Thus, in Chapter 2 it was assumed that, if an office could not afford male labor, it would turn by default to adult women, while in Chapters 3 and 4 it was assumed that, if there were disadvantageous positions within a firm, women would be recruited for such positions.

In reality, employers who are looking for cheap labor have a wide variety of options open to them. They may hire minority workers, illegal immigrants, juveniles, or members of the white male casual labor force, all of whom work for substandard wages. Each of these groups suffers from a limited demand for their labor, which intensifies the competition among group members for employment. The overcrowding hypothesis works for other forms of secondary labor besides women (Fawcett 1918; Edgeworth 1922). Adult white males can compete for any job in the national labor market; other workers can compete for only a select few. For these groups, the supply of labor is greater than the demand, and the market wage is lowered. Blacks, hispanics, and members of other disadvantaged ethnic groups suffer from overt racism and cultural discrimination. Illegal immigrants experience both these handicaps and the additional burden of not being protected by minimum wage legislation.

Juveniles represent another important source of secondary labor. Teenagers are hurt by their low human capital attainments. Not only do they lack formal training and job experience, but they often lack work discipline and show an extremely high natural propensity to turnover (Price 1977). The lack of these more social forms of human capital can be just as harmful as the lack of years of education.

An important and often neglected component of the secondary labor force is the population of marginal white men. Many majority members find their employment opportunities severely constrained by either low human capital stocks or by permanent blemishes in their career records. The white casual labor force consists of many individuals who are uneducated or unskilled or who are persistent nonperformers. This latter group includes both the incompetent and the criminally inclined. Besides these objectively poor workers, there are other individuals who despite reasonable levels of ethics and proficiency are barred from many jobs because of their past records. The employment difficulties faced by ex-convicts, ex-mental patients, or recovering alcoholics are well known. Since all of these groups face the prospect of low wages brought on by reduced labor demand, the fundamental question for the student of occupational sex-typing is to explain why any given low-status job goes to women rather than to one of these other types of workers.

This chapter cannot provide an exhaustive model of the allocation of jobs among alternative sources of secondary labor. However, some components of such a model are suggested here, and their utility is demonstrated by their relevance to the feminization of clerical work. Among the factors that help determine which groups are hired for low-status positions are the relative supply of different kinds of workers, the human capital required for adequate job performance, and the length of employee tenure that the employer prefers.

Mechanisms for Affecting Job Allocation

Relative Supply

Since employers have to choose their workers from the labor market in which they are located, they cannot always find workers of a given socio-demographic category. Regional labor markets have different ethnic mixes. These differences involve not only what kind of disadvantaged ethnic group is present but what percentage of the working population is made up of minorities of any kind. Some inner cities are primarily black, while others are divided evenly among blacks and hispanics. A suburban employer may have limited recourse to either of these groups and thus must work with a predominantly anglo labor force. The suburban employer, however, has access to a large supply of white teenagers and adult women who may not be available in certain urban neighborhoods. Some of the change in the hiring patterns of women and minorities may have come from the transformation of urban neighborhoods from white middle class to non-white lower class, with an attendant change in the population of workers available to local firms. There are non-geographical determinants of supply as well. Certain workers may be legally barred from certain jobs. Mandatory schooling has severely constrained the supply of child labor. College students become more available in the summer; there is a comparable seasonality to the industrial availability of those laborers who also work in agriculture. All of these factors will reduce the choices open to an employer seeking cheap labor.

Human Capital

Despite the fact that many secondary occupations are relatively menial, some jobs have legitimate requirements that new entrants possess particular capacities or skills. Positions that require educational skills such as spelling or arithmetic, or social skills such as work discipline, are unlikely to be open to the white male casual labor force. Jobs that require fluency in the English language will not be appropriate for many illegal immigrants. Labor-intensive jobs with extremely high human capital requirements may be filled with specially trained women or college students. On the other hand, there are jobs that are sufficiently undemanding that even the white male marginal labor force can fill them adequately.

Ideal Tenure Length

Occupations differ in which length of employee career produces the greatest economies in staffing. Some jobs are fundamentally seasonal in nature. In these cases, virtually anybody can be hired. However, it may be convenient to use employees whose voluntary job tenures will be short. The amount of on-the-job training can also affect the desirability of long tenures, as was discussed in Chapter 4. The different secondary labor forces are each associated with distinctive turnover patterns. A college student taking a summer job is likely to work for only two months and quit. High school students are likely to last only one or two years. High school or college graduation is likely to produce some job change; furthermore, many adolescents vacillate between one interest and another, producing relatively intense but short-term commitments. Marginal males might have even shorter job tenures, while women and minority heads of families might be expected to stay somewhat longer. Career lengths cannot be predicted perfectly, since turnover depends somewhat on labor market conditions (Price 1977). Nevertheless, turnover rates are sufficiently predictable for them to have an impact in hiring decisions.

Alternative Sources of Secondary Labor in the Office

Clerical work provides an excellent example of how feminization can occur as a dynamic of the changing preferences of employers for different secondary labor forces. Clerical work feminized because of the increasing difficulties associated with the use of teenaged boys in office positions. In Chapter 3, we saw that clerical work did not significantly de-skill from 1870 to 1940. There were a substantial number of marginal office jobs throughout the entire period. Women came to occupy those positions that had previously been held by workers called "office men," "office boys," "copyists," and "messengers." As other groups became increasingly impractical for use as low-level office workers, women became by default the employees of preference in labor-intense, high-turnover positions.

Casual males, disadvantaged ethnic minority members, and juveniles had all been used for secondary office labor. Casual males served as male copyists and office men. The Great Western Railway gave such individuals the job title "wage clerks," although in the depots they could also be known as "checkers" or "callers-off." Wage clerks differed from salaried clerks in that all the terms of their employment were substantially inferior. Their pay rates were lower; their hours were worse; they lacked any guarantee of job security. Because of these relatively unattractive terms of employment, the better candidates applied for the salaried positions, leaving the wage positions to be filled with more marginal candidates.

Clerical work is not well performed by individuals with low levels of education or intelligence. A letter that is misspelled cannot be sent out. Arithmetic errors can add hours to the work involved in balancing accounts; if these errors are undiscovered, they can be very expensive. The savings that can be obtained by hiring casual men can be obliterated by the expenses of ruined work. In the Victorian era, when clerical labor costs were not a large component of total costs, such inefficiencies could be tolerated by the patriarchical employer with a preference for men. However, with the increasing administrative intensity of business, clerical labor intensity increased, and the resulting efficiency movement helped doom the male wage clerk.

The Taylorites on the Great Western Railway were dedicated opponents of temporary male clerks. In the early 1920's the Clerical Work Committee, a collection of in-house scientific office managers, systematically reviewed the staffing of many of the offices of the GWR. In general, they found most staffing levels satisfactory and thus made relatively few systematic recommendations. However, there was one policy change they strongly advocated: the substitution of women for male wage clerks. In most of the offices they examined, they found that temporary males lacked the qualifications for efficient clerical performance and that the work they did was of very low quality. This was of especial concern because the duties that were being mishandled were not especially demanding in the first place. In each office where they studied the performance of male wage clerks, the most common recommendation was that a woman be employed (Goods Stations 1922).

At the time these studies were done, the Great Western Railway was using very few wage clerks. Although the Taylorite studies did not cover every office in the GWR, wage clerks comprised less than 5 percent of the staffs of those offices the Clerical Work Committee examined. This suggests that the Taylorite recommendations actually reflected current management practice. By 1933, the use of unskilled male office help had become negligible. Wage clerks comprised less than 2 percent of the clerical force of those departments that had no factories. Wage clerks made up a third of the clerical force of the factory departments, but even here their use was strictly confined to the shop floor, having disappeared from the main offices (Staff Charts 1914–37; GWR Staff Census 1933).[1]

Ethnic minorities seem to have played a minor role in nineteenth-century Victorian staffing. B. G. Orchard's 1870 monograph on the

---

1. The General Post Office also used temporary male wage clerks; their job title was "male writer." They were largely eliminated by the 1890's, which could have been due to the inefficiencies of using casual men. However, official civil service policy was to give all employees permanent tenure and avoid the use of temporary personnel. Thus, the elimination of the wage clerks may have been caused by the special circumstances involved with public employment, rather than by any deficiency of the writers themselves.

clerks of Liverpool features a discussion of English clerks' being undercut by cheap German immigrants, suggesting that the use of immigrants was not wholly unknown. Little is known about the role of ethnicity in either the United States or Britain. However, there are few other mentions of such phenomena either in the historical literature or in the internal documents of the GWR or the GPO. The best guess would seem to be that the impact of ethnicity was fairly small and that minority members tended to become full-fledged clerks rather than constituting an office underclass per se.

In England, one of the most important sources of secondary clerical labor was teenaged boys. In the late Victorian era, boys made up between 20 and 40 percent of the clerical staff of most offices, and in particular cases the share could be much higher. The most accurate global estimates of the use of juvenile clerks come from the British census. In 1871, in England and Wales, approximately 30 percent of the clerks were under twenty years of age. Being under twenty does not necessarily imply juvenile status. Many offices paid their clerks an adult wage at the age of eighteen or nineteen. Thus, in the fifteen-to-nineteen age group, some clerks would have been receiving full wages while others would have been paid at the junior rate, making the percentage of juveniles in the labor force somewhat less than 30 percent. However, 1870 data from Liverpool suggest that the 30 percent estimate may not be far off the mark for the late nineteenth century.

In 1870, Orchard collected data on the office personnel of over three thousand firms in Liverpool. He divided the staffs of his offices into three categories: adults, lads, and apprentices. The exact definition of these terms is not easy to discern. Obviously adults are full adults, and lads are juvenile boys; however, the composition of the apprentice category is ambiguous. In some cases in the text, Orchard describes the apprentices as youths. However, some industries show an enormously high percentage of apprentices. If all of these were youths, some industries would have been over 85 percent juvenile. Probably the apprentice ranks included some younger adults as well as juveniles and thus had the same ambiguous interpretation as clerks aged fifteen to nineteen.[2]

2. It is likely that different respondents probably defined the term "apprentices" in different ways. The Great Western Railway had a Liverpool sales office that would have

In Liverpool in 1870, between 18.4 and 44.0 percent of the clerical force was juvenile, depending on how one interprets the age of the apprentices (see Table 8.1). With the exception of banks, loan offices,

Table 8.1
Age Composition of Clerks in Liverpool by Industry, 1870

Industry*	Appren-tices (no.)	Lads (no.)	Adult clerks (no.)	Total clerks (no.)	Appren-tice and lad (%)	Lad only (%)
Accountants	60	50	220	330	33.3	15.1
Banks	30	0	200	230	13.0	0.0
Brewers-distillers	60	60	160	280	42.9	21.4
Coal	100	160	700	960	27.1	16.7
Corn	90	100	300	490	38.8	20.4
Cotton	950	200	420	1,570	73.2	12.7
Forwarding agents	90	70	260	420	38.1	16.7
General brokers	1,000	800	300	2,100	85.7	38.1
Grocers (wholesale)	212	150	700	1,062	34.1	14.1
Insurance	50	32	475	557	14.7	5.7
Lawyers	54	1,000	484	1,538	68.5	65.0
Merchants-shops	350	150	1,050	1,550	32.6	9.7
Money dealers-loans	0	10	110	120	8.3	8.3
Newspapers-printers	0	30	135	165	18.2	18.2
Railways-carriers	50	200	527	777	32.2	25.7
Shipbuilder-foundry	35	120	300	455	34.1	26.4
Shipping	401	159	1,029	1,589	35.2	10.0
Ship's stores	20	60	120	200	40.0	30.0
Stockbrokers	15	70	135	220	38.6	31.8
Timber	180	75	230	485	52.5	15.4
Wine-spirit merchant	70	150	480	700	31.4	21.4
Total	3,817	2,737	8,355	14,909	44.0	18.4

*Closely related industrial categories in the original have been merged for simplicity of presentation.
Source: Adapted from Orchard (1870).

been in Orchard's sample. The GWR had no employees called apprentice per se. They had lad clerks, who were apprentices in every reasonable sense of the term, and they had starting-level senior clerks. How the manager of the Liverpool sales office would have divided his staff between lads and apprentices on his form is a matter of guesswork.

and insurance companies, the office staff of every industry was at least 10 percent juvenile. Some industries were especially heavy users of boys. Without even considering the apprentices, the offices of ships' stores suppliers, stockbrokers, general brokers, and lawyers used boys for at least 30 percent of their clerical staff. In law offices, boys made up nearly two-thirds of the clerical force. Other industries seem to have been heavy users of apprentices. Even if these individuals were entirely young adults, a claim that is probably incorrect, they were still an age-based secondary labor force. Over 25 percent of the staff of corn concerns, cotton concerns, forwarding agencies, general broker-ages, shipping companies, and timber concerns were made up of apprentices alone.[3]

These data are consistent with the claim that roughly 30 percent of the clerical labor force was juvenile. The use of juvenile clerks was not universal, and industries differed dramatically in their dependence on such labor. Furthermore, it is not implausible that more boys may have been used in Liverpool than in other clerical labor markets. Neverthe-less, regardless of the precise percentages involved, boy labor seems to have been an important component of the clerical secondary force and a large component of the office population overall.

The Demise of Boy Labor in the Great Western Railway and the General Post Office

Both the Great Western Railway and the General Post Office made extensive use of juveniles. Boys had been introduced in 1862 as part of the creation of the GWR's internal labor market. Use of the boys had been sparing at first; they made up less than 5 percent of the clerical force after the first year of the program. However, once the savings of not paying adult salaries became apparent, the traffic department

---

3. The conclusions that are drawn from these materials must be tempered to some extent by a consideration of the quality of the data. The statistics that Orchard generated are somewhat suspect; there is a high percentage of crudely rounded numbers, and the data show a number of arithmetic inconsistencies. Although these materials are prob-ably not accurate enough for elaborate statistical analysis, however, they are probably acceptable as rough estimates of the labor force composition. The errors that were the product of rounding, arithmetic error, and informal estimation are likely to have been random.

began to hire over one hundred boys a year, quickly raising the percentage of juveniles to a third of the clerical staff. According to the 1870 GWR staff census of the traffic department, 35.2 percent of the clerical force was made up of boy clerks. Boys constituted nearly 25 percent of the ticket collectors and were extensively used as van boys, stable lads, machine watchers, depot attendants, and messengers. Nearly 97 percent of all positions that had been created by organizational growth were filled with boy clerks. The Great Western management calculated that the use of juveniles saved the company over £2,300 a year (GWR Staff Census 1870).

The Post Office was a very uneven employer of boys. Some offices used large numbers of boy writers, sorters, and clerks. Others maintained a virtually all-adult labor force. In 1871, 22 percent of the Savings Bank clerks were lads. Thirty-seven percent of all central London sorters were boys, as well as 50 percent of all District sorters.[4] In contrast, the Secretary's Office, the Money Order Department, and RAGO used relatively few boys; those that were hired were used as messengers.

In 1881, a substantial number of juveniles were added to the postal force. The secretary's office obtained a budget line for copyists that included boys. A new intelligence division was created to facilitate news delivery whose clerical force was over 80 percent juvenile. The money order department hired forty-eight boys, who comprised over 25 percent of the total office staff. The percentage of boy sorters in central London declined to 27 percent; however, in the districts, the percentage rose to a striking 66 percent. The new telegraph service used very few boys for either signalling or office work, although they did hire over two hundred for telegraph delivery. RAGO continued to rely exclusively on adults, while the percentage of juveniles in the Savings Bank actually declined. As in the Liverpool case, the use of boys was not universal; however, a very large subset of offices made intensive use of juveniles, making boys a major component of overall postal staffing.

---

4. Central London here refers to the London EC district, which is the main sorting office for the country; it also processes deliveries for the City of London. The districts include most of the central areas that are not in the City of London, such as Piccadilly Circus, Whitehall, or Knightsbridge, as well as more distant areas such as Clapham and Hammersmith.

By the 1930's these boy clerks had virtually disappeared. On the Great Western Railway in 1933, only 0.8 percent of the clerical force were junior clerks. This low figure was virtually the same for males and females, suggesting that the GWR had become an all-adult labor force.[5] In the Post Office, the same thing occurred. In 1931, only 2.9 percent of the Savings Bank was juvenile, with the figures for RAGO and the Money Order office being 1.9 percent and 0.7 percent respectively. Significantly, boys were no longer employed in any of these positions. The only juvenile job title left in these offices was "girl probationer." In the sorting offices, boys had been eliminated entirely. All of the work of sorting was now done by adult males. Juvenile clerks having disappeared, the only remaining concentration of juvenile labor was in telegram delivery. With the general decline in demand for telegraph service, however, even these workers were being eliminated.

One possible explanation for the declining use of boy labor is that an increased supply of women eliminated the need to use boys. If women were in all cases more economical than boys, then an exogenous increase in the availability of women would have led to automatic substitution by employers of women for boys. The elimination of the youngest males from employment would produce an aging of the male clerical force, as this population became composed exclusively of adult workers. It is unlikely, however that the decreased use of boys was caused by an exogenous process of feminization. For one thing, boys' salaries were traditionally lower than women's. An employer seeking to use the cheapest workers available would have chosen an all-boy labor force. Furthermore, such an explanation would be inconsistent with the empirical patterns of change in the use of juveniles. Both the Great Western Railway and the postal sorting offices dramatically curtailed their use of boy labor, but neither of these work settings underwent significant feminization.[6] If juvenile labor declined, it was because of some factor endogenous to the mechanics of hiring youth, rather than because of the availability of substitutes.

5. The figures for the GWR as a whole are identical to those of the traffic department considered separately, making these statistics comparable to those calculated for 1870.

6. In the traffic department in 1870, 32.5 percent of all clerks were boys, while in 1933, 0.7 percent of all clerks were boys. Since 9.6 percent of the clerks were female, this suggests that the remaining 22.2 percent of the clerical positions, which in 1871 had been filled with boys, were in 1931 being filled by adult men.

There were two problems associated with boy labor that led to its ultimate disuse. The first was that the supply of skilled boys began to decrease significantly, forcing employers to turn to alternative sources of labor. The second problem was that boys began to create serious problems of absorption as they matured into adult males. Both of these situations were created by the high human capital stocks employers required for their secondary clerks. As was argued in the case of casual adult males, clerical workers needed to be both good spellers and arithmetically competent, a requirement that limited potential recruits to those workers who were both well educated and naturally intelligent. Children of the middle class were particularly sought after because of their superior educational attainments.

One indicator of the value office employers put on educational attainments is that both the GWR and the GPO had an elaborate formal testing program with which they evaluated all potential clerical recruits. Candidates for entry-level jobs were tested in spelling, arithmetic, and the taking of dictation, with occasional extra sections in geography, foreign language, typing, and shorthand, depending on the job (GWR Women 1906; Hobhouse 1906; GPO Women 1908; Salaried Recruitment 1912). These exams were more than mere formalities. Between 1868 and 1870, over 60 percent of the candidates who sat for the GWR junior clerk exam failed (Staff Statistics 1870). The *Railway News* reported that in 1910, 40 percent of all job candidates for railway clerkships were disqualified from taking the exam. Subsequently, 60 percent of those who were left did not pass (Railway News, Oct. 8, 1910). In 1895, between 89 and 97 percent of all applicants to the Post Office failed the telegraphists' and sorters' exams (Telegraph Chronicle, Sept. 27, 1895). The outcome of the clerical exams is not known, but they were designed to be much harder. The fact that the failure rates were high does not establish that these firms had high human capital requirements. Any candidate selection process with a large number of applicants and a small number of openings will have a relatively high failure rate. What is significant, however, is that these exams were the main criteria by which job candidates were evaluated. This supports the claim that these organizations valued language and mathematical skills.

They also valued middle-class origin. Observers of the Great Western Railway in 1914 noted that recruitment for clerical positions seemed to have been limited entirely to the middle class (Salaried Recruitment 1912). Dorothy Evans noted that postal clerical positions were reserved for children of the middle class, although sorter and telegraph positions were open to more lower-class entrants (Evans 1934). To some extent, this may have been due to elitist prejudice; however, middle-class candidates may also have been the only reasonable source of those educational skills clerical employers valued. Telegraph authorities in 1873 noted that there were difficulties in finding qualified candidates in Hull, Lancaster, Leicester, Sheffield, Nottingham, Birmingham, and Manchester. They explained this in the following way: "It is hard to find learners where the severer forms of labour predominate. Towns in which a large proportion of the population belongs to the lower section of the middle class will always provide us with a plentiful supply of learners" (Telegraph Report 1873). It is unlikely that this scarcity was caused by working-class people being uninterested in the high pay and permanent job security the telegraph service offered. The shortage of candidates probably reflected the Post Office's own selectivity.

An important consequence of this preference for high-quality recruits was that a potential clerk would have had a wide variety of alternative career possibilities. The parents of the prospective boy clerk would have been assessing all the possible forms of activity that could reasonably lead to a remunerative occupation for their son. Thus, the parents would have been choosing among clerical employment in different industries, employment in careers that did not require holding a clerkship as a first post, such as the military, and delaying entering the labor force to invest in formal education. For the better candidates, taking a boy clerkship would only have been a reasonable option if it could be expected to lead to some form of lucrative lifetime employment. The very best candidates would expect some promise of managerial employment; the next best would expect a promise of a permanent adult clerkship; only the most marginal would accept a purely temporary position.

This meant office managers had to have a coherent plan concerning the long-term prospects of their boy clerks. A teenaged boy could only be expected to receive a juvenile salary for a limited number of years. At the age of eighteen, he would qualify for an adult salary and no longer be inexpensive. One option would have been to fire all boy clerks at the age of eighteen and replace them with a set of younger recruits. This approach would have saved money, but would have discouraged the better candidates from applying for those positions. If the employer wanted a high-quality labor force, he had to guarantee permanent employment after age eighteen at an adult rate. This meant the employer had to be able to absorb an adult male with a prime salary. Over time, if an employer hired the same number of boys every year and then kept them for the full duration of their worklives, his adult male labor force would swell with each class of graduating boys. Thus, over time, there would be a gradual increase in total expenditure that would come both from the increase in the total size of the organization and from the fact that secondary labor would be making up an even smaller proportion of the total staff. The juveniles would become outnumbered by the adults.

The absorption problem is not by itself prohibitive. There are a number of conditions under which increasing the number of full adult clerks will not be a significant concern to management. If the firm is not clerical-labor-intensive, or if it is somehow buffered from office personnel costs, the increase in salaries over time will be considered acceptable. Furthermore, there are some economic situations in which even cost-conscious employers can tolerate absorption. If the skill distribution of an office is being upgraded, there may be less need to depend on secondary labor. The increasing percentage of adults will parallel the growing need for skilled labor. Likewise, if the organization is growing, the absorption will be economical. An expansion in scale will create a new set of adult positions that the graduates can fill. If there is a need to maintain a constant ratio of youths to adults, the size of the boy cohort can be increased at the same rate that the organization as a whole is growing. When organizational growth stops, the firm will have a serious absorption problem with the final cohort of boys, but such a regime could work under conditions of long-term growth. Finally, if turnover is high among adult males, the loss of highly paid employees will both stem the size of the labor force and reduce the ratio of adults to juveniles, compensating for the problem of graduating junior clerks. However, a cost-conscious employer with stagnant or declining skill demands, low organizational growth, and low turnover will find the absorption of his boy clerks prohibitively expensive. He will either have to stop promising permanent employment to his youths or seek an alternative source of secondary labor.

It can be seen that the conditions under which an apprentice system of boy labor can exist are fragile. The Great Western Railway and the General Post Office generally failed to meet these conditions, particularly in the twentieth century. As Chapter 3 showed, it is extremely unlikely that there was any kind of dramatic upgrading of skill levels in these firms. Neither stable nor declining skill levels could provide a solution to the problem of absorption. Adult male exits were unlikely to create a supply of senior vacancies. As the actuarial records demonstrated, male turnover was extremely low. Exit rates were close to zero for most age categories.

The only source of openings that was realistically available to both firms was organizational growth. Both firms grew dramatically from 1870 to 1930. In the nineteenth century, this growth would have been sufficient to support a modest percentage of boy clerks. Growth rates reached their natural limit by the end of the century, however, after which it became impossible for either firm to support a large apprenticeship system.

Tables 8.2 and 8.3 show the rates of growth for total employment in the Great Western Railway and the General Post Office. Since clerk/staff ratios are roughly constant in both firms, these figures provide a good index to the overall size of the clerical force.[7] The Great Western Railway more than quadrupled between 1860 and 1884, nearly doubled again between 1884 and 1911, and then grew by less than a half between 1911 and 1931. The growth in this last period is overstated, since much of the new staff that was added during this period came from the national amalgamation of the GWR with other regional carriers. This growth thus represented absorption of existing personnel rather than the creation of new vacancies. This pattern of rapid growth slowing first to intermediate growth and then to relative stagnation is also noticeable in the Post Office, where a growth rate of

Table 8.2
Total Employment on the Great Western Railway, 1860–1931

Date	Total employment (no.)	Exponential annual growth rate (%)
1860	9,013	—
1884	39,547	5.8
1911	70,014	3.4
1931	96,436	1.6

Source: Railway Return (1860, 1884, 1911); GWR Staff Census (1933).

7. Reliable estimates of the size of the Great Western Railway clerical force are not available for all dates.

Table 8.3
Total Employment in the General Post Office, 1871–1931

Date	Total employment (no.)	Exponential annual growth rate (%)
1871	28,078	—
1891	113,550	7.0
1911	212,814	3.1
1931	196,762	−0.4

Source: Postmaster General (1871, 1891, 1911); Civil Service Return (1931).

7 percent in the 1880's declined to 3 percent at the turn of the century and to negative growth in the post-war years.[8]

Table 8.4 shows the rates of organizational growth that would be necessary to absorb the supply of graduating boys while maintaining the ratio of boys to total staff at any given level. The details of its construction can be found in Appendix F. The table is based on the turnover behavior of the GWR and GPO males and makes a number of simplifying assumptions. It thus only applies to the junior clerk programs of these two firms, and even with this limitation its estimates should be treated as approximate.

Small percentages of boys were easy to maintain, even with zero

Table 8.4
*Rates of Annual Growth Required to Sustain Given Percentages
of Boy Labor with the Terms of Employment and Turnover Rates
of the Great Western Railway and the General Post Office*

In order to sustain this percentage of boy labor:	The organization must grow annually at this percentage rate:
5	0.0
10	3.7
20	7.8
30	10.5

Source: See text and Appendix F.

8. The exponential growth rate is the rate of increase that if applied continuously would provide the change in absolute employment observed in the data. It is in many ways analagous to a compound interest rate (Shyrock and Seigel 1975).

growth. However, any significant increase in the ratio of boys to staff could only be maintained by extraordinary increases in the levels of total staffing. The GWR and the GPO could have maintained a junior clerk program with 5 percent of their staff without requiring any growth to create vacancies. However, expanding the percentage of youths to 10 percent would have required an organizational growth rate of 3.7 percent. Having a labor force of only 10 percent boys would have meant that fully 90 percent of the workforce would have been full-priced males. However, an annual growth rate of 3.7 percent implies a doubling of the size of the organization every twenty years. Not every firm can rely on its staff's doubling in this period of time. To allow 20 percent of the staff to be juvenile, a 7.8 percent growth rate is required, and to allow 30 percent requires over a 10 percent growth rate. These imply a doubling of size in ten and seven years respectively. Such rates of growth can only be maintained for fairly short periods of time.

The only period in which the GWR and the GPO could have tolerated an apprenticeship program involving more than 15 percent of their staffs would have been in the 1870–90 period. A staff that was 10 percent juvenile could have been maintained over the turn of the century. In the post-war period, the percentage of juveniles could not have been much more than 5 percent. These firms thus experienced a clearly declining capacity to absorb the graduates from their junior clerk programs. Even in the heyday of these programs, there were limits on the ratios of juvenile clerks that could be tolerated. The 33 percent figure that characterized the GWR Traffic department in 1870 was clearly a short-term aberration. As organizational growth declined, these firms would have had to search elsewhere for their secondary labor. This meant either abandoning the job-guarantee programs and accepting a lower quality of boy, turning to casual adult males, or using women. Only educated women could have provided the numerical and linguistic skills that employers preferred in their clerical forces.

The problems of absorption, while serious, would not have been sufficient to eliminate boys from clerical positions completely. Some clerical positions, such as sorter, required less human capital than others. Presumably, poorly educated youths could have filled these less demanding positions; such youths would not have required a permanent guarantee of employment and thus would have not posed absorption problems. Furthermore, juvenile clerks came to represent less than 2 percent of the clerical employees of these firms, despite the fact that a force that was 5 percent juvenile could have been carried quite easily.

An equally fundamental problem was that boy clerks of any quality were becoming increasingly scarce. Levels of educational attainment were consistently rising during this period. While, on the one hand, this would have increased the number of boys who were capable of doing clerical work, it reduced the number who were willing to take such positions. This was not particularly due to mandatory school attendance laws. Between 1870 and World War II, the age of compulsory school attendance never rose higher than fifteen, a year younger than the customary recruitment age for junior clerks. The greater problem was that many of the more talented youths were voluntarily delaying their labor force entry in order to further their education. Increasingly, from the boys' point of view, the way to obtain a high-paying job was not to take a clerical apprenticeship but instead to graduate from college. With the loss of college-bound individuals from the clerical recruitment pools, private employers found the quality of their applicants steadily deteriorating.

For the Great Western Railway, this problem seems to have become particularly acute in the early years of the twentieth century. Discussions of recruitment during this period centered around the poor quality of the available junior clerks. On two different occasions, 1901 and 1912, the GWR management circulated memos among itself seeking solutions to the problem of under-qualified clerks. In 1901, they tightened the standards for moving from junior to senior clerk by providing a more difficult senior clerk exam; in 1912, they extended the period of probation to facilitate the expulsion of unsatisfactory recruits (Salaried Recruitment 1912; GWR Petitions 1914).[9] Such plans would have encouraged further study among those junior clerks who were already employed; however, it did little to improve the quality of the candidate pool. As one GWR manager put it, "The service has ceased to attract youths educated at higher class schools"

---

9. There were two efficiency checks for junior clerks. There was a probationary period of three to twelve months, during which time a youth could be dismissed summarily. Subsequently, at the end of two years, there was a senior clerk exam, which determined eligibility for promotion to an adult position. The overwhelming majority of junior clerks passed both requirements.

(GWR Petitions 1914). The response taken in 1912 was to raise the salaries for entry-level junior clerks. It was felt that by providing a better level of initial remuneration, the GWR would at least become financially competitive with other employers.

One alternative that was considered at the time was the recruitment of university graduates. If the best candidates were all attending college, it made sense to hire them when they finished their education. Despite the presence of strong advocates of hiring university men, the GWR never followed this course of action until after World War II. In part this was due to a somewhat exaggerated concern for preserving traditional chains of promotion. However, an important factor in this decision was that university men could hardly serve the function of providing secondary labor that motivated the original use of boys. To summarize the objections of two managers who considered the use of college graduates for the Audit department, the university men would be quite expensive, and since the work given to entry-level clerks involved "care and accuracy rather than great intellectual power," the use of university graduates could only be considered in those settings where trainees would be immediately involved in technical and substantive decision-making (Salaried Recruitment 1912). At one time, talented individuals had had to wait for responsible positions, and while they waited they could be put to work copying receipts and filling inkwells. Now, they had to be promoted directly, and someone else would have to be found for the preliminary duties.

It is significant that complaints about the quantity and quality of junior clerks became an issue only in the twentieth century. Complaints about a shortage of juvenile labor can be found in the 1930's as well as the 1900's and teens (Labour Report 1930). However, there is no mention of scarcity in any discussion of juvenile labor in the nineteenth century. The 1870 GWR Staff Statistics report an ample supply of qualified junior examination candidates. The 1912 Salaried Recruitment file contains documents from both the nineteenth and twentieth centuries. Although the nineteenth-century documents in this folder were explicitly selected by 1901 managers for their relevance to the current shortage of qualified juveniles, none of these records makes any mention of a tradition of supply problems. No mention of a shortage appears in any other personnel records either. The fact that scarcity problems only started to emerge when education was on the rise strongly supports the claim that competing opportunities were hampering the viability of boys as a secondary clerical force.[10]

The reduction in the supply of boy clerks played an important role in facilitating the feminization of office work. The elimination of boys did not automatically produce a female labor force. The Great Western Railway placed adult males in many of the former juvenile positions. The Post Office Engineers replaced boys with women only in certain circumstances. Typing positions continued to be predominantly male, particularly in the Engineer in Chief's office. Many boy clerks would have been trained on the typewriter during their apprenticeships; now the Engineers hired male graduates of the typing schools. However, some of the duties of the former boy clerks were transferred to clerical assistants, an entry-level position for adult women (Engineering Clerks 1919).

A significant blue-collar illustration of the effect of the supply of boy labor on women's opportunities can be found in the Post Office Savings Bank Printing Shop. The Savings Bank used an extremely large volume of passbooks, certificates, and pre-printed forms. To produce these materials as needed, the Post Office maintained a print shop that employed over fifty people. In the nineteenth century, the staff had consisted of a number of male adult printers and a large staff of boys. The boys did all of the unskilled work associated with form production, such as cutting and separating forms or removing finished work from the press. The Post Office did not run a printing apprenticeship program, its printers being hired fully trained from the outside world. Therefore, being a boy helper was a dead-end job without any prospects of internal promotion or absorption by other departments. Since the human capital requirements for being a helper were low, the Savings Bank staffed the print shop with temporaries. A boy would be hired with the understanding that he must resign at the age of eighteen.

10. The absence of a reference to scarcity could also be due to an idiosyncratic survival pattern among the GWR documents. While the presence of such a methodological artifact cannot be wholly discounted, it is nevertheless significant that an enormous body of personnel records and correspondence survive from this period. Since the GWR archives are far more reliable and complete than most corporate archives, it seems likely that any major staffing problem that merited systematic attention would show up somewhere in the documentation.

After 1910, it became official civil service policy not to hire any boys who could not be absorbed. This policy came from a national political concern with unemployment. Boys who took dead-end apprenticeships were often burdened with skills that had no future labor market value and were subsequently very difficult to re-employ. In attempting to reduce the national supply of such unhirables, the British government decided to act as a model employer and only hire those juveniles to whom a permanent job could be promised.

The foreman of the print shop was therefore informed that he no longer would be allowed to use boy labor. Since the budget for printing was extremely restricted, it would have been impossible to run the shop with a full complement of men. The foreman vehemently resisted the suggestion that he use female labor. Fully a year and a half was absorbed in a bureaucratic battle similar to that fought by the Savings Bank Controller in the 1870's. The foreman's main tactic was to seek out offices that used blue-collar men that would have been willing to commit themselves to creating job openings for print shop graduates. When this failed, the foreman accepted the inevitable and converted most of his staff to women. Thus the Savings Bank Print Shop became one of the few British printing establishments in 1914 that was nearly 60 percent female. The key was the artificial reduction of the supply of boys from which most private printers would have been exempt (Savings Bank Print Shop 1914).

The Decline of Boy Clerks in Britain as a Whole

Although the decline in the use of boy clerks in the GWR and the GPO was especially dramatic, a similar if more modest decline occurred in Great Britain as a whole. Table 8.5 shows the percentage of commercial clerks in England and Wales who were under the age of twenty from 1871 to 1931. During this period, the percentage of clerks under twenty declined only from 31.4 percent to 26.5 percent. These gross figures are somewhat misleading, however, since they conflate two phenomena: the decline in the use of juvenile male clerks and the increase in discrimination against older female clerks. The female clerical force became significantly younger between 1871 and 1931. This is quite likely to have been the result of an increase in the use of synthetic turnover. The selective recruitment of single teenagers, combined with the non-retention of married women, would have had the

Table 8.5
Commercial Clerks in England and Wales under Age Twenty by Year

Sex	1871 (%)	1881 (%)	1891 (%)	1901 (%)	1911 (%)	1921 (%)	1931 (%)
Males	31.5	29.5	29.9	28.1	26.2	20.0	20.3
Females	22.6	27.0	30.6	37.8	35.6	36.6	35.0
Total	31.4	29.4	30.0	29.6	27.2	27.2	26.5

% of Total Clerical Force Made Up of Male Clerks under Age 20:

	31.0	28.6	27.7	23.9	19.8	18.6	11.7

effect of driving older women from the labor force and lowering the average age of female clerks.

The data for male clerks, which is free from such influences, show a clear trend away from the hiring of juveniles. Of all male clerks, 31.5 percent were twenty or younger in 1871. This figure fell to 20.3 percent in 1931. Boy clerks had lost fully a third of their relative share of male employment. The most dramatic reduction occurred between 1911 and 1921, but most of the other periods saw some degree of relative decline. While a drop from 30 to 20 percent is noteworthy, it is not nearly as striking as the complete elimination of boy labor that occurred in the GWR and GPO.

These figures exaggerate the number of juveniles working in Britain. In 1931, only 8.2 percent of all male clerks were aged fourteen to seventeen. The overwhelming majority of clerks under twenty-one were aged eighteen to twenty and were, for employment purposes, adults. Data limitations prevent the calculation of comparably corrected figures for earlier periods. Given that the Orchard data suggest that a third of all male clerks in 1871 were juveniles, while in 1931 we know for certain that this figure was 8.2 percent, if anything the decline in boy clerkships was even more dramatic than is suggested by Table 8.5. This drop, however, would have been less than the decline that was experienced by the two main firms in the study. While the figures in Table 8.5 are misleading in an absolute sense, the bias they introduce is conservative. What remains to be explained is why these figures declined, and why this decline was less steep than that observed in the two-case analysis.

The more modest nature of the national changes can be attributed to two factors. First, non-railway commercial firms would have been able to absorb a higher percentage of their boy clerks than would have been possible for the GWR or the GPO. The Great Western Railway and the General Post Office had very low turnover rates. Employees were reluctant to leave voluntarily because both firms paid premium wages. Furthermore, the policy of lifetime employment that was practiced by both organizations virtually eliminated involuntary turnover among males. Because other private employers paid lower wages and were more willing to lay off employees, there would have been more circulation of staff in this sector, which would have created vacancies that could be filled by rising boy clerks.

Second, the GWR and the GPO had completed their growth by the end of the nineteenth century. They were thus incapable of absorbing boy clerks through expansion. Other industries would not have been subject to this kind of restraint. Both banking and insurance saw substantial growth in the twentieth century. The number of manufacturing clerkships would have increased both from economic expansion and from the increasing clerical labor intensity of the administration of production. It would have been much easier to maintain large apprenticeship programs in those industries undergoing steady long-term organizational growth.

The pressure to eliminate boy clerks would have come from the supply side. Qualified candidates for boy clerkships would have become increasingly scarce as the brighter youths turned instead to higher education. This would have been exacerbated by the bifurcation of internal labor markets within the office. As employers learned to differentiate between managerial and clerical career paths and started to recruit potential executives to the managerial track only, school-leavers would have become increasingly reluctant to accept clerical positions. Faced with a growing scarcity of educated boys willing to do menial work, employers would have had little choice but to abandon their apprenticeship programs and staff their low-level positions with someone else. Although boy clerk programs were not as severely threatened in Britain generally as they were in the GWR and the GPO, there was still enough of a supply crisis to make the widespread use of boy clerkships problematic. This is why the percentage of male clerks under twenty declined between 1871 and 1931.

Conclusion

We have seen the importance of other secondary labor forces in determining the opportunities that are open to women, with considerations of relative supply, human capital, and ideal tenure length influencing the relative attractiveness of competing sources of cheap labor. The most detailed discussion has been of the trade-off between women and boys, but the same logic could be applied to casual white males or to members of disadvantaged minority groups.

There is suggestive evidence that these factors apply to other occupations besides clerical work. Thomas Dublin has documented a trade-off between the employment of women and the employment of Irish in the Lynn textile mills of the nineteenth century. Originally Yankee farm girls were hired as cotton spinners. While natural training with textiles may have had something to do with this allocation, an equally important consideration was their relative cheapness. In the company houses near the factories, however, a tight occupational community formed that was capable of generating a strong sense of solidarity. This resulted in a dramatic strike by the women operatives against the Lynn mill owners. Subsequently, the owners began to phase out female employment. A new wave of Irish immigration provided an alternative supply of labor that promised docility as well as low wages (Dublin 1979). In this case, women were rejected for Irish, but there is no reason why this history could not have been reversed, with women undermining a group of militant Irish.

An important example from the quantitative literature comes from the work of David Snyder, Mark Hayward, and Paula Hudis. In an investigation of the relationship between sex-typing and location in core versus peripheral industries, Snyder et al. had a striking finding. Over time, the sex composition of the primary sector was generally stable; however, counterintuitively, the second sector was undergoing sex change in both directions. Some occupations were feminizing quickly, while others were de-feminizing. The robustness of these findings is slightly suspect, since the measurement of sectors was fairly crude; however, if these findings are right, they are suggestive. It is unlikely that, in the secondary sector, women were being replaced by white men. It is more probable that women were being replaced by teenagers or ethnic workers of either sex. Since change was occurring in both directions, Snyder et al. suggested that the secondary sector represents a continual flux of recirculating labor forces. It seems quite likely that some of these transformations can be explained by the changing preferences of employers, as they shuttle from one secondary labor force to another looking for marginal advantages (Snyder et al. 1978).

9

Conclusion

A question that emerges after completing any empirical analysis is the degree to which the immediate findings are representative of larger social regularities. Every dataset from the narrowest case study to the largest set of cross-national statistics is going to have some quirks and idiosyncrasies that will introduce a degree of bias. Therefore it is important for any sociologist to step back from her material at the end of her investigation and ask what can be inferred about her dependent variable in general. This particular analysis has been a case study that has attempted to draw some larger theoretical conclusions about the determinants of women's economic opportunities. Most of the material has come from two relatively unusual firms, the Great Western Railway and the British General Post Office, two Victorian British clerical employers who were extremely large, monopolistic, and unionized as well. Other material came from a larger consideration of the history of office work. These analyses are free from the biases associated with the GWR and GPO, but are still colored both by the limited time frame of the analysis, in this case the years 1870 to 1940, and by the peculiar problems of clerical work, which are different from those of other occupations. Studying a sample of occupations from 1970 to 1980 would hardly have eradicated these problems, since no sample of occupations can ever be complete, and the modern era with its legal changes and its tumultuous transformations in gender roles is certainly no less idiosyncratic than any other. Nevertheless, some explicit attempt should be made to place this study's findings in a larger context and to speculate on how they relate to an economic structure that is filled with work situations that are totally dissimilar from early twentieth-century offices.

218

In the present analysis, a fairly large number of arguments have been made on a variety of different topics. It is important to summarize these coherently and identify the major themes that bind together the argument before integrating them into a larger theory of occupational sex-typing. Then these principles will be applied to two larger questions: first, why did clerical work feminize? and, second, how does white-collar work differ from blue-collar work and why are women disproportionately concentrated in the former? The study of the GWR and the GPO suggests answers to both these questions and these hypotheses parallel each other to a significant degree. Third, the conclusion explicitly considers what kind of variables might be significant to a theory of sex-typing that might be obscured by a study of Victorian offices. In particular, the roles of law and of organizational vacancies are explored, although the analysis remains strictly at the level of speculation. Lastly, the question of women's concentration in low-status jobs is addressed. While this study provided some answers to this question, the theoretical structures that have been suggested cannot account for the universality of female subordination. An alternative hypothesis is put forward that is not immediately and obviously testable but is consistent with the domination of men over women in settings where the synthetic turnover hypothesis would not apply.

The Main Findings of the Analysis

Buffering from Labor Costs

In Chapter 2, it was shown that an important determinant of the percentage of women in a firm is the capacity of an employer to tolerate discrimination. This capacity to tolerate discrimination is affected by many different factors. Discrimination is less likely to occur in firms which are labor-intensive and, all other things being equal, is less likely to be tolerated among occupations that make up the bulk of a firm's labor force. Thus, firms and offices that are clerical-labor-intensive are more likely to use women clerks, while firms and offices that are non-clerical-labor-intensive are more likely to use male clerks. Organizations that are under pressure to maximize profits are less likely to tolerate discrimination than are organizations whose success is determined by other considerations. In the Post Office, offices whose political duties freed them from the necessity of cost-cutting were more likely to hire male clerks than were offices that were administered strictly by criteria of economic efficiency.

De-Skilling

Women were generally confined to low-status positions within each firm. Nevertheless, in these cases, the overall feminization of clerical work cannot be attributed to an increase in the percentage of low-status positions. Real clerical salaries did not decline in this period, either in Britain as a whole or in these particular firms. Furthermore, neither firm experienced a decrease in the ratio of promotions to entry-level jobs. Although there were dramatic changes in the technology of clerical work, individual innovations varied in their implications for the substantive complexity of office work. Thus, in the aggregate, technological change had little net impact on the overall distribution of skills, since the various reforms tended to cancel each other out.

Synthetic Turnover

The exclusion of women from high-status positions in these firms cannot be explained using human capital theory in either its pure or its modified forms. Human capital theory argues that women's anticipated careers are too short to allow them to be profitably trained for skilled or supervisory positions. In these firms, women worked for an average of twelve years, a period sufficiently long to justify training them for nearly any position. Furthermore, management seems to have been less concerned with conserving scarce human capital than with artificially increasing turnover. In firms where there is a pre-existing supply of skilled labor, where employees do not significantly increase their productivity over time as they gain experience, and where these employees are paid on tenure-based salary scales, there will be a strong incentive for employers to prefer newer workers to older workers, since newer workers will be considerably less expensive. Under such conditions, employers will attempt to maximize their quit rates by hiring employees whom they believe are unstable or, if this fails, by imposing tenure bars. Both the Great Western Railway and the General Post Office used marriage bars. These policies were explicitly defended by management as ways of keeping wages low and promotion chains fluid. Similar policies were instituted by other white-collar employers, as was shown by surveys of firms in the United States, Britain, and other developed nations. White-collar employers were particularly prone to using marriage bars because they paid with · tenure-based salary scales.

Legitimating Ideologies

Women are often excluded from particular jobs on the basis of organization-specific policies whose primary functions seem to be patriarchical in nature. Although the initial motivation behind the implementation of these policies may have been sexist, their persistence depends on the degree to which they can be made compatible with the requirements of efficient organizational and economic functioning. Two specific examples on the GWR and GPO were night work bans and sex segregation. Both policies were initially implemented out of a managerial concern with traditional sex roles. The ban on night work survived because it forced a significant proportion of men to serve late shifts. This facilitated the functioning of internal labor markets in each firm by intensifying the competition over day jobs. Sex segregation did not survive in most firms, since it seriously impeded communication between employees working on closely related jobs. It survived in the Post Office only due to a rare set of conditions that allowed the GPO to make extraordinary adjustments to the demands of such a regime. Furthermore, once the policy had been in place for a long time, eliminating sex segregation might have allowed experienced women to be promoted over younger high-level men.

Employee Discrimination

The patterns of feminization that occurred in the Great Western Railway and General Post Office cannot be explained in terms of employers' being prevented from hiring women due to pressure from sexist male employees. Most unions were not sufficiently strong to be able to force management to make concessions on sex issues. This condition almost certainly applied to the white-collar unions on the GWR and the GPO. Nearly every explicit demand concerning women's employment that was made by these unions was disregarded by management; this applies both to those demands for the exclusion of women that were made by the sexist unions and the demands for the preservation of female employment made by the feminist unions. Informal employee discrimination does not appear to have affected hiring either. Strong workers should have been more capable of informally excluding women than should weak workers. Nevertheless, there was no correlation between the percentage of female clerks and the bargaining strength of male workers.

Women as Labor Control

The patterns of hiring in these two firms can not be explained in terms of the use of women to control male white-collar militancy, since there seems to have been no tendency for women to be less strike-prone than men. The telegraph service of the Post Office attempted such a strategy in 1870 by filling strategic offices with women clerks. However, the female strike rate was essentially the same as the male strike rate, and the Post Office abandoned feminization as a strategy of labor control. Women were no more prone to docility on the Great Western Railway; after controlling for occupational composition, the differences between men and women in their participation in the General Strike of 1926 were trivial.

Alternative Sources of Secondary Labor

Both the Great Western Railway and the General Post Office increased their use of female clerks because of difficulties associated with the use of other sources of inexpensive labor. In the nineteenth century, duties that are now given to female clerks were given to temporary adult male clerks and boy apprentices. Male wage clerks fell into disfavor during the twentieth century because they lacked the human capital required for office work. They were doomed by the rationalization of office management that emerged during the Taylorite era. High human capital requirements also reduced the demand for boy clerks. Firms were only willing to use those boys with relatively high levels of intelligence and education. Victorian firms attracted such individuals by offering them full adult positions after they reached the age of eighteen. However, there were demographic limitations on the percentage of positions that could be given to boys, because of this obligation to absorb male graduates. Rapidly growing firms had no absorption problems, but as growth rates decreased, firms would be obligated to turn elsewhere for their cheap labor. This problem was exacerbated by a growing scarcity of qualified boys as higher education and introductory lower managerial positions drew off boys who previously would have taken clerical positions. Feminization in both the GWR and the GPO was accompanied by some sort of limit on the availability of acceptable juvenile job candidates.

The Feminization of Clerical Labor Overall and the
Concentration of Women in White-Collar Jobs

The preceding analyses have important implications for two related larger questions in the study of occupational sex-typing. The first question is why clerical work changed its sex-type from male to female. The traditional explanation is that clerical feminization occurred as a response to several different social and economic changes. Among the most important of these were the increase in the supply of educated women seeking employment, the de-skilling of office work, and the reduction in both managerial and employee resistance to female employment that came from a change in societal norms (Davies 1975). While the increased supply of educated women undoubtedly facilitated feminization, it is unlikely that a scarcity of female job candidates ever inhibited the use of female clerks. The Post Office in 1870 had no problem obtaining a nearly unlimited supply of women telegraph recruits. The only supply difficulties they reported were with finding men. When the Great Western Railway chose not to hire women in 1876, the availability of female candidates did not even emerge as an issue in the debate. The continued use of men both by the GWR and by other private employers in the 1870's and 1880's would seem to have been due primarily to demand-side considerations.

De-skilling does not seem to have been a factor either. Many of the technological innovations that were associated with feminization, such as typing, actually represented upgradings rather than downgradings of clerical skill. Women entered clerical work not because there was an increase in the proportion of unskilled jobs, but because managers changed their strategies for filling these unskilled jobs.

There can be little question that male resistance to the use of women clerks represented a very significant obstacle to the progress of clerical feminization. Virtually in every instance that women clerks were introduced to a new setting, there was intensive protest by both managers and workers. The managerial objections were far more important than those of rank-and-file workers on the office floor. Although male clerks protested vigorously, their attempts to restrict or eliminate female employment came to nothing. Since the firms in these studies had unions that were unusually strong and successful, it is not likely that other male clerks were more effective at excluding female workers. In a sense, the feminization of clerical labor can be attributed in part to the overall weakness of clerical workers that prevented them from being able to control entry into their occupation.

Managerial sexism, on the other hand, remained the most potent barrier to clerical feminization. The degree to which this sexism was tolerated depended to a large extent on the degree to which offices had to economize on clerical labor costs. Over the course of the nineteenth and twentieth centuries, firms became increasingly clerical-labor-intense, which forced them to pay greater attention to the expenses of office management. In the era of the Victorian counting house, when the administrative staff of many concerns consisted of fewer than a dozen clerks, it was not terribly economically significant whether these positions were filled by men or women. A firm's fortunes were generally determined by its performance in other areas. The growing clerical labor intensity of industry came from two sources. On one hand, the growing sophistication of accounting and financial analysis in business necessitated the collection and processing of large amounts of data to facilitate more rational decision-making. This dramatically increased the percentage of staff in manufacturing concerns engaged in administrative rather than substantive duties. At the same time, the development of the service sector created a new set of industries that were almost entirely composed of clerical labor. Banking, insurance, and public administration each employed workforces that were nearly entirely white collar. The growing clerical labor intensity of industry promoted a global concern with efficient office administration. In the twentieth century, managers eagerly adopted many of the reforms of the office Taylorites and reworked their procedures for correspondence, calculating, and data retrieval. At the same time, they began to staff their offices economically and hired women clerks instead of men.[1]

---

1. An interesting empirical illustration of the importance of clerical labor intensity in promoting clerical feminization is the persistence of the male shipping clerk. Shipping clerk is perhaps the only clerical occupation that has remained predominantly male (Garfinkle 1975). The work of filling out bills of lading and receipts is similar to work done by female clerks in offices; furthermore, the physical demands of the job are not great, since, in most firms, loading and unloading freight is handled by packers or warehouse staff. What differentiates a shipping clerk from an office clerk is that the shipping clerk is usually the only clerical worker in a staff that is primarily blue collar. Although the employer of the shipping clerk, namely a warehouse supervisor or fore-

Synthetic turnover also contributed to the feminization of clerical work. Most clerical employers would have suffered from the joint problem of tenure-based salary scales and relatively flat productivity curves over time. They would not have had the extreme problems of overannuation of the Great Western Railway and General Post Office, since those firms paid above prevailing market rates, but many of them would have wanted to increase their rates of turnover, and, as was seen in Chapter 4, it was quite common for clerical employers to use marriage bars. The use of gender as the criteria for differentiating between short-term and long-term employees virtually guaranteed that a significant share of low-status office jobs would henceforth be reserved for women. It is hard to imagine any other demographic classification besides gender that could have been used for a tenure bar that would have been at all practical in an office setting. Hiring juveniles and then dismissing them upon reaching adulthood provides a career of only two or three years in length. Dismissing people at age sixty-five is a common practice but hardly solves the particular problems of clerical work. Hiring sixteen-year-old women and forcing them to retire at marriage ensures careers anywhere from six to ten years long. This is long enough to ensure the conservation of any firm-specific skills, but not so long as to create a severe crisis of productivity. Thus, ironically, even as tenure bars diminished the opportunities for older women, they gave younger women a near monopoly on clerical positions, since their tenures could be more easily manipulated to fit the needs of office employers. Synthetic turnover thus helped ensure that clerical work would become a female sex-typed job.

Finally, clerical work feminized because of the growing problems inherent in using other sources of cheap labor. There was no increase in the problems associated with using casual males. Undereducated clerks had been a problem in Victorian Britain, and concerns with clerical quality control date back at least to the 1870's. However, since temporary men were a suboptimal solution to the problem of staffing routine clerical jobs, one would expect that their use would diminish

---

man, may claim that women cannot handle the physical demands of such a position, this is really no different from the claims that were made by the Postal Engineers or the Great Western Railway management. What all of these managers have in common is a clerical force that is sufficiently small relative to their total staff that the luxury of male clerks can be afforded.

over time, as managers became more sophisticated in the business of office management. Each wave of office rationalization should have made further inroads into the numbers of temporary male clerks until they finally disappeared altogether. For boys, the problem would have been the growing scarcity of qualified candidates as more and more boys turned instead to higher education and starting jobs with explicitly managerial job titles. Increasingly, women represented one of the few sources of highly educated skilled inexpensive labor that would have been available to employers.

A second closely related question is why women are predominantly concentrated in white-collar rather than manual positions. To some extent, this question asks why jobs similar to clerical work became feminized as well, and the answer closely parallels the above discussion. White-collar occupations tend to be labor-intensive rather than capital-intensive. Factories tend to expend a substantial proportion of their budgets on raw materials and technology. Offices devote their budgets entirely to labor. White-collar employers are less capable of tolerating discrimination against women and are more likely to make use of their relative cheapness. White-collar occupations are also relatively poorly unionized. As such, male workers in these positions are less capable of acting in their own behalf to restrict the supply of labor and forbid employers from using secondary sources of labor. White-collar jobs tend to pay on tenure-based salary scales, thus making them more apt than blue-collar jobs to require some form of synthetic turnover. Blue-collar occupations are paid on piece rates or with job-specific wage rates that do not vary by the demographic attributes of the jobholder. Since, in these situations, older workers are not necessarily more expensive than younger workers, employers have no incentive to increase turnover, and there is no motivation to create an underclass of female employees. Lastly, most white-collar jobs require a non-trivial amount of formal education. These jobs are likely to require the verbal and intellectual skills that are taught in schools, unlike blue-collar occupations, where the training often occurs in extracurricular settings, or occurs on the job itself. Because of the high value that is placed on formal education, employers reserve white-collar jobs for workers with a college degree or better. In general, minority members, juveniles, and casual males are less likely to have the educational qualifications that are available in the adult white female labor force. Thus, women should receive a disproportionate share of white-collar positions, while workers in other categories of secondary labor should find more employment in manual occupations, where education is a less important barrier to entry.

The Operation of Occupational Sex-Typing
at the National Level

Some of the arguments that were elaborated in the main analysis are of direct relevance to the quantitative literature on occupational sex-typing that has examined national occupational structures. A full-scale empirical test of these theories using national data has not been attempted. Nevertheless, the existing studies do provide an opportunity to examine individual propositions to see how they fare.

The quantitative literature provides further evidence of the relationship between buffering from labor costs and the percentage of females in an occupation. Labor intensity has generally been a significant predictor of occupational sex type. Michael Wallace and Arne Kalleberg, as part of a larger investigation of the structure of dual labor markets, estimated the determinants of the percentage of females among 68 industries. They found that capital intensity was negatively correlated with the percentage of females in an industry. Furthermore, capital intensity was the only variable in their model that was statistically significant at the .05 level (Wallace and Kalleberg 1981).[2] Bridges obtained similar findings in his analyses of 80 primary and secondary industries and 320 "industry strata."[3] In his earlier research, the only analytic variable that consistently predicted the percentage of women was capital intensity. Fixed assets per worker had the strongest zero-order relations with the use of women and was the only variable besides industry dummies that survived the inclusion of other variables. In his later work, Bridges used a variable called "classic capitalist organization," which was a combination of firm size

---

2. This relationship was not robust to controlling for occupational composition. However, that finding comes from an equation that used fully fifteen variables to predict variance in only sixty-eight cases. The uncontrolled equation used only six independent variables. The small N available in most analyses of industrial attributes makes data attrition a real methodological concern.

3. In Bridges' terminology, an industrial stratum is either the white-collar or the blue-collar staff of an industry considered separately.

and fixed assets per worker. Out of eleven independent variables, classic capitalist organization was the third best predictor of the percentage of females. The best predictor was white collar–blue collar, which, as was argued above, can also be viewed in part as a proxy for labor intensity. The raw correlation between fixed assets per worker and the use of women was much weaker for tertiary industries, with the relationship being insignificant in multivariate analyses (Bridges 1980, 1982). This may have been due to the presence of financial and insurance firms in this sector. Such firms tend to own a lot of assets but have operating budgets that are entirely labor intensive. Except for those tests involving the tertiary sector, the performance of measures of buffering from labor costs generally has been very impressive.[4]

The percentage of females in an industry is also affected by the demographic composition of the rest of the workforce. In some cases, this can be explained in terms of a trade-off between primary and secondary labor. If the use of women was positively correlated with the use of other disadvantaged workers, this would suggest the presence of some factor that was benefiting both groups at the expense of white adult men. If the use of women was negatively correlated with the use of these other groups, it would suggest a trade-off between alternative sources of secondary labor such as was discussed in Chapter 8. In general, one would expect that if one did not control for attractiveness of employment, there would be a positive correlation between female and minority hiring, since the zero-order relationship would primarily capture the overall advantages white males enjoy in the labor market. As one controls for attractiveness of employment and other variables affecting white male employment, the inverse relationship between female and minority employment should become more apparent. In Bridges' models, both types of relationships make an appearance. In his early work, Bridges found a negative relation between female employment and that of blacks. The zero order relationship was relatively weak, while as one would expect, the relationship after secondary sector was controlled was much stronger. In Bridges' later

4. A labor cost buffering theory would also imply that secondary sector firms would be more likely to hire women than would primary firms because of their generous supply of organizational slack. This proposition has been disconfirmed in several preliminary analyses. There are several methodological reasons for questioning these findings, and the most that can be said is that the relation between patterns of gender hiring and dual labor markets is empirically unknown. For a discussion of the complex measurement issues involved, see Appendix G.

work, the second most important predictor of the percentage of females was the percent of males who are between twenty-five and fifty-four. Women are less likely to work in industry sectors whose men are predominantly in their prime working years. The direction of the relationship is embarrassing at first glance, since in a model that included numerous controls for attractiveness of employment, there was a positive rather than a negative relationship with the percentage of juveniles. Nevertheless, the strength and significance of the relationship suggests that the dynamics of trade-offs between these groups needs further study and that there appears to be a very definite relationship between female employment and the dynamics of the hiring of other types of labor.

Bridges' work also illustrates the relative unimportance of employee exclusion in determining occupational sex type. After controlling for other variables, the path between unionization and the percentage of females was virtually zero. Furthermore, unionization significantly decreased the amount of sex segregation within industries. If unions were restricting female employment, one would have expected the opposite—that is, that in unionized industries, women would be more likely to be confined to a small subset of occupations.

These findings are consistent with the historical evidence on male exclusionary campaigns presented by Alice Kessler-Harris. Male unionists have consistently been opposed to female employment. However, there have been relatively few cases of an employer's attempting to introduce women but being forced to abandon such plans in the face of organized resistance from labor. Unions have frequently barred women from union membership, only to find that employers have ignored this lack of certification and hired the women anyway. In the nineteenth century, the National Typographical Union banned women from membership and steered work away from female printers. Women printers set up their own union and seem to have prospered throughout the remainder of the century.[5] Cigar-makers originally excluded women from their union, but were forced to reverse their policy in the face of an overwhelming feminization by an unsympathetic management. When Detroit streetcar conductors refused to give union cards to female conductors, the women were able to overturn this policy by appealing to the National War Labor Board

---

5. By the twentieth century, printing had become a male-dominated occupation. A closer examination of the decline of the female printer would be an excellent test of union exclusion theories as well as a fascinating case study in its own right.

(Kessler-Harris 1982). It is true that many employers claim that they are unable to hire women due to the policies of their unions. However, many of these statements can be easily interpreted as rationalizations by managers whose own interest in feminization is lukewarm. Thus Bridges' findings of no significant union effects are likely to be relatively robust.

Environmental Constraints on the Rates of Change of Occupational Sex-Type

The analysis thus far has implicitly assumed that occupational sex-type is determined largely by the desires of management. Most of the arguments that have been made to explain the persistence of relatively expensive male clerks involve either countervailing advantages (synthetic turnover), buffering from the requirement to maximize profits (clerical labor intensity), or the availability of sources of relatively inexpensive male labor (boy clerkships). The only environmental constraint that was discussed was resistance from organized labor, and the position taken was generally negative. Nevertheless, there are some important environmental constraints on the ability of a firm to set its sex-type at will that did not play a role in this study. One of these is law and government policy. The other is the supply of vacant positions.

Postal hiring was subject to a wide variety of political constraints. Nevertheless, most of these tended to be idiosyncratic and were not typical of the problems felt by the average firm in the private sector. The most important legal constraints that have affected the hiring of women have been protectionist legislation and affirmative action. Neither of these was terribly important to the feminization of clerical labor, but each have had obvious consequences in the blue-collar and professional sectors. Any quantitative study of contemporary American sex-typing would have to take such considerations into account. Net of whatever variables are suggested by this analysis, the design should include explicit measures of the timing and enforcement of affirmative action policy. Firms in industries or regions where enforcement activity has been especially rigorous should be more likely to hire women, even if the firms themselves have not received any direct pressure.

The role of vacancies in determining sex-type is less obvious. The discussion has implicitly assumed that an employer can immediately adjust his labor force to reflect current economic and social conditions.

In fact, he can only introduce new workers into positions for which there are vacancies. If the number of openings is relatively small, his current sex-type may reflect past rather than present economic conditions. This was graphically illustrated in the Post Office by the length of time it took to get the political appointees out of office. The Orders in Council banning patronage were passed in 1870. The last political hires finally left the Post Office in 1911, fully forty years after the original decision to dispense with patronage was made. Most organizations are somewhat more adaptable than the Post Office. Nevertheless, the effect of this inertia must be factored in when considering any cross-sectional employment data.

The speed at which vacancies arise is determined by three factors: the secular rate of organizational growth; the effect of cyclical factors on organizational growth; and the rate of voluntary quitting by employees. If a firm is growing steadily, there will be an ample supply of new positions that can be filled with members of a new socio-demographic category. If a firm is stagnating, the employer will only be able to put new workers in those positions that arise from attrition. If the firm is shrinking, there will be no new vacancies at all. Furthermore, employers generally have less autonomy over who they fire than they do over who they hire. The employer may not be able to lay off individuals in such a manner as to control the demographic composition of the resulting workforce.

Cyclical firms should be particularly responsive to current needs. Firms that fluctuate in size go through phases of releasing older workers and then obtaining new ones. Even if some institutional arrangement exists allowing former employees to get their jobs back, there are usually enough workers who do not return to create a supply of vacancies that management can fill with a free hand. In the case of extremely unstable employment, such as seasonal labor or casual work, the labor force itself is sufficiently transitory to allow for nearly complete restaffing with every wave. There should be no lagged adjustment at all in these situations.

The role of voluntary turnover in creating vacancies is obvious and need not be belabored. This implies that life-tenure bureaucracies, relatively high-paying firms, and firms that refrain from hiring juveniles will all suffer from some form of inertia in their hiring, since all three types of firm are particularly likely to have low turnover. Internal labor markets thus have the effect of reinforcing a pre-existing in-group's statistical domination of employment by reducing the number of vacancies for which an outsider can be hired.

An illustration of the importance of these principles comes from Snyder, Hayward, and Hudis (1978), who found that, in the secondary sector, occupations were more likely both to increase and to decrease their percentage of women workers. Secondary sector industries are more likely to be highly cyclical, are more likely to be low-paying, causing workers to leave, are more likely to hire juveniles who tend to quit for personal considerations, and are less likely to have well-developed internal labor markets. Furthermore, to measure secondary status Snyder et al. used the percentage of workers that were part-year and the percentage of workers that were part-time. Both of these measures are particularly sensitive measures of the overall supply of vacancies.

The effect of legal changes is likely to be relatively permanent. Even if future governments were to stop enforcing affirmative action, the bureaucratic procedures that were created for initial compliance are likely to persist, albeit with reduced efficiency. However, the effects of vacancy shortages are relatively transitory. Over the middle term, most employers should be able to make some adjustment in the composition of their labor force, even if the change is less than they might desire. Lag models can make a contribution to the study of occupational sex-typing, but only within the context of a larger theory that specifies the changes that employers are attempting to achieve.

Women and Low-Status Jobs

One of the fundamental questions in the study of women's work is why women are concentrated in low-status jobs. A major goal of this study was to develop an alternative to the natural turnover hypothesis. This second explanation, the synthetic turnover model, was extremely useful in explaining women's subordination in the Great Western Railway and the General Post Office. It is also quite helpful in explaining women's subordination in the white-collar sector. However, the model only works under a fairly narrow range of economic conditions. If the employer does not pay with tenure-based salary scales, or if labor is scarce, or if employees significantly improve their productivity with increased experience over the long term, or if there are efficient sex-neutral mechanisms for eliminating workers whose pay increases have exceeded their productivity, then there will be either no advantage to increasing turnover or no need to use gender to differentiate the labor force and the synthetic turnover model will not hold. The general predictive power of the synthetic turnover model is based on the fact that the complex conjuncture of events that sets the model into action occurs relatively frequently in practice. Many women's jobs are characterized by tenure-based salaries, a labor surplus, minimal on-the-job training, and an absence of practical sex-neutral tenure bars. However, another explanation must be sought for women's economic subordination in the extremely large number of empirical settings where the terms of the synthetic turnover model do not apply.

The most compelling explanation of women's concentration in low-status jobs involves employee discrimination. Most forms of employee discrimination do not directly affect occupational sex-type, since most employees do not control entry into their own occupations. However, there is a significant exception to this principle. A particularly important set of workers who do control entry into their occupation is managers. Managers fundamentally control the setting of occupational sex-type by determining who gets hired for virtually every kind of job. This study has followed the traditional practice of viewing discrimination by managers as being a form of employer discrimination, which can be explained in terms of pure sexism and patriarchical ideology. However, discrimination by managers can also be viewed as employee discrimination.

The exclusion of women from high-status positions benefits the managerial class by restricting the supply of replacement labor for these positions and increasing the economic returns to managers as a whole. Employee discrimination is very easy to ground in economic rationality. Effective discrimination restricts the supply of candidates for any given occupation. This provides job security for pre-existing workers by making it less likely that they will be replaced by an alternative job candidate. This difficulty of replacement in turn gives them bargaining power that they can use to increase the wages for their occupation. Managers are employees just like operatives or laborers, with a rational concern for protecting their careers and economic prospects. Executives defend the overall salary levels of their occupation by restricting the supply of entrants to the entry-level positions in administrative job chains. By hiring only men for junior-level jobs, employers make qualified managerial trainees artificially scarce. This raises the salaries of entry-level positions through simple market competition. Upper-level executives benefit from this inflation because their salaries are generally set to be higher than those given to entering trainees. Thus, if discrimination raises the salaries of entry-level managers, it will put upward pressure on the entire executive salary structure.

A somewhat related argument can be made for professionals. Professionals also control entry into their own occupations. They control entry into whatever academic institutions provide the basic training in the field; they control the accreditation process by which students are allowed to practice the profession; and most importantly, they control the hiring of professionals in the firms in which they themselves are employed. Most professional firms are administrated in a collegial fashion, with all senior partners having a significant vote in determining both hiring and advancement within the organization. Even when professionals work within a corporate or bureaucratic setting, it is unusual for anyone to be hired who does not meet the approval of the pre-existing professional staff.

The motivation for professional discrimination is somewhat different from that of managers. Professional incomes are largely determined by the volume of fees that has been earned by the firm. Although most professionals do receive a nominal salary, a significant proportion of their remuneration comes in the form of a bonus, which is entirely dependent on the prosperity of the firm. Thus professionals do not benefit in the same way managers do from internal labor markets that ensure a positive differential between the salaries of entering and advanced workers in an occupation. Instead, professionals benefit from discrimination because it increases the price they are able to charge for their services. If successful discrimination drives women or minority practitioners from the labor market, there will be a reduced number of firms capable of providing professional services. This reduces competition among the firms already in the labor market and maintains an inflated schedule of fees.

Most managers and professionals do not have such overtly economic motives explicitly in mind when they institutionalize policies of discrimination. In general, the non-hiring of women would be motivated by sincerely held beliefs in patriarchical ideology and a genuine concern with the compatibility of gender and professional roles. However, the fact that discrimination is likely to raise managerial and professional incomes helps to eliminate a potential check on the operation of sexism in hiring. When managers think about the economics of hiring non-managerial workers, their patriarchical concerns are tempered by a consideration of larger economic considerations. Because managers are interested in obtaining the lowest rather than the highest possible salaries for these workers, they have to consider the relative cheapness of women in their calculations. This provides a continual pressure to feminize and create labor economies. When managers or professionals hire themselves, they become concerned not with lowering but with raising the standard of living for their occupation. Any policy that will be consistent with maintaining levels of remuneration will tend to be accepted rather uncritically by employers. Sexism survives because it serves a latent economic function for this class of individuals.

These tendencies are exacerbated because the hiring for both types of positions is relatively buffered from a concern with using sex to minimize labor costs. Managers and executives make up a very small percentage of the labor force of most firms. If levels of executive remuneration were to become extremely high, this would have almost no bearing either on the labor costs or on the overall profitability of the firm. As a result, most corporations tend to be relatively generous in their executive benefits. Six- and seven-figure salaries, stock options, and expensive perks such as private planes are all affordable because the absolute expense they represent is trivial compared to the total corporate budget. Given that these rewards are approved by trustees and directors who would like to see comparable remuneration given to themselves, it is not hard to see why such generosity continues to persist.

A related argument can be made for professionals. One cannot claim that the profits of professional firms are independent of labor costs. Professional fees make up the lion's share of the budget in most of these firms. However, doctors and lawyers cannot save money by hiring female partners rather than male partners. The professions are one of the few occupations where the fifty-nine cent to the dollar rule does not apply. Female professionals still make less money than male professionals because they are barred from practicing in the more lucrative specialties. Nevertheless, once a women professional is hired by a firm, she is paid the same rate as a man. It is more difficult for a professional firm to deny a woman comparable worth than it is for a corporate employer. Corporations are large authoritarian organizations that can mask pay inequities in a welter of different job titles. The presence of bureaucratic administration provides companies with the ability to segregate women workers by arbitrary job title providing different rates of return to similar work. Professional partnerships are less capable of practicing this kind of discrimination. Because they are small, they do not have the same semantic differentiation of their staff. This tends to provide comparable treatment for all workers within broad categories, such as "summer intern" or "senior partner." Furthermore, most professional partnerships are run under norms of collegiality. This reduces the viability of having separate regimes for ostensibly equal workers. These factors keep professional firms from paying women less than the male rate for doing equal work. However, they also destroy whatever economic incentive there may be for hiring women in the first place. Since women work at the same rate as men, there is no pressure for professionals to seek economies through feminizing. As a result, they can indulge their sexist fantasies, or they can act to restrict the supply of women into the profession. Both of these will tend to limit female employment.

Thus, although the synthetic turnover model cannot serve as a general explanation of why women are concentrated in low-status jobs, the various arguments of the book provide tools to help fill in this gap. Employee discrimination can only work when workers have the power to control entry into their occupations. High-status workers are the only cases of such exclusion's being effective. Women are generally excluded from occupations when such exclusion benefits their employers. Thus, women are barred from the occupations of the employers themselves so as to preserve upper-level salaries. Women are excluded from settings that are buffered from the need to use cheap female labor to reduce labor costs. Both professional and managerial occupations enjoy the benefits of such buffering. Thus, the propositions that were derived from a study of variance in female employment can be used to explain the relatively universal phenomenon of women's economic subordination.

Further Research in Women's Work

A final lesson of this study is methodological. Those who have taken a radical or critical perspective on gender have in general been too reluctant to test their theories rigorously with either historical evidence or statistical methods. There is generally a despair on the part of progressive writers on women's status that their problems are particularly intractable to the use of quantitative social science analysis. Sometimes this suspicion comes from the perception that large sample analyses tend to use individuals as the unit of analysis and thus become biased towards micro-level rather than macro-level strategies of explanation. In other cases, the suspicion is based on a despair with the quality of historical data. Archives are often seen as only providing scraps of anecdotal evidence that relate to particular and unique social occurrences. Some fear that the analytical clustering of incidents will do violence to the individuality of each event. Others fear that the data is so incomplete as to make any program of systematic measurement or sampling practically impossible.

These reservations are real, but can be readily overcome by the analyst who is willing to be creative with what the data have provided. The pitfall of perpetually sliding into an individual-level analysis can be avoided by relentlessly seeking larger units of analysis. Instead of comparing particular workers, one can compare firms, industries, or any other aggregation that makes employers rather than workers the key decision-making actors. The analyst who is concerned about riding roughshod over the individual characteristics of his cases can devote careful scholarly attention to the historical context surrounding each. Such systematic attention to the historical record can suggest unanticipated sociological regularities that in fact were operating unobserved in the other cases. The plea of historical individualism is often a disguised argument for the necessity of rich multivariate analyses. Finally, the data that is available in public archives are far richer than most social scientists have realized. Most of the major corporate archives in the United States are unidentified, let alone unexplored. Furthermore, the most banal, useless-looking document can be found on second analysis to contain a wealth of analytical possibilities. The turnover data in this study came from actuarial analyses in pension files. The dependent variable for the Post Office came from personnel lists, which often contained no more information than the name and job title of an office's clerks. The only data a name will provide is whether that clerk is male or female. A lot of archival data is not quantitative in and of itself. However, there are a lot more numbers out there than most people realize. The decision makers and bureaucrats of earlier eras kept accounts, took censuses, kept membership lists, took inventories, counted errors, and estimated costs in a fashion that allowed them to quantify the problems they faced in their daily lives. Sometimes these accounts were kept voluntarily by the organization; other times they were kept as a requirement of the local or national government, and a copy can be found in the public archives.

These figures combined with the qualitative leavings of letters, reports, and public announcements can provide historical reconstructions that are remarkably detailed. An archive will not always generate information on precisely what an investigator is looking for. However, it often contains a wealth of information on important topics that one might have never even considered examining. By being willing to consider what an archive has to offer, and by making special efforts to consider what can be quantified from this material, one can uncover some fascinating and bizarre historical processes that have direct relevance for the intellectual questions of today.

Appendixes

Appendix A
The Postal and Railway Samples

General Post Office

Most of the data from the Post Office comes from the Post Office Establishment Books. These are annual listings of the staff of every department of the Post Office along with statistical breakdowns by sex and job title. The Establishment Books also provide information on the pay scale associated with each position and provide both the names and career summaries of the top job holders in each department. Although the data is available on an annual basis, for economy's sake analysis was confined to the following years: 1871, 1876, 1881, 1886, 1891, 1896, 1901, 1906, 1911, 1914, 1918, 1921, 1926, 1931, and 1936. In general, every effort was made to preserve even five-year panels except during World War I, when the dates were selected to represent the last pre-war observation, the middle of the war, and the first year after the immediate post-war adjustments.

The data set is not a neat rectangular one of N departments times M years. The number of departments in the Post Office fluctuated over time, with new departments being created as the Post Office diversified and old departments being eliminated through merger or loss. In 1921, for example, all the Dublin offices were lost due to Irish independence. Furthermore, the percent female in very small offices is subject to dramatic and somewhat random fluctuations due to the addition or subtraction of one individual. As a result, the analysis is confined to all departments with a staff of at least ten, a fact that

239

produces some mild fluctuations in the number of cases from year to year.

The departments used in the analysis are the Secretary's Office, the regional secretaries in Dublin and Edinburgh, the Registry, the Receiver and Accountant General's Office (RAGO), the Money Order Department, the Savings Bank, the regional accounts offices in Dublin and Edinburgh, Central Telegraph Control, the Central Telegraph Signalling Gallery, the Central Telegraph Cable Section, the Central Telegraph Intelligence Section, the London East Central (EC) Telegraph Office, the West London Telegraph Office, the telegraph departments of Dublin and Edinburgh, the Telephone clerical section, the Telephone operating force, both types of telephone offices in Dublin and Edinburgh, the Engineering Department, the Factory Department, the Stores Department, the Returned Letter Offices in London and Edinburgh, London Postal Control, the main London East Central (EC) sorting office, the West London Sorting Office, and the sorting offices of Dublin and Edinburgh.

The West London Telegraph and Sorting offices are used as proxies for the policies of the London postal service for staffing the district offices as a whole. The correlation between the levels of variables calculated for the West London office alone and those for the entire Metropolitan District are above .90. Using the West London office to represent trends in the Metropolitan District provided extremely substantial economies in data-collecting and processing. The Money Order Department includes data from the Postal Order section. In some periods, the Postal Order section was under the supervision of the Money Order Department, but in other years it was under the control of the Receiver and Accountant General's Office. In order to prevent department scores from fluctuating randomly due to changes in the possession of a division that was in itself rather constant, it was decided to allocate the Postal Order section to the Money Order Department for all dates. Excluded from the analysis are the Medical Department and the Surveyor's clerks, due to their small size and extremely irregular reporting procedures in the data. Furthermore, the only postal employees included in the analysis are those employed in London, Dublin, or Edinburgh. Data are only available for clerks in other locations for selected dates in the twentieth century, and the scanty quantitative data is matched by an even greater paucity of supporting archival materials. A crude examination of the provincial data for those years for which they are available suggests patterns very similar to those reported for London, Dublin, and Edinburgh.

Great Western Railway

There are actually three sources of personnel statistics for the railway. The first is the series of staff censuses discussed in the text. Data are provided for every department, and within departments they are disaggregated where appropriate into three categories: headquarters staff, divisional office staff, and depot staff. In this study, each of these divisions within the department is treated as a separate unit. The second source of data is the annual series of organizational charts of the salaried staff of the railway. These charts are lists of the clerical staff of every department by name, sex, and salary grade. These are clustered by individual office within each department; for example, within the Goods Department Headquarters one can find listings for the wages office, the scheduling office, and the rates office among others. The office staff lists are accompanied by brief descriptions of the work done in each office, allowing for crude analysis of the relation between job duties and staffing patterns. The last source of data is a set of strike statistics compiled after the General Strike of 1926 for the Chief Mechanical Engineer's Department. For every office within the Chief Mechanical Engineer's Department, there are data on the sex composition of the office and its strike rate. One particular advantage of these data is that they include material on the wage clerks of the shop floor. Wage clerks are included in the GWR census but are excluded from the organizational charts of salaried staff.

The departments used in the analysis are as follows:

	Headquarters	*Divisional*	*Depot*
Secretary	x		
General Manager	x		
Traffic	x	x	x
Goods	x	x	x
Chief Accountant	x		
Engineering	x	x	x
Chief Mechanical Engineer	x	x	x
Signal	x		x
Docks	x	x	
Stores	x	x	x
Road Transport	x	x	
Estate and Rating	x	x	
Hotel and Refreshment Room	x	x	
Stationery	x		
Police	x		

Appendix B
The Occupational Composition of the
Postal and Railway Samples

The statistical records for the Post Office and the Great Western Railway contain data on a wide variety of employees, of whom some were clerical, some non-clerical, and some borderline. The following criteria were used to determine who would be within the sample and who would be excluded. All employees whose job title was "clerk" were included. Unfortunately, the title "clerk" also includes some personnel who were clearly managerial. It is desirable to exclude top executives from the study, and the only systematic basis for defining executives was by salary. Therefore all employees who in 1870 were earning £500 a year or more were excluded from the study. The £500 cut line usually identified a clear occupational border between clerks and non-clerks, which was then used in subsequent years. This definition is reasonably generous in allowing upper-level employees into the sample; thus the study clearly includes many workers who would be called administrative assistants or first-line managers today. Workers who had been given a job title with "clerk" in the 1870's but were renamed in later years were kept in the sample. Furthermore, workers with obviously clerical job duties, such as bookkeepers, paper sorters, or writers, were included. Many workers at the bottom of the office hierarchy were excluded. All janitorial and security personnel were removed, as well as messengers and office boys. Messengers and office boys performed substantial amounts of clerical work in the nineteenth century, but their primary duties tended to be non-clerical. Itinerant workers were also kept out of the analysis. This includes canvassers, inspectors, surveyors, traveling sales personnel, and members of the Travelling Post Office. The normal conception of office work involves sedentary personnel. A variety of blue-collar clerks were excluded as well. These were workers hired within a manual chain of command to do primarily clerical duties. An example would be a worker on the Great Western Railway called a "caller-off," whose job is to identify all of the packages entering or leaving a freight car and check them off against a bill of lading. Ideally such workers would have been included and their work settings considered as additional units of analysis. The problem is that the job titles of most of these workers are somewhat arcane and are not easily identified by the modern-day observer. Because these workers are easy to miss, there is a very real danger that only some of these workers would be included in the sample and the resulting description of this population would be seriously distorted. Stationmasters were generally excluded as being managerial. Technical and scientific personnel were removed whenever possible. Because of the ambiguities of nineteenth-century terminology, a high number of technicians were included in the engineering sample. Repetition of the main analyses of the book excluding all the disputed cases provides findings similar to those presented in the text, suggesting that the effect of including the hidden technical personnel is not substantial.

Appendix C
Estimating the Gender Wage Differential for Jobs of Comparable Content

The gender wage differential correction is designed to eliminate that component of the lowering of wages that is strictly due to the fact that women get paid less than men for doing identical work. The overall goal is to calculate a set of rates that reflect how much would have been paid had all the work been done by men. This entails calculating an average salary for an office that uses the observed male salary rates and a set of female rates that have been inflated by a factor measuring the differences in pay for men and women doing jobs of comparable worth.

To quantify the sex-discrimination factor, I searched the job classifications to locate jobs where men and women did work that was close to identical. Such assessments inevitably involve subjective judgments. Five pairs of jobs were selected for the sex-discrimination index. These are male and female shorthand typist, male paperkeeper and female sorting assistant, male and female counter clerk/telegraphist, male and female executive officer, and male and female high-grade clerk. Of these five, the closeness of fit of the first three pairs is easier to establish than is the case with the last two.

The meaning of the term "shorthand typist" was the same in the Post Office as it is today. Both men and women did the same sorts of duties; men, however, were employed in settings such as the engineering office that preferentially hired male employees. The paperkeepers and sorting assistants were essentially filing clerks. "Paperkeeper" is merely an older term for the job. To some extent, the female sorting assistants were more skilled. They were expected to rotate from office to office doing whatever putting away was required. Thus, they had to learn the filing systems of many different departments. The paper-keepers were limited to one department and could confine themselves to a single system. Counter clerks/telegraphists were the clerks who served at postal windows. They were also expected to transmit local telegraph messages using Morse code. Since local post offices were either all male or all female, and the work of each post office was fundamentally similar, the work of these two classes can be viewed as identical.

The situation for the two pairs of supervisory grades is somewhat more ambiguous. The executive clerks were management trainees. They were started at a very low salary and given broad pre-management training. Their scales allowed them to by-pass the bulk of the clerical force and advance quickly to responsible positions within the bureaucracy. It is unclear whether female executives got to the same levels of authority as their male counterparts. The high-grade clerks were supervisors who were promoted up from the ranks. Their primary responsibility was the supervision of large bodies of single-sex subordinates. The nature of the advanced substantive tasks involved with their jobs is unclear.

The ratio of male to female pay in these job categories was as follows:

Shorthand typists	1.49
Paperkeeper/sorters	1.39
Counter clerk/telegraphists	1.44
Executive officers	1.25
High-grade clerks	1.32

All of these figures are within .12 of each other, and the three most similar jobs are all within .05 of each other. This suggests a relatively consistent pattern of bias in pay scales.

Note also that the discrimination coefficients for the supervisory jobs is lower than those for the rank-and-file positions. One would normally expect higher-level jobs to show more discrimination; had these jobs been "truly" dissimilar, the reasonable bias one would expect would be that men would have jobs having significant responsibilities and remuneration, while women would have had more limited positions with a lower ceiling on pay. This would have produced a greater gap between male and female earnings. The reverse bias that we observe suggests that the jobs were in fact "truly" identical and that the lower-grade positions overestimate the global degree of discrimination involving jobs of comparable worth.

The rhetorical goal of Chapter 3 is to argue that real wages increased in the Post Office. Findings of high levels of sex discrimination allow for the calculation of higher estimated "true" wages. To allow a conservative bias into my calculations, I have included the supervisory categories, for a low sex-discrimination correction factor and a comparatively modest estimate of real trends in postal wages.

Appendix D
The Estimation of the Percentage of Non-entry-Level Jobs under Assumption B in 1870

Under Assumption B, the percentage of non-entry-level jobs is defined as all clerks with a status equal to or lower than the highest grade 5 male clerk. In 1933, there was a standard salary that represented the cutting line between a grade 5 and a grade 4 clerk: £210 per annum. The strategy used here is to calculate the percentage of clerks in 1870 who had the same relative salary or less. An equivalent 1870 salary was calculated by estimating the range of salaries in 1933 from minimum to maximum. Most salary distributions are highly skewed at the upper end. To reduce the skew, the top 2 percent of salaries were removed from the distribution. It was then determined that £210 was on the 47.8th percentile of this range of salaries. Note that this range is not the actual distribution of observed salaries; the range is the distance between the minimum and maximum salaries. The 47.8th percentile was then calculated for the 1870 salary range (after first removing the top 2 percent as before). This produced a cut point for 1870, £150 per annum. The top 2 percent was then added back into the distribution, and the observed percentage of all salaries greater than £150 was the measure of the percentage of non-entry-level jobs.

Appendix E
Bibliography of Taylorite Materials

Center, Stella, and Herzberg, Max
  1929 *Secretarial Procedure*. New York: Ronald.
Darlington, George
  1942 *Office Management*. Rev. ed. New York: Ronald.
Dicksee, Lawrence, and Blain, Herbert
  1906 *Office Organization and Management Including Secretarial Work*. London: Pitman.
Gardiner, Glenn
  1929 *Practical Office Supervision*. New York: McGraw-Hill
Leffingwell, William
  1917 *Scientific Office Management*. Chicago: Shaw.
  1918 *Making the Office Pay*. Chicago: Shaw.
  1925 *Office Management: Principles and Practice*. Chicago: Shaw.
  1926 *Office Appliance Manual*. N.p.: National Association of Office Appliance Manufacturers.
Leffingwell, William, and Robinson, Edwin
  1950 *Textbook of Office Management*. New York: McGraw-Hill.
McClelland, Frank
  1920 *Office Training and Standards*. Chicago: Shaw.
McCord, James
  1923 *Textbook of Filing*. New York: Appleton.
Nichols, Frederick
  1934 *Personal Secretary: Differentiating Duties and Essential Personal Traits*. Cambridge, Mass.: Harvard University Press.
Schulze, J. William
  1913 *The American Office: Its Organization, Management, and Records*. New York: Key.
  1919 *Office Administration*. New York: McGraw-Hill.

Appendix F
The Calculation of the Organizational Growth Rates Required by Various Percentages of Juvenile Clerks

The calculation of the growth rates that the GWR and GPO would have needed to absorb their graduating junior clerks can be easily calculated using stable population techniques. Each organization was assumed to hire incoming recruits as junior clerks for the first two years of their careers. Subsequently, such clerks would graduate to senior clerkships, where they would work for thirty-eight years. It was assumed that between hiring and the fortieth year of employment, there would be no resignations or exits. Furthermore, at the fortieth year, all clerks were assumed to retire. These simplifying assumptions are comparatively similar to the turnover behavior suggested by the actuarial data in Chapter 4. There was a very slight amount of turnover in the first few years of employment, and some mild deviations from retiring after the fortieth year. However, the absolute differences between the observed rates and the simplifying assumptions is not large. The actuarial data come from the 1910–25 period and may not be typical of what was experienced in earlier periods. Given this room for ambiguity, the errors in using the observed actuarial data to represent the experience of the whole 1870–1930 period are probably greater than those caused by a cosmetic simplification of the mathematical model.

For the present discussion, an adult is defined as anyone with more than two years of experience, while a junior has two or fewer years of experience. Then, using stable population techniques, one can estimate what rate of population growth is necessary to keep a fixed percentage of the population with two years of experience or less. The formula for the growth rate is

$$r = \frac{ln(g(r)/g(0))}{MJ(0) - MA(0)}$$

where r is the rate of population growth; $g(r)$ is the ratio of adults to juniors that is to be maintained by management; and $g(0)$ is the rate of adults to juniors that would cause no population growth. Put differently, $g(0)$ is the ratio of individuals above the age of two to people below the age of two in a hypothetical stationary population. In this case, a completely rectangular age distribution will produce zero population growth, so $g(0)$ is 38/2, or 19. $MJ(0)$ is the mean age of juniors in the stationary population, while $MA(0)$ is the mean age of adults in the stationary population. These figures are 1 and 21 respectively.

I am extremely grateful to Alberto Palloni of the University of Wisconsin Sociology Department for generating these equations and explaining their use.

Appendix G
Women and the Secondary Sector

Labor cost buffering theory would suggest that those firms that have a lot of organizational slack should be less likely to attempt to cut costs. Relatively prosperous firms should be less concerned with minimizing wages, and thus more tolerant of hiring adult male workers. Thus Francine Blau and Carol Jusenius (1976) and R. D. Barron and G. H. Norris (1976) are probably correct in arguing that women are more likely to be concentrated in the secondary sector and less likely to appear in the primary sector.

This is a controversial claim because statistical tests of this hypothesis have generally been unsuccessful. Bridges found that out of six measures of primary sector status only capital intensity had any consistent predictive power in explaining the percentage of females in American industries. Wallace and Kalleberg, using slightly different measures of industrial structure, were only able to explain 9 percent of the variance among industries in the use of women using dual sector-related variables. Most of their measures of primary sector status had no significant relation with sex. While these initial findings are discouraging, they should not be viewed as definitive. Bridges is probably correct that some of the variables used in dual sector models have little relation to occupational sex-typing. However the effect of others has been seriously underestimated, due to methodological limitations of the data.

Most of the quantitative studies of both occupational sex-typing and dual labor markets have used industries as units of analysis. This strategy has been necessitated by the practical consideration that the economic data upon which these studies depend is available in industrial aggregates. As is often noted even in these very studies, however, most dual labor market theories operate at the level of the individual firm. Most of the propositions in dual labor market theory are designed to contrast relatively monopolistic firms with more marginal firms. The contrasts between firms in a single industry are likely to be far more dramatic than the contrast across industries. General Motors and Weyerhauser have far more in common with each other than they do with Red Star Auto Parts and Tuscaloosa Plywood. Nevertheless, General Motors and Red Star Auto Parts are defined as being in transportation equipment and are thus primary sector, while

Weyerhauser and Tuscaloosa Plywood are defined as lumber companies and are thus secondary sector. It is true that there should be compositional effects that allow industry attributes to be inferred from the average attributes of its firms. Nevertheless, most industries are somewhat heterogeneous, so the potential for measurement error is extremely non-trivial.

The unit of analysis problem does not mean that all of the findings of these studies should be discarded. Some of the relationships under consideration should be robust to whether firms or industries are being considered; others should be more sensitive. In general, the effects of economic concentration and economic scale are likely to be misrepresented by industry-level variables, while the firm size, state intervention, and capital intensity can tolerate the higher level of aggregation. Let us consider each of these measures in turn.

Economic Concentration

Economic concentration is the aggregate measure of whether firms in a given industry have oligopolistic power through their domination of market share. This variable is, by its very nature, zero-sum. If four firms control 70 percent of an industry's market, the other one hundred firms must be competing for the remaining 30 percent. Thus, in a primary sector industry, the peripheral firms should be more marginal than those in a secondary sector industry, and one would expect substantial improvements in the performance of this variable if one had access to good-quality firm-level data.

Economic Scale

Economic scale is a measure of financial resources; it is based on such measures as the average amount of assets per firm and reported levels of profitability. In some respects, this variable can be viewed as a measure of financial "size." Economic scale is quite likely to be distorted by the use of grossly aggregated units of analysis. Within any industry, there should be fairly substantial differences in absolute wealth and profitability between the major and minor producers.

Firm Size

The number of employees per firm is also likely to be distorted by industry-level measures. However, attempts to remeasure firm size at a smaller level should not improve its poor ability to predict sex-type. The number of employees per firm has always been a questionable indicator of primary sector status. If a firm is underfinanced, competing for market share, and burdened with a labor-intensive technology, it is hard to see why its employment policies would be any different for a labor force of a hundred workers or a labor force of ten thousand workers. In the latter case, it is managing more employees but does not have any additional resources for paying them. Bridges is undoubtedly right in suggesting that firm size will be a poor predictor of female employment, but the behavior of size net of economic scale, concentration, and capital intensity should be irrelevant to a dual sector model of female employment.

State Intervention

The extent to which the state serves as a market for a firm's goods is likely to vary significantly from firm to firm within an industry. This factor is less likely to be a problem with state regulation, since this tends to apply across the board within industries. As is the case with firm size, however, it is not clear that re-estimating the variable at a lower level of aggregation would improve its predictive power. This is because state intervention has a secondary effect that is likely to counteract the exclusionary effects of governmentally induced financial security. In recent years, the government has vigorously enforced affirmative action laws. One of the most common strategies for doing this has been to put strict minority hiring requirements on employers holding government contracts. Firms that are regulated by the state have also been vulnerable to government pressure and have had incentives to cooperate with affirmative action. If the economic security that comes from government support has had any exclusionary effect on women, this would only have occurred before 1965, when equal opportunity programs were not vigorously enforced.

Capital Intensity

Capital intensity, like state regulation, is not seriously mismeasured by using data at the industry level. This is because capital intensity is to a large extent determined by technological considerations that are common to all firms within the industry. Most factories in the lumber industry are sawmills with a fairly standard ratio of capital to labor. Most steel mills are capital-intensive, regardless of their modernity or level of technological sophistication. There are some industries where firms do differ in the extent of automation; core automobile factories use assembly lines, robots, and other forms of mechanized production, while the peripheral firms are traditional machine shops. Nevertheless, the within-industry variance in labor intensity is probably far less than the between-industry variance, a statement that is not true for monopoly power or economic scale.

Conclusion

This long methodological discussion has important implications for interpreting the results of Bridges, and Wallace and Kalleberg. Capital intensity is likely to remain as a significant and important predictor of the percentage of females in a firm. Firm size is likely to be unrelated to sex while the relationship between sex and levels of state intervention is likely to be extremely complex and unstable over time. Market share and economic scale should correlate with the use of white adult males. These findings would support the claims that buffering from labor costs reduces the use of women. Those firms that are relatively wealthy and have financial surpluses can afford to hire an expensive labor force.

References

This bibliography refers to a large number of unpublished archival sources, as well as more generally available published documents. These archival sources have been identified with a three-letter abbreviation and a reference number. The three-letter abbreviation refers to the archive where the document may be found. The reference number is an identifier used by the archive itself to index and locate the document. It is analogous to a Library of Congress classification number on a printed book. The archival abbreviations are as follows:

GPO General Post Office Archives
     General Post Office Headquarters
     Saint Martin-le-grand
     London
LSE The Library
     London School of Economics
     Portugal Street
     London
MRC Modern Records Centre
     The Library
     University of Warwick
     Coventry, West Midlands
PRO Public Record Office
     Ruskin Street
     Kew, Richmond, Surrey

Aigner, Dennis, and Cain, Glen. 1977. "Statistical Theories of Discrimination in the Labor Market." *Industrial and Labor Relations Review* 30: 175–87.

Aldcroft, Derek. 1968. *British Railways in Transition*. New York: Macmillan.

Anderson, B. W. 1974., "Empirical Generalizations on Labor Turnover." Pp. 33–59 in Richard Pegnetter, ed., *Studies in Labor and Manpower*. Iowa City: University of Iowa Press.

Anderson, Gregory. 1976. *Victorian Clerks*. New York: Kelley.

Anderson, Michael. 1971. *Family Structure in Nineteenth-Century Lancashire*. New York: Cambridge University Press.

Antos, Joseph; Chandler, Mark; and Mellow, Wesley. 1980. "Sex Differences in Union Membership." *Industrial and Labor Relations Review* 33: 162–69.

Armknecht, Paul, and Early, John. 1972. "Quits in Manufacturing: A Study of Their Causes." *Monthly Labor Review* 95: 31–37.

Aron, Cynthia. 1980. "To Barter Their Souls for Gold: Female Clerks in Federal Government Offices, 1862–1890." Unpub. paper.

Averitt, Robert. 1968. *Dual Economy: The Dynamics of American Industry Structure*. New York: Norton.

Bagwell, Philip. 1963. *Railwaymen: A History the of National Union of Railwaymen*. London: Allen and Unwin.

Bain, George. 1970. *The Growth of White Collar Unionism*. Oxford: Clarenden.

Baker, Elizabeth Faulkner. 1964. *Technology and Women's Work*. New York: Columbia University Press.

Bank Introduction. 1875. *Introduction of Women to the Savings Bank*. GPO, E3613/1875.

Barkin, Solomon. 1961. *The Decline of the Labor Movement and What Can Be Done about It*. Santa Barbara, Calif.: Center for the Study of Democratic Institutions.

Barron, R. D., and Norris, G. H. 1976. "Sexual Divisions and the Dual Labor Market." Pp. 47–69 in Diana Leonard and Sheila Allen, eds., *Dependence and Exploitation in Work and Marriage*. New York: Longman.

Becker, Gary. 1957. *Economics of Discrimination*. University of Chicago: Chicago Press.

———. 1964. *Human Capital: A Theoretical and Empirical Analysis with Special Reference to Education*. New York: National Bureau of Economic Research.

Beechey, Veronica. 1978. "Women and Production: A Critical Analysis of Some Sociological Theories of Women's Work." Pp. 155–97 in Annette Kuhn and AnnMarie Wolpe, eds., *Feminism and Materialism: Women and Modes of Production*. London: Routledge and Kegan Paul.

Begnoche Smith, Catherine. 1979. "The Influence of Internal Opportunity Structure and Sex of Worker on Turnover Patterns." *Administrative Sciences Quarterly* 24: 362–81.

Benet, Mary Kathleen. 1972. *Secretary: An Enquiry into the Female Ghetto*. London: Sedgwick and Jackson.

Best, Doris. 1938. "Employed Wives Increasing." *Personnel Journal* 17: 212–20.

Bevan Letter. 1914. *Letter from Bevan to Walkden Concerning Women on Railways*. MRC, 55B/3/WEH-1.

Blackburn, Robert. 1967. *Union Character and Social Class: A Study of White Collar Unionism*. London: Batsford.

Blau, Francine. 1978. "Data on Women Workers: Past, Present and Future." Pp. 29–62 in Ann Stromberg and Shirley Harkess, eds., *Women Working: Theories and Facts in Perspective*. Palo Alto, Calif.: Mayfield.

Blau, Francine, and Jusenius, Carol. 1976. "Economists' Approach to Sex Segregation in the Labor Market: An Appraisal." Pp. 181–200 in Martha Blaxall and Barbara Reagan, eds., *Women and the Workplace: The Implications of Occupational Segregation*. Chicago: University of Chicago Press.

Blau, Francine, and Kahn, Lawrence. 1981. "Race and Sex Differences in Quits by Young Workers." *Industrial and Labor Relations Review* 34: 563–77.

Bliss, William Dwight Porter, and Andrews, John. 1911. "History of Women in Trade Unions." Vol. 10 of *Report on Conditions of Women and Child Wage Earners in the United States*. S. 645, 61 Cong., 2nd Sess. Washington, D.C.: Congressional Printing Office. Rpt., New York: Arno, 1974.

Blum, Albert. 1971. "Office Employees." Pp. 3–45 in Albert Blum et al., eds., *White Collar Workers*. New York: Random House.

Braverman, Harry. 1974. *Labor and Monopoly Capital: The Degradation of Work in the Twentieth Century*. New York: Monthly Review.

Brenner, Johanna, and Ramas, Maria. 1984. "Rethinking Women's Oppression." *New Left Review* 144: 33–71.

Bridges, William. 1980. "Industry Marginality and Female Employment: A New Appraisal." *American Sociological Review* 45: 58–75.

———. 1982. "Sexual Segregation of Occupations: Theories of Labor Stratification in Industry." *American Journal of Sociology* 88: 270–95.

Brower, F. Beatrice. 1937. *Personnel Practices Governing Factory and Office Administration*. New York: National Industrial Conference Board.

Burton, John, and Parker, John. 1969. "Interindustry Variations in Voluntary Labor Mobility." *Industrial and Labor Relations Review* 22: 199–216.

Caplow, Theodore. 1954. *The Sociology of Work*. Minneapolis: University of Minnesota Press.

Center, Stella, and Herzberg, Max. 1929. *Secretarial Procedure*. New York: Ronald.

Chandler, Alfred. 1977. *The Visible Hand: Managerial Revolution in American Business*. Cambridge, Mass.: Belknap.

Christmas Pressure. 1912. *Correspondence File on the Employment of Women as Sorters during Christmas and New Year Pressure*. GPO, E20693/1912.

Clerical Appointments Committee. 1924. *Minutes of the Clerical Appointment Committee of the Great Western Railway*. PRO, Rail 250/148–151.

Clerical Work Committee. 1916–28. *Minutes of the Great Western Railway Clerical Work Committee*. PRO, Rail 250/147.

Cohen, Emmeline. 1941. *Growth of the British Civil Service*. London: Allen and Unwin.

Cohn, Samuel. 1981. "The Feminization of Clerical Labor in Great Britain: 1857–1937." Unpub. Ph.D. dissertation, University of Michigan.

Cole, Robert. 1979. *Work, Mobility, and Participation: A Comparative Study of American and Japanese Industry*. Berkeley, Calif.: University of California Press.

Colours. 1920. *Great Western Railwaymen Called to the Colours*. PRO, Rail 258/728.

Contract Talks. 1919–20. *Transcripts of Negotiations: Negotiating Committee and Railway Clerks Association*. MRC, MSS/55/AG/1/1–46.

Convention. 1946. *Transcript of the Annual Convention of the Railway Clerks Association*. MRC, MSS/55/1/BR/CON/49.

Cook, Alice, and Hayashi, Hiroko. 1980. *Working Women in Japan: Discrimination, Resistance and Reform. Ithaca, N.Y.: New York State School of Industrial and Labor Relations, Cornell University*.

Coyle, Grace. 1929. "Women in Clerical Occupations." *Annals of the American Academy of Political and Social Sciences* 143: 180–87.

Creighton, W. B. 1979. *Working Women and the Law*. London: Mansell.

Curtin, Edwards. 1970. *White Collar Unionization*. National Industrial Conference Board Study in Personnel Policy no. 220. New York: National Industrial Conference Board.

Cyert, Richard, and March, James. 1963. *Behavioral Theory of the Firm*. Englewood Cliffs, N.J.: Prentice-Hall.

Darlington, George. 1942. *Office Management*. Rev. ed. New York: Ronald.

Davies, Margery. 1975. "Women's Place Is at the Typewriter: The Feminization of the Clerical Labor Force." Pp. 279–96 in Richard Edwards et al., eds., *Labor Market Segmentation*. Lexington, Mass.: Heath.

———. 1982. *Women's Place Is at the Typewriter*. Philadelphia: Temple University Press.

Dicksee, Lawrence, and Blain, Herbert. 1906. *Office Organization and Management Including Secretarial Work*. London: Pitman.

Dinerman, Beatrice. 1969. "Sex Discrimination in the Legal Profession." *American Bar Association Journal* 55: 953.

Dublin, Thomas. 1979. *Women at Work: Transformation of Work and Community in Lowell, Massachusetts, 1826–1860*. New York: Columbia University Press.

Dubnoff, Steven. 1978. "Inter-occupational Shifts and Changes in the Quality of Work in the American Economy, 1900–70." Paper presented at the annual meeting of the Society for the Study of Social Problems, San Francisco.

Edgeworth, F. Y. 1922. "Equal Pay to Men and Women for Equal Work." *Economic Journal* 32: 431–57.

Edwards, Richard. 1979. *Contested Terrain: Transformation of the Workplace in America*. New York: Basic Books.

Engineering Clerks. 1904. *Report of the Committee on the Organization of the Engineer in Chief's Office*. GPO, E18135/1904.

———. 1919. *Report of the Committee on Engineering Clerical Establishments*. GPO, E2451/1919.

Epstein, Cynthia Fuchs. 1981. *Women in Law*. New York: Basic Books.

Evans, Dorothy. 1934. *Women and the Civil Service: A History of the Development and Employment of Women in the Civil Service and a Guide to the Present-Day Opportunities*. London: Pitman.

Ex-servicemen's Employment. 1921. *Report on the Appointment and Employment of Ex-servicemen*. GPO, M19938/1921.

Fawcett, Millicent. 1918. "Equal Pay for Equal Work." *Economic Journal* 18: 1–6.

Feldberg, Roslyn. 1980. "Union Fever: Organizing among Clerical Workers, 1900–30." *Radical America* 14: 53–67.

Female Pension. 1927. *Papers on the Great Western Railway Female Clerks Superannuation Scheme*. PRO, Rail 258/523.

Foner, Philip. 1979. *Women and the American Labor Movement: From Colonial Times to the Eve of World War I*. Glencoe, N.Y.: Free Press.

———. 1980. *Women and The American Labor Movement: From World War I to the Present*. Glencoe, N.Y.: Free Press.

Freeman, Richard and Medoff, James. 1979. "New Estimates of Private Sector Unionism in the United States." *Industrial and Labor Relations Review* 32: 143–74.

Fry, Fred. 1973. "Behavioral Analysis of Economic Variables Affecting Turnover." *Journal of Behavioral Economics* 2: 247–95.

Gallie, Duncan. 1978. *In Search of the New Working Class: Automation and Social Integration within the Capitalist Enterprise*. New York: Cambridge University Press.

Gardiner, Glenn. 1929. *Practical Office Supervision*. New York: McGraw-Hill.

Garfinkle, Stuart. 1975. "Occupations of Women and Black Workers, 1962–74." *Monthly Labor Review* 98: 25–35.

General Strike. 1926. *Great Western Railway Documents on the General Strike*. PRO, Rail 253/451.

Gladden, Edgar Norman. 1967. *The Civil Services of the United Kingdom: 1855–1970*. London: Cass.

Glenn, Evelyn Nakano, and Feldberg, Roslyn L. 1977. "Degraded and De-skilled: The Proletarianization of Clerical Work." *Social Problems* 25: 52–64.

Goods Stations. 1922. *Report of the Clerical Work Committee of the Great Western Railway on the Accounts Organization of the Goods Depots of*

Bristol, Paddington, Gloucester, Swansea, Reading, and Plymouth. PRO, Rail 250/783.

GPO Establishment Books. 1857–1937. *The Establishment of the General Post Office with Returns of the Provincial, Dublin, Edinburgh, and Colonial Establishments.* GPO, entire PO 59 series.

GPO Women. 1908. *Recruitment of Women and Girls to the Post Office.* GPO, E12171/1908.

Grand Classification. 1920. Grand Classification of Salaried Staff on Every British Railway Showing the Percentages in Each Class. MRC, *Railway Clerk*, Dec.

Great Britain Census. 1871. *Census of England and Wales.* London: Her Majesty's Stationery Office.

———. 1881. *Census of England and Wales.* London: Her Majesty's Stationery Office.

———. 1891. *Census of England and Wales.* London: Her Majesty's Stationery Office.

———. 1901. *Census of England and Wales.* London: Her Majesty's Stationery Office.

———. 1911. *Census of England and Wales.* London: His Majesty's Stationery Office.

———. 1921. *Census of England and Wales.* London: His Majesty's Stationery Office.

———. 1931. *Census of England and Wales.* London: His Majesty's Stationery Office.

Grimm, James. 1978. "Women in Female-Dominated Professions." Pp. 293–315 in Ann Stromberg and Shirley Harkess, eds., *Women Working: Theories and Facts in Perspective.* Palo Alto, Calif.: Mayfield.

Gross, Edward. 1968. "Plus Ca Change . . . ? Sexual Structure of Occupations over Time." *Social Problems* 16: 198–208.

GWR Petitions. 1914. *Great Western Railway Memorials and Petitions of Clerical Staff.* PRO, Rail 258/404.

GWR Staff Census. 1919. *Great Western Railway Census of Staff.* PRO, Rail 253/417.

———. 1933. *Great Western Railway Census of Staff.* PRO, Rail 253/454.

GWR Women. 1906. Great Western Railway Correspondence on the Employment of Women. PRO, Rail 258/405.

Hall, C. E. 1902. *Postal and Telegraph Clerks: Thirty Years of Agitation.* Liverpool: Pearl. GPO.

Hanami, Tadashi. 1965. "Women Workers and Retirement after Marriage." *Japan Labor Bulletin* 8: 37–56.

Hanham, H. J. 1960. "Political Patronage at the Treasury: 1870–1912." *Historical Review* 3: 75–84.

Hartman, Heidi. 1976. "Capitalism, Patriarchy, and Job Segregation by Sex." Pp. 137–69 in Martha Blaxall and Barbara Reagan, eds., *Women and the Workplace: The Implications of Occupational Segregation.* Chicago: University of Chicago Press.

Heritage, James. 1983. "Feminization and Unionization: A Case Study from Banking." Pp. 131–48 in Eva Gamarnikow et al., eds. *Gender, Class, and Work.* London: Heinemann.

Hirsch, Barry. 1980. "Determinants of Unionization: An Analysis of Interarea Differences." *Industrial and Labor Relations Review* 33: 147–61.

Hobhouse. 1906. *Report from the Select Committee on Post Office Servants with the Proceedings of the Committee, Evidence and Index.* House of Commons, Sessional Papers, vol. xii, pp. 11–1561.

Hoke, Donald. 1978. "Women and the Typewriter: A Case Study in Technological Innovation and Social Change." Unpub. paper.

Holcombe, Lee. 1973. *Victorian Ladies at Work.* Hamden, Conn.: Archon.

Horowitz, Morris, and Herrnstadt, Irwin. 1966. "Changes in the Skill Requirements of Occupations in Selected Industries." Pp. 223–87 in National Commission on Technology, Automation, and Economic Progress, *The Employment Impact of Technological Change: Appendix*, vol. 2 of *Technology and the American Economy.* Washington, D.C.: Government Printing Office.

Humphreys, B. V. 1958. *Clerical Unions in the Civil Service.* Oxford: Blackwell and Mott.

Hunt, Audrey. 1975. *Management Attitudes and Practices towards Women at Work.* London: Her Majesty's Stationery Office and Office of Population Surveys and Censuses, Social Survey Division.

Hunt, Pauline. 1980. *Gender and Class Consciousness.* New York: Holmes and Meier.

International Labor Office. 1962. "Discrimination in Employment or Occupations on the Basis of Marital Status." *International Labor Review* 85: 368–89.

Ireson, Carol. 1978. "Girls' Socialization for Work." Pp. 176–200 in Ann Stromberg and Shirley Harkess, eds., *Women Working: Theories and Facts in Perspective.* Palo Alto, Calif.: Mayfield.

Jenkinson, Lambert. 1914. *Organization of Goods Departments.* London: Railway Press.

Kalleberg, Arne; Wallace, Michael; and Althauser, Robert. 1981. "Economic Segmentation, Worker Power, and Income Inequality." *American Journal of Sociology* 87: 651–83.

Kanter, Rosabeth Moss. 1977. *Men and Women of the Corporation.* New York: Basic Books.

Kassalow, Everett. 1966. "White Collar Unionism in the United States." Pp.

305–64 in Adolf Sturmthal, ed., *White Collar-Trade Unions*. Urbana: University of Illinois Press.

Kessler-Harris, Alice. 1979. "Where Are the Organized Women Workers?" Pp. 343–66 in Nancy Cott and Elizabeth Pleck, eds., *A Heritage of Their Own*. New York: Simon and Schuster.

———. 1982. *Out to Work: History of Wage-Earning Women in the United States*. New York: Oxford University Press.

Kingsford, Peter. 1970. *Victorian Railwaymen: The Emergence and Growth of Railway Labour, 1830–70*. London: Cass.

Klingender, Francis Donald. 1935. *Condition of Clerical Labour in Great Britain*. London: Lawrence.

Labour Report. 1930–33. *Great Western Railway General Manager's Report on Labor Matters*. PRO, Rail 250/474–75.

Laws, Judith Long. 1976. "Work Aspirations of Women: False Leads and New Starts." Pp. 33–50 in Martha Blaxall and Barbara Reagan, eds., *Women and the Workplace: The Implications of Occupational Segregation*. Chicago: University of Chicago Press.

Leffingwell, William. 1917. *Scientific Office Management*. Chicago: Shaw.

———. 1918. *Making the Office Pay*. Chicago: Shaw.

———. 1925. *Office Management: Principles and Practice*. Chicago: Shaw.

———. 1926. *Office Appliance Manual*. N.p.: National Association of Office Appliance Manufacturers.

Leffingwell, William, and Robinson, Edwin. 1950. *Textbook of Office Management*. New York: McGraw-Hill.

Lockwood, David. 1958. *The Blackcoated Worker: Study in Class Consciousness*. London: Allen and Unwin.

London Branches. 1914. *Correspondence Concerning the London Postal Service's Proportion of Female to Male Force*. GPO, E14324/1914.

Lyle, Jerolyn, and Ross, Jane. 1973. Women in Industry: Employment Patterns of Women in Corporate America. Lexington, Mass.: Heath.

Macdermot, Edward Terence. 1927. *The History of the Great Western Railway*. London: Ian Allan.

Madden, Janice Fanning. 1973. *The Economics of Sex Discrimination*. Lexington, Mass.: Heath.

———. 1975. "Discrimination: A Manifestation of Male Market Power." Pp. 146–74 in Cynthia Lloyd, ed., *Sex, Discrimination, and the Division of Labor*. New York: Columbia University Press.

Male Pension. 1925. *Great Western Railway Male Clerical Superannuation Funds*. PRO, Rail 258/395.

Martindale, Hilda. 1938. *Women Servants of the State*. London: Allen and Unwin.

McClelland, Frank. 1920. *Office Training and Standards*. Chicago: Shaw.

McCord, James. 1923. *Textbook of Filing*. New York: Appleton.

McDonagh. 1912–13. *Evidence and Appendices of the First and Second Report of the Royal Commission on the Civil Service.* House of Commons Sessional Papers, vol. xv, 113–625.

Medoff, James, and Abraham, Katherine. 1980. "Experience, Performance, and Earnings." *Quarterly Journal of Economics* 95: 703–36.

———. 1981. "Are Those Who Are Paid More Really More Productive? The Case of Experience." *Journal of Human Resources* 16: 186–216.

Melman, Seymour. 1951. "Rise of Administrative Overhead in the Manufacturing Industries of the United States." *Oxford Economic Papers* 3: 62–112.

Milkman, Ruth. 1980. "Organizing the Sexual Division of Labor: Historical Perspectives on Women's Work and the American Labor Movement." *Socialist Review* 10: 95–150.

———. 1982. "Redefining Women's Work: The Sexual Division of Labor in the Auto Industry during World War II." *Feminist Studies* 8: 337–72.

Mills, C. Wright. 1951. *White Collar: The American Middle Classes.* New York: Oxford University Press.

Mincer, Jacob, and Polachek, Solomon. 1974. "Family Investment in Human Capital: Earnings of Women." *Journal of Political Economy* 82: S76–S108.

Mitchell, Brian R. 1962. *Abstract of British Historical Statistics.* Cambridge, U.K.: Cambridge University Press.

Molyneux, Maxine. 1979. "Beyond the Domestic Labor Debate." *New Left Review* 116: 1–27.

Montagna, Paul. 1975. *Certified Public Accounting: Sociological View of a Profession in Change.* New York: Scholars.

Moore, Kristin, and Sawhill, Isabel. 1978. "The Implications of Women's Employment for Home and Family Life." Pp. 201–25 in Ann Stromberg and Shirley Harkess, eds., *Women Working: Theories and Facts in Perspective.* Palo Alto, Calif.: Mayfield.

Moore, William, and Newman, Robert. 1975. "On Prospects for American Trade Union Growth: A Cross-sectional Analysis." *Review of Economics and Statistics* 57: 435–45.

National Manpower Council. 1957. *Womanpower.* New York: Columbia University Press.

National Whitley Council. 1945–46. *Report on Marriage Bars in the Civil Service.* House of Commons Sessional Papers, vol. x, pp. 871–94.

Nichols, Frederick. 1934. *The Personal Secretary: Differentiating Duties and Essential Personal Traits.* Cambridge, Mass.: Harvard University Press.

Nock, Oswald. 1963. *The Great Western Railway in the Nineteenth Century.* London: Ian Allen.

———. 1964. *The History of the Great Western Railway.* London: Ian Allen.

Noland, William, and Bakke, E. Wight. 1949. *Workers Wanted: A Study of Employers' Hiring Policies, Preferences, and Practices in New Haven and Charlotte.* New York: Arno.

Northern Recruitment. 1904. *Reports to Board of Great Northern Railway on Recruitment of Clerical Staff.* PRO, Rail 236/286/13.

O'Brien, Mary. 1981. *Politics of Reproduction.* London: Routlege and Kegan Paul.

O'Connor, James. 1973. *Fiscal Crisis of the State.* New York: Saint Martin's.

Oppenheimer, Valerie Kincaide. 1970. *The Female Labor Force in the United States.* Westport, Conn.: Greenwood.

Orchard, B. G. 1871. *Clerks of Liverpool.* Liverpool: Arthur Mason.

Parnes, Herbert. 1954. *Research on Labor Mobility: An Appraisal of Research Findings in the United States.* New York: Social Science Research Council.

Parsley, Clifford. 1980. "Labor Union Effects on Wage Gains: A Survey of Recent Literature." *Journal of Economic Literature* 18: 1–31.

Patterson, Michelle, and Engelberg, Laurie. 1978. "Women in Male-Dominated Professions." Pp. 266–92 in Ann Stromberg and Shirley Harkess, eds., *Women Working: Theories and Facts in Perspective.* Palo Alto, Calif.: Mayfield.

Pencavel, John. 1970. *The Quit Rate in American Manufacturing Industry.* Princeton, N.J.: Industrial Relations Section, Department of Economics, Princeton University.

Phelps, Edmund S. 1972. "A Statistical Theory of Racism and Sexism." *American Economic Review* 62: 659–61.

Phelps Brown, Henry. 1977. *The Inequality of Pay.* New York: Oxford University Press.

———. 1983. *The Origins of Trade Union Power.* Oxford: Clarendon.

Piore, Michael, and Doeringer, Peter. 1971. *Internal Labor Markets and Manpower Analysis.* Lexington, Mass.: Heath.

Pitman, Isaac. 1891. *A History of Shorthand.* London: Pitman.

Polachek, Solomon. 1979. "Occupational Segregation among Women: Theory, Evidence, and Prognosis." Pp. 137–57 in Cynthia Lloyd et al., eds., *Women in the Labor Market.* New York: Columbia University Press.

Pollard, Sydney. 1965. *Genesis of Modern Management.* Cambridge, Mass.: Harvard University Press.

Pollins, Harold. 1971. *Britain's Railways: An Industrial History.* Newton Abbott, U.K.: David and Charles.

Postmaster Report. 1871. *Seventeenth Report of the Postmaster General.* House of Commons Sessional Papers, vol. xvi, pp. 793–881.

———. 1890–91. *Thirty-Seventh Report of the Postmaster General.* House of Commons Sessional Papers, vol. xxvi, pp. 533–647.

———. 1906. *Fifty-Seventh Report of the Postmaster General.* House of Commons Sessional Papers, vol. xxxix, pp. 595–696.

———. 1930–31. *Statement Showing Staffs of Government Departments.* House of Commons Sessional Papers, vol. xxii, pp. 783–852.

Power, Marilyn. 1983. "From Home Production to Wage Labor: Women as a Reserve Army of Labor." *Review of Radical Political Economics* 15: 71–91.

Prather, Jane. 1971. "When the Girls Move In: A Sociological Analysis of the Feminization of the Bank Tellers' Job." *Journal of Marriage and the Family* 33: 777–82.

Pratt, Edwin. 1921. *British Railways and the Great War.* 2 vols. London: Selwyn and Blount.

Price, James L. 1977. *The Study of Turnover.* Ames, Iowa: Iowa State University Press.

Railway Clerk. 1907–37. *Railway Clerk.* Also known as *Railway Service Journal.* MRC, no identifying no.

Railway Report. 1860. *Number and Description of Persons Employed on Each Railway in England and Wales, Scotland and Ireland.* House of Commons, Sessional Papers, vol. lxi, pp. 153–64.

———. 1884. *Number and Description of Persons Employed on Each Railway in England, Scotland and Ireland.* House of Commons Sessional Papers, vol. lxx, pp, 307–19.

———. 1913. *Return Showing the Number of Staff Employed and the Amount of Salaries and Wages Paid Respectively by the Several Railway Companies of the United Kingdom in 1911.* House of Commons Sessional Papers, vol. lviii, pp. 475–550.

Railway Return. 1907. *Returns Relative to the Railways of the United Kingdom.* House of Commons Sessional Papers, vol. lxxiv, pp. 517–666.

RCA Annual Reports. 1903–28. *Annual Reports of the Railway Clerks Association.* MRC, MSS55B/4/AR/7.

RCA Contract. 1925. *National Agreements Respecting Rates of Pay and Conditions of Service.* Also known as Railway Clerks Association, *Negotiating Machinery Schemes.* LSE.

Reich, Michael. 1981. *Racial Inequality: A Political-Economic Analysis.* Princeton, N.J.: Princeton University Press.

Richards, Peter Godfrey. 1963. *Patronage in British Government.* London: Allen and Unwin.

Rotella, Elyce. 1981. *From Home to Office: U.S. Women at Work.* Ann Arbor, Mich.: UMI Research.

Salaried Recruitment. 1912. *Great Western Railway Appointment and Recruitment of Salaried Staff.* PRO, Rail 258/400.

Savings Bank Print Shop. 1914. *Introduction of Women to the Savings Bank Print Shop.* GPO, E13753/1914.

Sawhill, Isabel. 1973. "Economics of Discrimination against Women: Some New Findings." *Journal of Human Resources* 8: 383–96.

Schulze, J. William. 1913. *The American Office: Its Organization, Management, and Records.* New York: Key.

———. 1919. *Office Administration.* New York: McGraw-Hill.

Scudamore, Francis. 1871. *Report by Mr. Scudamore on the Reorganization of the Telegraph System of the United Kingdom.* House of Commons Sessional Papers, vol. xxxvii, pp. 703–852.

Secombe, Wally. 1974. "The Housewife and Her Labour under Capitalism." *New Left Review* 83: 3–24.

Shallcross, Ruth. 1940. *Should Married Women Work?* Public Affairs Pamphlet no. 49. N.p.

Shyrock, Henry, and Seigel, Jacob. 1975. *Methods and Materials of Demography.* Washington, D.C.: U.S. Department of Commerce.

Simon, Herbert. 1957. *Administrative Behavior.* Glencoe, N.Y.: Free Press.

Snyder, David; Hayward, Mark; and Hudis, Paula. 1978. "Locations of Change in the Sexual Structure of Occupations, 1950–70: Insights from Labor Market Segmentation Theory." *American Journal of Sociology* 84: 706–17.

Snyder, David, and Hudis, Paula. 1976. "Occupational Income and the Effects of Minority Competition and Segregation: A Reanalysis and Some New Evidence." *American Sociological Review* 41: 209–34.

Spenner, Kenneth. 1983. "Temporal Changes in the Skill Level of Work." *American Sociological Review* 48: 824–37.

Staff Charts. 1914–37. *Great Western Railway Organizational Charts of Salaried Staff.* PRO, Rail 253/789–803.

Staff Expenses. 1879. *Great Western Railway General Manager's Report on the Expenses of the Traffic Department.* PRO, Rail 250/690.

Staff Statistics. 1870. *Great Western Railway General Manager's Report on Staff Statistics.* PRO, Rail 267/33.

Stevenson, Mary. 1975*a*. "Women's Wages and Job Segregation." Pp. 243–256 in Richard Edwards et al., eds., *Labor Market Segmentation.* Lexington, Mass.: Heath.

———. 1975*b*. "Relative Wages and Sex Segregation by Occupation." Pp. 175–200 in Cynthia Lloyd, ed., *Sex, Discrimination, and the Division of Labor.* New York: Columbia University Press.

Stinchcombe, Arthur. 1964. "Social Structure and Organizations." Pp. 131–210 in James March, ed., *Handbook of Organizations.* Chicago: Rand McNally.

———. 1968 *Constructing Social Theories.* New York: Harcourt, Brace and Jovanovich.

Stoikov, Vladimir, and Raimon, R. L. 1968. "Determinants of Differences in Quit Rates among Industries." *American Economic Review* 58: 1283–98.

Swift, Henry G. 1900. *The History of Postal Agitation from Fifty Years Ago to the Present Day.* London: Pearson.

Telegraph. 1927. *Correspondence on the Telegraph Instrument and Counter Duties: Proportion of Males to Females.* GPO, M6085/1927.

Telegraph Estimates. 1872. *Postal Telegraph Estimates and Report on Permanent Establishments.* GPO, P082/58.

Telegraph Report. 1876. "Report on the Organization of the Telegraph Service with Minutes and Evidence." House of Commons Sessional Papers, vol. xi, pp. 1–368.

Telegraph Strikes. 1872. *1871 Telegraphists Strike*. GPO, E274/1872.

Telegraph Substitution. 1880. *Further Substitution of Male for Female Labour in the Central Telegraph Office*. GPO, E171/1880.

Thurow, Lester. 1975. *Generating Inequality: Mechanisms of Distribution in the United States Economy*. New York: Basic Books.

Tilly, Louise A. 1981. "Paths of Proletarianization: Organization of Production, Sexual Division of Labor, and Women's Collective Action." *Signs* 7: 400–417.

Tilly, Louise A., and Scott, Joan. 1978. *Women, Work, and Family*. New York: Holt.

Treiman, Donald, and Terrell, Kermit. 1975. "Women, Work, and Wages: Trends in the Female Occupational Structure since 1940." Pp. 157–99 in Kenneth Land and Seymour Spilerman, eds., *Social Indicator Models*. New York: Russell Sage.

Tucket, Angela. 1976. "Swindon." Pp. 283–311 in Jeffery Skellen, ed., *General Strike, 1926*. London: Lawrence and Wishart.

U.S. Bureau of the Census. 1870. Census of Population. Washington, D.C.: Government Printing Office.

———. 1930. Census of Population. Washington, D.C.: Government Printing Office.

———. 1970. Census of Population. Washington, D.C.: Government Printing Office.

U.S. Department of Labor, Bureau of Employment Security. 1956. *Older Workers' Adjustment to Labor Market Practices*. Bulletin no. R151. Washington, D.C.: Government Printing Office.

U.S. Employment Service, Occupational Analysis Division. 1942. *Occupations Suitable for Women*. Washington, D.C.: Government Printing Office.

Viscusi, K. P. 1980. "Sex Differences in Worker Quitting." *Review of Economics and Statistics* 62: 388–98.

Voos, Paula. 1983. "Determinants of U.S. Unionism: Past Research and Future Needs." *Industrial Relations* 22: 445–50.

Wagner, David. 1979. "Clerical Workers: How Unorganizable Are They?" *Labor Center Review* 2: 20–50.

Walkden, A. G. 1928. *The Railway Clerk and His Path of Progress*. London: Williams.

Wallace, Michael, and Kalleberg, Arne. 1981. "Economic Organizations of Firms and Labor Market Consequences: Towards a Specification of Dual Economy Theory." Pp. 77–118 in Ivar Berg, ed., *Sociological Perspectives on Labor Markets*. New York: Academic.

War Cabinet. 1919. *Report of the War Cabinet Committee on Women in Industry*. House of Commons Sessional Papers, vol. xxxi, pp. 241–849.

Weber, Max. 1958. *The Protestant Ethic and the Spirit of Capitalism*. Trans. Talcott Parsons. New York: Scribner.

Wertheimer, Barbara, and Nelson, Anne. 1975. *Trade Union Women: A Study of Their Participation in New York City Locals.* New York: Praeger.

Whitley Council. 1919. *Report of the Subcommittee Appointed to Consider the Position after the War of Women Holders of Temporary Appointments in Government Departments.* House of Commons Sessional Papers, vol. xxix, pp. 153–60.

Wigham, Eric. 1980. *From Humble Petition to Militant Activism: A History of the Civil and Public Servants Association.* Tunbridge Wells, Eng.: Civil and Public Servants Association.

Wilensky, Harold. 1968. "Women's Work: Economic Growth, Ideology, Structure." *Industrial Relations* 7: 235–48.

Williamson, Oliver. 1975. *Markets and Hierarchies: Analysis and Antitrust Implications.* New York: Free Press.

Wolf, Wendy, and Fligstein, Neil. 1979a. "Sexual Stratification: Differences of Power in the Work Setting." *Social Forces* 58: 94–107.

———. 1979b. "Sex and Authority in the Workplace: The Causes of Sexual Inequality." *American Sociological Review* 44: 235–52.

Wright, Erik Olin, and Singelmann, Joachim. 1982. "Proletarianization in the Changing American Class Structure." Pp. 176–209 in Michael Burawoy and Theda Skocpol, eds., *Marxist Inquiries.* Chicago: University of Chicago Press.

Wrigley, Edward Anthony. 1969. *Population and History.* New York: McGraw-Hill.

WWI Nightwork. 1918. *Employment of Women at Night.* GPO, E2200/1918.

WWI Sorters. 1915. *London Postal Service Employment of Temporary Female Force on Sorting Duties during Wartime.* GPO, E14412/1915.

Zaretsky, Eli. 1973. *Capitalism, the Family and Personal Life.* New York: Harper and Row.

Zellner, Harriet. 1975. "Determinants of Occupational Segregation." Pp 125–45 in Cynthia Lloyd, ed., *Sex, Discrimination and the Division of Labor.* New York: Columbia University Press.

Zimbalist, Andrew. 1979. *Case Studies on the Labor Process.* New York: Monthly Review.

Index

267